Praise for Wit, Virtue, and Emotion

"With a deft hand, Elizabeth Tasker Davis rewrites traditional understandings of the European Enlightenment by tracing protofeminist acts of persuasion across a range of rhetorical ecologies during Britain's long eighteenth century. Royal women and ladies of court, actresses, elite socialites, middle-class club women, professional authors, educators, and teenage girls—all emerge in *Wit, Virtue, and Emotion* as intriguing practitioners and theorists of the arts of persuasion. With this monograph, Tasker Davis has issued a powerful call to historians of women's rhetorics to look more deeply and more expansively into the roots of our twenty-first-century feminisms."

—JANE GREER, editor of *Girls and Literacy in America: Historical Perspectives to the Present*

"Tasker Davis's engaging work fills an important and significantly underexplored gap in rhetorical history: women's rhetorical activity in the eighteenth century. This book challenges and reframes current rhetorical histories by examining the presence of the active, speaking female body in places such as salons, debate societies, and clubs, as well as women's proliferation of written documents. While people do not usually think of the eighteenth century as a significant period of rhetorical activity for women, this book reminds us that not only were women rhetorically active at this time but this activity helped to shape and define both enlightenment rhetoric and the rhetorical practices of the nineteenth century."

—LISA S. MASTRANGELO, author of *Writing a Progressive Past: Women Teaching and Writing in the Progressive Era*

"While the Enlightenment is often depicted as an era dominated by the voices of male intellectuals, Tasker Davis has persuasively argued that social, intellectual, and economic change during this period created space for women's rhetorical intervention in public life. Tasker Davis's careful analysis of women's roles in the theater, salons, debating societies, and newly accessible print media illuminates the varied and complex ways in which the rhetorical presence of women significantly shaped the Enlightenment's intellectual landscape. This book makes a strong contribution to the study of women's rhetoric and, more broadly, Enlightenment rhetorical history."

—LOIS PETERS AGNEW, author of *Outward, Visible Propriety: Stoic Philosophy and Eighteenth-Century British Rhetorics*

"Defining and adopting a lens of 'progressive protofeminist women's rhetoric,' Elizabeth Tasker Davis deftly redirects attention to sites of British women's rhetorical activity (the stage, clubs, debating societies, tea rooms, and the page). Doing for the long eighteenth century what Nan Johnson's *Gender and Rhetorical Space in American Life, 1866–1910* did for the subsequent American period, *Wit, Virtue, and Emotion* relies on accessible archival materials to expand conceptions of what counts as Enlightenment rhetoric. Tasker Davis offers the postures of wit, virtue, and emotion as feminist counterparts to Aristotle's conceptions of *logos, ethos,* and *pathos*—and in the process provides contemporary readers with another lens for refiguring issues of gender (in)equality, social class, and rhetorical activity."

—LYNÉE LEWIS GAILLET, coeditor of *Remembering Women Differently: Refiguring Rhetorical Work*

Studies in Rhetorics and Feminisms

Series Editors, Cheryl Glenn and Shirley Wilson Logan

Wit, Virtue, and Emotion

British Women's Enlightenment Rhetoric

Elizabeth Tasker Davis

Southern Illinois University Press
Carbondale

Southern Illinois University Press
www.siupress.com

24   23   22   21   4   3   2   1

COVER illustration: Beauty in Search of Knowledge, December 1782, Sayer
& Bennett. Hand-colored mezzotint of a print by John Raphael Smith, published in 1781 (1902,1011.5058; BM, Exhibition of English Art, 1934, no. 180).
Lettered on plate with title and publication line, "London printed for R.Sayer
& J.Bennett, Map, Chart & Printsellers, No. 53 Fleet Street, 3oth Decr 1782."
https://www.britishmuseum.org/collection/image/377223001. © The Trustees
of the British Museum, 2001,0930.33.

Library of Congress Cataloging-in-Publication Data
Names: Davis, Elizabeth Tasker, 1962- author.
Title: Wit, virtue, and emotion : British women's Enlightenment rhetoric
/ Elizabeth Tasker Davis.
Description: Carbondale : Southern Illinois University Press, [2021]
| Series: Studies in rhetorics and feminisms | Includes bibliographical
references and index.
Identifiers: LCCN 2020046331 (print) | LCCN 2020046332 (ebook)
| ISBN 9780809338276 (paperback) | ISBN 9780809338283 (ebook)
Subjects: LCSH: Women—Great Britain—Social conditions. | Feminism
and Rhetoric—Great Britain | Women--Great Britain—Language.
English Language—Rhetoric—History. | English wit and humor. | Virtue
in literature. | Emotions in literature. | Enlightenment—Great Britain.
| Great Britain—Intellectual life—18th century.
Classification: LCC HQ1593 .D43 2021 (print) | LCC HQ1593 (ebook)
| DDC 305.420941--dc23
LC record available at https://lccn.loc.gov/2020046331
LC ebook record available at https://lccn.loc.gov/2020046332

To Troy, Bonnie, and Jesse

Contents

Contents

Figures

Acknowledgments

My work on this project spans over a decade, and many have helped me along the way. My first giant thanks goes to Troy Davis, my husband, best friend, sounding board, and most excellent proofreader. Secondly, I offer heartfelt thanks to the faculty of Georgia State University, including Lynée Lewis Gaillet, Tanya Caldwell, and Malinda Snow, all of whom inspired my love of all things eighteenth century, and Beth Burmester and George Pullman who gave me a solid foundation in classical rhetoric. I am deeply grateful to Cheryl Glenn, Shirley Wilson Logan, Kristine Priddy, and Lisa Marty for their strong and insightful editorial guidance. I am also indebted to the generosity of feminist scholars and colleagues, including Lindal Buchanan, Jackie Cowan, Lisa Mastrangelo, and Courtney Adams Wooten, who provided feedback on early and very rough drafts, as well as Kate Adams and Lois Agnew whose guiding commentary on later drafts helped me to elevate and clarify my analyses. I was fortunate to have the assistance of three excellent graduate students, Athena Hayes, Melissa Hutchens, and Hollis Thompson, who assisted with research and copyediting tasks at various points. My ongoing work on this project was made possible by a faculty research grant, a sabbatical, and multiple mini-grants from Stephen F. Austin State University through the administrative support of Mark Sanders, Brian Murphy, Kenneth Untiedt, and Matthew McBroom. I also thank my colleagues at SFA for their support and encouragement, including Ericka Hoagland, Tom Reynolds, Marc Guidry, Kevin West, Steve Marsden, Michael Martin, Michael Given, Christine Butterworth-McDermott, John McDermott, Andrew Brininstool, Jessie Sams, Chris Sams, and Megan Condis. For the use of their archived visual images, I acknowledge with gratitude the British Museum, London; the Bodleian Libraries, the University of Oxford; National Portrait Gallery, London; Lilly Library, Indiana University; and the Metropolitan Museum, New York. I am deeply thankful for the support and patience of my family, especially my parents, Jesse and Bonnie Lyons; my three children, Rebecca, Sean, and Austin; and my Aunt Trudy and Uncle Tom, who were with me through the many hours, days, weeks, and years of my research and writing. Finally, I want to acknowledge that Mary Wollstonecraft and I share the same birthday. Cheers!

WIT, VIRTUE, AND EMOTION

Introduction

We shall say what has not been said before, or if the substance
is old, the mode & figure shall be new.
—Elizabeth Montagu, "Letter to Elizabeth Carter," 1769

$\mathcal{D}$ESPITE MASS SUBORDINATION and suppression under centuries of patriarchy, women throughout history have spoken out on a wide range
of subjects through the means available at their times. During the age of Enlightenment, in the seventeenth and eighteenth centuries, these means increased significantly for British women. Rising levels of literacy and increased
accessibility to intellectual venues led women to pursue many diverse forms of
persuasive discourse. Myriad writings and artifacts—such as the large corpus
of letters by and to famous Bluestocking leader Elizabeth Montagu—stand as
evidence of women's Enlightenment rhetoric. In Montagu's letters, we can discern her own personal style as well as her appropriation of classical rhetorical
theory. As Tania Smith argues, Montagu's construction of her own rhetorical
identity reflects a careful study of Cicero's moral character and his blending
of public and private rhetoric ("Elizabeth Montagu" 165). Certainly, Montagu
was a highly educated woman and a member of the late eighteenth-century
British intellectual elite. However, middle-class eighteenth-century women also
engaged in self-reflexive rhetorical practices, such as those documented in the
1721 charter of the Fair Intellectual Club of Edinburgh—an intellectual society
of teenage girls. Unsurprisingly, these types of intellectual rhetorical acts did
not elevate women to equal public standing with men. Montagu could not
hold a seat in parliament (as her husband Edward Montagu did), and the Fair
Intellectuals felt the need to keep their society secret, to protect the reputations
of their members. Regardless of restrictions and taboos, women's rhetorical
practices were ubiquitous.

Contextualizing the contributions of British women to the history of rhetoric during the age of Enlightenment is the mission of this book. The scope of
this history includes spoken, written, and embodied rhetoric and rhetorical
theory by women as individuals and as an impactful demographic within British Enlightenment culture. In providing the background necessary to set up
this conversation, this introduction starts with a gendered description of the

Enlightenment followed by a brief review of cultural studies scholarship on British women intellectuals during this era. I then move into the disciplinary subfield of Enlightenment rhetoric and review the scholarship on women's rhetorical activities within the context of eighteenth-century Britain.

A Gendered Enlightenment

In the context of world history, the Enlightenment refers to the evolution of progressive socioeconomic and scientific ideas that emerged across Western Europe and North America from the early seventeenth to the early nineteenth century. Forming a segue between the Renaissance world of church and state and the modern world of science and industry, the Enlightenment worldview privileged individual experience and inductive reasoning over the auspices of classical authority and deductive logic. Enlightenment thought coheres around the premises that humans are rational, sentient beings; relatively equal in cognitive capability; and alike enough to work together on social, scientific, and economic projects for the progress of society. Along these lines, Enlightenment philosophies and theories of rhetoric are greatly concerned with cognition of empirical evidence; moral reasoning and benevolence; capitalist models of government and commerce; and new appraisals of social class, education, religion, and gender roles.

The umbrella term European Enlightenment includes both the English and Scottish Enlightenments (among other national subdivisions), and also encompasses the subdiscipline of Enlightenment rhetoric, which occurred in Britain during what is called the *long eighteenth century*—from 1660 to approximately 1800. During this era, people in Britain held strong but evolving ideas about sex and gender identity, including qualities of masculinity and femininity. Some of these assumptions were based on biology—male strength and female softness were considered part of nature—and oftentimes perceptions of these biological differences extended to religious and moral antecedents, such as the notions of males possessing God-given rationality and females being driven by emotion and intuition. Many people believed that these qualities were, indeed, biological facts, the laws of nature as designed by God. Contradicting these stereotypes of biological and religious predeterminism, many people within eighteenth-century British society also recognized gender identity as a social construct. Furthermore, it was widely acknowledged that people could possess qualities of gender deemed opposite their biological sex (although divergencies were not encouraged). In fact, gender identities and proper gendered behaviors (especially for girls and women) constituted a topic of ongoing discussion. As

Karen O'Brien explains, "The issue of the 'distinction of sex' was central to the Enlightenment attempt to understand the role of women . . . , yet it was also one of the areas of most fundamental disagreement" ("Sexual Distinctions" 3). Popular opinion tended to conflate gender identity with the two recognized biological sexual identities (male and female), but many people—especially intellectuals and scholars—also recognized gender as a multiplicity of socially constructed gender roles.[1]

The textual legacy of the Enlightenment, however, has long exhibited a male bias. The Enlightenment canon consists of ideas and works by a group of geographically dispersed, white, Western European and American men—philosophers and professors whose diverse theories find unity in their views of modern social progress. Historical narratives about the Enlightenment, although usually focused on the eighteenth century, often begin earlier with Francis Bacon's *Essays* (1597) and *Nova Organon* (1605), Descartes's *Discourse on Method* (1637), and Hobbes's *Leviathan* (1660). From these seventeenth-century roots, a diverse group of modern philosophers emerged across Europe and America, including John Locke, Isaac Newton, and Anthony Ashley Cooper in England; Denis Diderot, Jean le Rond d'Alembert, Marquis de Condorcet, and Jean Jacques Rousseau in France; David Hume, Adam Smith, Francis Hutcheson, George Campbell, and Hugh Blair in Scotland; Baruch Spinoza in Holland; Gottfried Wilhelm Leibniz in Germany; and Thomas Paine and Benjamin Franklin in America.[2]

Broad as this international list of elite historic figures seems, participation in the Enlightenment was even broader and included intellectual performances of women as well as men. As Barbara Taylor and Sarah Knott explain in *Women, Gender, and Enlightenment,* "Enlightenment was a living world where ideas were conveyed not only through 'high' philosophical works but also through novels, poetry, advice literature, popular theology, journalism, pornography, and that most fluid of eighteenth-century genres, the 'miscellaneous essay'" as well as "conversation, reading (both private and communal), pedagogy," and many sociable contexts (xvii–xviii). The conveyance of Enlightenment ideas naturally partook of rhetoric in many forms: persuasive appeals, argumentation, oratory, composition, and the training and theory necessary to underpin these performances and practices.

In *The Rhetoric of Blair, Campbell, and Whatley,* James Golden and Edward Corbett call the Enlightenment "one of the most prolific eras in rhetorical history" (7). Their landmark collaboration analyzes the masculine lineage of Enlightenment rhetoric from its classical Greek and Roman foundations, to its branching out in the eighteenth century (in Britain and North America) to encompass more modern, empirically based theories of human interaction, both for oratory and written composition, and its hybridized blossoming into the new scholarly disciplines of psychology, composition, and speech communications in the late eighteenth and nineteenth centuries. Golden and Corbett's study of eighteenth-century rhetoric as a hybrid and cross-disciplinary field is further supported by Mark Longaker, who more recently has argued that a major innovation of British Enlightenment rhetoric was its alignment with the disciplines of economics and ethics into a "cohesive vision of free-market capitalism, rhetorical style, and bourgeois virtue" (2). Longaker's term "bourgeois virtue" emphasizes Enlightenment rhetoric's dual focus on social class and moral value. I would add that the era's notion of virtue also included considerable discourse on gender definitions, which in turn created new opportunities for women to theorize and practice rhetoric.

This book excavates British women's Enlightenment rhetoric—by which I mean protofeminist genres, methods, and acts of persuasion—in a variety of sites across the social spectrum of eighteenth-century British society. To take a feminist, multigendered view of Enlightenment rhetoric requires rethinking received notions about the discipline. While I agree with Miriam Brody's description of Enlightenment rhetoric as adhering to the classical "tradition of rhetoric and its long-standing project of discovering probable truths with the tools of human language," I also challenge the current historical depiction of Enlightenment rhetoric as an elite intellectual activity strictly "empowered by a male body" (Brody 106, 111). The Enlightenment not only revised classical masculine rhetorical theory and produced new academic fields, it also significantly expanded women's situated ethos (*phronesis*) as well as their rhetorical practices (*techne*). As Tania Smith describes, the classical term *phronesis*, or acknowledged possession of practical wisdom, refers to "a meta-rhetoric" that includes "social contexts, rhetorical intentions, and ethos," while she describes *techne* as "strategic rhetoric" consisting of "discursive tools and conventions for achieving rhetorical aims" ("Elizabeth Montagu" 166–67). Over the course of the long eighteenth century, increased literacy fostered significant enhancements to British women's phronesis and techne and kindled the slow process of women's large-scale transformation from subalterns to fully participating citizens—an end goal that would take two more centuries to reach fruition.

Although women did not realize equal legal and political rights in Britain until the twentieth century, during the long eighteenth century, British women engaged vocally in the major Enlightenment debates. Women intellectuals, or learned ladies as they were known, brought a feminine perspective to the forefront in their engagement with elite discourses on individual cognition, virtue, taste, feelings, and economic independence. Serious philosophical writings from English intellectuals of the early eighteenth century, such as John Locke and Mary Astell, energized British public discourse about human nature, the rights of individuals, virtuous citizenship, and gender-role prescriptions. The idea that women had the capacity to excel intellectually and professionally took hold among mixed-gender circles of the intellectual elite, within middle-class venues of education and sociability, and even in private, feminine, and domestic settings. The later eighteenth-century emphasis on feelings and sympathy, as found in the work of Shaftesbury, Adam Smith, and David Hume, perpetuated an even more multigendered view of modern civilization (DeLucia 9). With the influential voices of the earlier English and later Scottish Enlightenments encouraging more egalitarian social theories and practices, ignoring concerns of gender and social class increasingly came to be perceived as immoral. These developments of Enlightenment philosophy perpetuated developments in women's rhetoric.

Nevertheless, locating evidence of British women's Enlightenment rhetoric presents difficulties, mainly because women's communicative and persuasive practices in the seventeenth and eighteenth centuries did not occur within traditional venues of rhetoric. Prior to the very late nineteenth century, British law barred women from attending universities where rhetoric was taught, and, even into the twentieth century, cultural customs discouraged women from participating in professional disciplines, especially in activities involving public speech, written argumentation, and other displays of so-called masculine reasoning. Nevertheless, historical evidence shows that, in eighteenth-century Britain, girls did study the style and mechanics of writing and elocution, and it was not uncommon for educated women to participate in a variety of intellectual and rhetorical activities within feminine and mixed-gender venues and genres.

Mary Astell (1666–1731), for example, was well versed in neoclassical theories of rhetoric, and her numerous published treatises, pamphlets, and letters written in a variety of rhetorical styles on a wide variety of social and philosophical subjects demonstrate her ability to put rhetorical theory into practice. Best known for *A Serious Proposal to the Ladies, For the Advancement of Their True and Greatest Interest, Part I* (1694) and *A Serious Proposal to the Ladies, Part II: Wherein a Method Is Offer'd for the Improvement of Their Minds* (1697), Astell's writing synthesizes the influential epistemological and moral philosophies of her times and applies them to women's needs and situations. *Part II* of *Serious Proposal* is where she most directly details her rhetorical theory and advocates for feminine rhetorical practices. Just about a century after Astell, Mary Wollstonecraft (1759–97) gained notoriety for her politically radical publications and henceforth achieved lasting fame for her arguments on the rights of women and men. In her progressive treatises, most notably her *Vindication of the Rights of Woman* (1792), Wollstonecraft critiques the rhetoric of patriarchy and espouses protofeminist models for gendered conduct, education, and interpersonal communication. Bracketing the start and close of the eighteenth century, Astell and Wollstonecraft are the best-known protofeminist British women intellectuals of the Enlightenment era. A few other seventeenth- and eighteenth-century British women appear in current anthologies on the history of rhetoric and in scholarship examining women's rhetorical activities within intellectual circles and theatrical performance. However, the volume of scholarship on British women's Enlightenment rhetoric is extremely small in comparison to the substantial body of work on the rhetoric of nineteenth- and twentieth-century American women.

In *Wit, Virtue, and Emotion: British Women's Enlightenment Rhetoric,* my aim is to delineate a protofeminist ecology of British women 's Enlightenment rhetoric, which, I argue, is currently a buried cornerstone of modern feminism. British women's rhetorical activities were instrumental in expanding the role and the reach of the female individual in the age of Enlightenment. The accumulated acts of embodied, spoken, and written protofeminist rhetoric by and for seventeenth- and eighteenth-century British women translated to a groundswell of persuasive power, which set in motion new developments in feminine gender roles and education and created opportunities for women within British society in the age of Enlightenment and beyond. Examining artifacts of these mediated activities by British women in the long eighteenth century reveals numerous protofeminist historical precedents—before the first wave of feminism in Britain (or anywhere else). Women's Enlightenment rhetoric prefigures feminist arguments for gender equality and future legal and moral reforms, including the formalized campaigns for women's civil rights, abolition, standardized education, child-labor protections, and suffragism that were to come in the nineteenth and early twentieth century in Britain and America.

This narrative, then, elucidates the origins of Anglo-feminist rhetoric, thereby highlighting an understudied and very significant era in the historical development of women's persuasive voices and feminine power. This book addresses feminist scholars and advanced students in the field of rhetoric and composition and urges them to attend more closely to the Enlightenment era within the broad history of women's rhetoric. Feminist rhetorical methods of analysis provide a novel lens for analyzing seventeenth- and eighteenth-century women writers, intellectuals, education theorists, and actresses as purveyors of Enlightenment rhetoric. Students in a variety of fields in the liberal arts—including literature, rhetoric and writing, history, theater, and women's studies—can gain insight and inspiration from rhetorical analyses of eighteenth-century British protofeminism and the many women writers and performers this book describes.

Many of the themes addressed by eighteenth-century British women— restrictive gender roles; the inequities for women in courtship, marriage, divorce, and childrearing; the need for comprehensive education for girls; and women's desire for more fulfilling professional opportunities—still persist today as relevant feminine rhetorical topoi, and thus resonate strongly with twenty-first-century readers. This cultural relevance helps explain the reason for the present (booming) state of scholarship on eighteenth-century British women in literary and cultural studies. In contrast, the lack of women's representation within current histories of Enlightenment rhetoric stems partly from the legacy of classical rhetoric as a masculine discipline ensconced in elite intellectual history. As preparation for approaching and remedying this scholarly void, I will first review the current historical model of Enlightenment rhetorical theory and then suggest the application of feminist methodologies for studying Enlightenment rhetoric, particularly for analyzing women's rhetorics of this era.

Entering the Conversation

Geological metaphors convey the possibility of change even amid deeply entrenched habits of mind. Writing in 2001, Derek Hughes used the phrase "fissuring a monolith" to describe the impact of seventeenth- and eighteenth-century women writers on the British Enlightenment (8–9). Appearing for centuries as a solidly masculine body of cultural history, the Enlightenment upon closer study is heavily veined with traces of the feminine. The vast hegemony of the modern West has viewed the outcomes of the Enlightenment as enabling democratic capitalist civilization and life as we know it today, but a trend to question whether or not Enlightenment progress has been ethical or desirable has emerged over the last fifty years or so, as postmodern, Marxist, and feminist theorists have contested the validity of Enlightenment thinking. Although its critics claim that the Enlightenment's replacement of religion and monarchy with the newer authorities of science and business merely traded one set of biased, positivist narratives for another, many cultural historians of the Enlightenment believe these critical assessments are too narrow.

In the field of eighteenth-century studies over the past few decades, the notion of the Enlightenment as a monolithic intellectual movement of prominent white male philosophers has received further scrutiny (Roy Porter, J. G. A. Pocock, Clifford Siskin and William Warner, Sankar Muthu). As Porter has argued, it is now possible to see the Enlightenment writ large as "a revolution in mood . . . advanced by a range of protagonists, male and female, of various nationalities and discrete status, professional and interest groups" (3). Porter states, "In place of the old emphasis on superstars" scholars need to consider "wider enlightened circles" (11). But there are also reasons that the Enlightenment has been historicized as a tenaciously male-centric movement. As Rebecca Merrens explains, the culture of seventeenth-century England encompassed "the seemingly disparate discourse communities of literature, science, theology, and political philosophy [that] all worked to create a stable space for patriarchal authority by variously constraining, rejecting, and dissecting the feminine" (32). Countering these stable masculine spaces, feminist historians and literary scholars have re-visioned the European Enlightenment to more accurately portray the cultural contributions of women working, writing, socializing, and participating in public activities in the seventeenth and eighteenth centuries (Margaret Hunt, Michele Cohen, Karen O'Brien, Clarissa Orr, JoEllen DeLucia, and Anna Clark).

Recovery of the European women's Enlightenment has been a major project spanning many academic disciplines (literature, cultural history, women's studies) and national cultures (British, French, Spanish, for example). Publications, such as Taylor and Knott's magisterial collection *Women, Gender, and Enlightenment* and volumes 4 and 5 of *The History of British Women's Writing* series by Palgrave Macmillan have expanded our knowledge of the professional, political, intellectual, and social opportunities open to British women of the era while also emphasizing the limitations dictated by the combination of gender and social class.[3] There has been a recent surge in scholarship examining the multigenerational bluestocking culture and its connections to the English, Scottish, and French Enlightenment in works such as Elizabeth Eger's *Bluestockings: Women of Reason from Enlightenment to Romanticism,* Karen O'Brien's *Women and Enlightenment in Eighteenth-Century Britain,* JoEllen DeLucia's *Feminine Enlightenment: British Women Writers and the Philosophy of Progress, 1759–1820,* and Deborah Heller's collection *Bluestockings Now!: The Evolution of a Social Role.*[4] Many of these works touch on rhetorical theory and practice, although their primary focus is cultural and literary history.

Meanwhile, feminist historians working in the field of rhetoric and composition have expanded the coverage of women in the history of rhetoric. These scholars also have used geological metaphors to describe women's contributions to the history of rhetoric. In 2011, Jacqueline Jones Royster and Gesa Kirsh in *Feminist Rhetorical Practices* compared the changes wrought by feminist scholarship within the field of rhetoric and composition to "tectonic shifts" (17). As Royster and Kirsh explain, geological metaphors "offer generally familiar language for describing a historically under-interrogated academic terrain" (15). Expanding upon these geological metaphors, researchers in the history of rhetoric recently have adopted the metaphor of ecology to emphasize the human agents and actors within a cultural terrain. In *Rethinking Ethos*, Kathleen Ryan, Nancy Myers, and Rebecca Jones define *rhetorical ecology* as a method of rhetorical analysis focused on how "the rhetor accounts for her subject position relative to others, as well as shifting material, cultural, and historical situations circulating around rhetorical acts" (viii). In *Rhetorical Feminism and This Thing Called Hope*, Cheryl Glenn further develops the ecological model by surveying the history and present state of feminist rhetoric and rhetorical feminism as a vast and expanding organic continuum, characterized by cresting waves (first, second, third, fourth) of feminist activism, dialogue, and scholarly inquiry over time and across cultures.[5] This scholarship has allowed many advances in the history of rhetoric, especially of the nineteenth and twentieth centuries.

It is logical to imagine small waves of protofeminism appearing before the so-called first wave of feminism. Yet, the methods of feminist rhetorical ecology, which reimagine the conditions, methods, and practices of women and other subaltern speakers in broad cultural contexts, have yet to be applied to studies of Enlightenment rhetoric. Despite the recent surge in feminist scholarship in the history of rhetoric, researchers in the field of rhetoric have not tapped the immense mass of primary and secondary resources available on seventeenth- and eighteenth-century women writers, even as researchers working in Enlightenment literary and cultural studies are culling these materials meticulously. A sizable rift separates rhetoric from other areas of eighteenth-century studies. Evidentiary of this divide, the traditional masculine model of European Enlightenment rhetoric, as it was defined by twentieth-century scholars, such as Golden and Corbett, remains largely intact and exclusive of women.

Current anthologies and collections of rhetoric include only a few seventeenth- and eighteenth-century women who worked in traditional rhetorical genres, such as the treatise and the sermon—including Bathsua Makin on rhetorical education, Margaret Fell on women preaching in public, and Hannah More on conversation practices. In Michael Moran's *Eighteenth-Century British and American Rhetoricians*, which claims to cover "all major and many minor eighteenth-century British and American rhetoricians," for example, of the thirty-four brief academic biographies presented, only two are of women: Margaret Askew Fell and Mary Wollstonecraft (1). However, this assessment is far too narrow. As Linda Ferreira-Buckley notes in her article "The Eighteenth Century" in *The Present State of Historical Scholarship in the History of Rhetoric*, during the eighteenth century, the study of rhetoric extended beyond politicians, attorneys, clergy, and scholars to an activity practiced by "an increasing number of gentlewomen and gentlemen, and of course, the teachers, tutors, and governesses responsible for instructing them at home or at sundry educational institutions," as well as by "individuals—indeed whole factions" in formal and informal oral and written venues (115). New mixed-gender rhetorical venues and practices emerged in urban centers and spread across Western Europe. As historian Margaret Hunt explains, women's older oral traditions, including storytelling, competitive singing, and popular healing, existed "side-by-side" with the new "world of reading, writing, books, newspapers, commercialized concert going, opera, fine art, and the like," with the newer traditions rapidly dominating in urban areas while the older traditions persisted in rural areas (263). Consequently, evidence of women's rhetorical activity lies preserved in a wide variety of eighteenth-century manuscripts and print media, including treatises, letters, lecture notes, periodicals, pamphlets, petitions, plays, dedications, prologues, epilogues, poems, novels, and memoirs, and in other artistic and cultural artifacts of the period.

Scholars of the history of rhetoric know there is a gap to be filled and have clearly stated that women's contributions to Enlightenment rhetoric remain an understudied area. Tania Smith speculates that "a subculture favoring women's rhetorical education and practice was stronger than previously supposed" (351). As Thomas Miller notes, the "unprecedented number" of women who began to write and speak publicly in the eighteenth century offers myriad opportunities to study "the rhetorical practices that oppressed groups used to speak against prevailing conventions" (235). Linda Ferreira-Buckley recommends that the recovery of eighteenth-century women's rhetorics "should be a clear priority in the years ahead" (118). Jane Donawerth concurs and explains that "the trends and categories advanced by canonical histories of eighteenth- and nineteenth-century British and American rhetoric do not adequately account for the genres and strategies emphasized in women's rhetorical theory" (*Conversational Rhetoric* 41). In "Conversation and the Boundaries of Public Discourse in Rhetorical Theory by Renaissance Women," *Rhetorica (journal)*, Donawerth cites over a dozen scholarly studies on the history of women's speech-making and composition during the period 1600 to 1900; however, most of the studies Donawerth names cover nineteenth-century American women, and none focus on eighteenth-century British women (185.n1–5).

Although the volume of scholarship on eighteenth-century British women's rhetoric is slim, a small group of feminist scholars have made inroads. In her chapter on Hannah More's conversation theory, Donawerth contextualizes parameters for the bluestocking model of conversation and delineates it as eighteenth-century British women's rhetorical practice. Other scholarly studies on eighteenth-century British women's rhetoric include Christina Mason Sutherland's *Eloquence of Mary Astell;* multiple essays by Tania Smith on the rhetoric of Elizabeth Montagu, Hannah More, Hester Thrale Piozzi, Elizabeth Carter, and Catherine Talbot; and Miriam Brody's work on Mary Wollstonecraft, most specifically her article "The Vindication of the Writes of Women: Mary Wollstonecraft and Enlightenment Rhetoric." Additionally, Lindal Buchanan, Angela Escott, and I have contextualized eighteenth-century British actresses and women playwrights as protofeminist rhetors, and Lynée Gaillet has examined the rhetorical legacy of Susannah Wesley. Also, studies on the rhetoric of Mary Wollstonecraft, particularly her *Vindication of the Rights of Men* (1790) and *Vindication of the Rights of Women* (1792), have been done by Jamie Barlow, Anne K. Mellor, and Julie Monroe.[6] The body of work currently theorizing British women's Enlightenment rhetoric is a good start, but there is much more to do.

To further uncover the rhetorical activities of eighteenth-century British women, this study draws from and extends recovery efforts of feminist scholars working in eighteenth-century literary and cultural studies. A vast corpus of British women's writing, including an extensive body of rare published books and unpublished archived manuscripts increasingly available in digital form, awaits scholarly study for its rhetorical theories and practices. The twenty-first century has seen the publication of new critical editions and anthologies of eighteenth-century women authors, as well as databases and online tools such as Gale's Eighteenth Century Collections Online (ECCO), Adam Matthew Digital, and Texas A&M's 18thConnect, which provide access to numerous eighteenth-century texts in a wide array of genres, including essays, treatises, dialogues, defenses, letters, magazines, and other miscellaneous writings. The task of the scholar in search of women's Enlightenment rhetoric is also facilitated by numerous works of cultural and literary criticism in specialized journals and on websites dedicated to eighteenth-century studies and women's writing. With the ubiquity of digital access, scholars interested in women's Enlightenment rhetoric can now locate and view primary sources online and read about the social contexts surrounding these sources. The sheer volume of primary documents represents a massive and complex rhetorical ecology.

To help contextualize this body of historical material into a coherent textual terrain, this book relies on a set of specialized terms, starting with the phrase *progressive protofeminist women's rhetoric,* which I will break down and define here. By *progressive,* I am referring to a dual trend in Enlighten-ment thought toward liberatory and commercially motivated ideas and insti-tutions. Progressive thinking connoted both the movement toward the ideal of social class and gender equality and the pursuit of new capitalist economic models. I use the second term, *protofeminist* or *protofeminism,* to describe activities and ideas supporting women's rights and opportunities during the long eighteenth century (1660–1800) because this period obviously precedes the so-called first-wave of feminism that began in Britain in the latter half of the nineteenth century. As for the third term, *women,* this word collectively describes a socially constructed gender identity with a deep set of connota-tions, including a complexity of social roles and practices, that in eighteenth-century usage (and even today) maintains an underlying association with the female biological sex.[7] *Rhetoric,* the final term in the phrase, I define broadly as any nonviolent act of communication. Taking these words collectively as a term, by *progressive protofeminist women's rhetorics,* I mean any spoken, written, or embodied public performance, document, or display that occurred prior to the feminist movements of the nineteenth and early twentieth cen-turies and that argued for expanding the roles, rights, and opportunities for women within society. In other words, protofeminist women's rhetorics con-sist of pro-woman acts of persuasion before 1800, which were ideologically or economically motivated.

Another key term that I refer to throughout this text is *feminizing* or *femi-nization.* Cultural and literary scholars in eighteenth-century studies use *fem-inizing* to describe a modernizing trend "in which emotions are tempered by a feminine desire to reflect on the needs and feelings of others" (DeLucia 8). Similarly, *feminization* refers to a notable rise in the cultural significance of the woman. The usage of *feminization* as a term—at least as I have encountered it in the field of eighteenth-century studies—usually does not hold the negative connotation of something being devalued or weakened (although this conno-tation exists today).[8] Rather, the feminization of British culture in the early to mid-eighteenth century refers to a move toward virtue, a consideration of in-dividual feelings, and a civilizing influence on society. The eighteenth-century emphasis on the importance of feelings reflects not only the Enlightenment focus on cognition and sympathy but also a new type of feminine influence on mainstream cultural practices.[9] The feminization of Enlightenment culture is a well-documented phenomenon in the fields of literary and cultural history, but it has received little attention in the history of women's rhetoric.[10]

The gradual but steady feminization of the eighteenth-century British rhe-torical ecology is highlighted in this book's title: *Wit, Virtue, and Emotion.*

These words emphasize the appeals, or postures, that gained respect and became focal points of the rhetorical landscape. I argue that wit, virtue, and emotion are the primary postures of women's Enlightenment rhetoric and that they echo the Aristotelian elements of logos, ethos, and pathos. Through a wide range of writings across literary, ephemeral, public, and personal genres, the three postures of wit, virtue, and emotion built upon each other in a trajectory of overlapping, gendered rhetorical appeals.

The first posture, *wit,* originated as a masculine appeal denoting clever wordplay and evidence-based reasoning. Witty wordplay and solid reasoning were both considered masculine skills and essential displays of intellectual capital throughout the long eighteenth century. As Manushag N. Powell explains, "Wit happens, in part, when an author embraces his or her ability to construct a 'creditable' written expression of him or herself as an author worth hearing" (28). Thus, wit forms the mainstay of eighteenth-century ethos. Masculine wit, in the form of logical evidence, is the backbone of the treatise genre. Wit also denotes a confident style of conversing and punning, which often involves power metaphors, such as in this dialogue between two male libertine characters, Harcourt and Dorilant, in William Wycherley's outrageous comedy *The Country Wife* (1675):

> Harcourt: *Mistresses are like books:* if you pore upon them too much, they doze you and make you unfit for company, but if used discreetly, you are the fitter for conversation by 'em.
> Dorilant: *A mistress should be like a little country retreat near the Town,* not to dwell in constantly but only for a night and away, to taste the Town the better when a man returns.
> (Wycherley 1.1.236–42, italics added)

These misogynistic similes exhibit the swaggering and cavalier style of libertine wit and masculine domination. As I will show in chapters 1 and 2, women in the late seventeenth century purposefully appropriated this masculine rhetorical style and flipped it into powerful acts of protofeminist persuasion. In seventeenth- and eighteenth-century British culture, wit was a dangerous but important appeal for a woman to possess. Displays of wit were essential to feminine power; however, any woman who exuded wit, logic, and learning ran the risk of appearing unladylike.

The second posture of British women's Enlightenment rhetoric, *virtue,* was a universal, and increasingly multigendered, appeal. Virtue describes the demonstration of one's moral worth and lack of corruption, and, thus, was an intrinsic measure of credibility. Reversing the early modern trend of perceiving women as Eve-like (weak and depraved by original sin), over the course of the eighteenth century, virtue increasingly came to symbolize feminine strength. The combination of masculine wit and feminine virtue denoted a high capacity for moral reasoning. Women aspired to demonstrate wit balanced by virtue in their conversations and in their writings. This dual appeal became the tone and the path for women who desired to make and publish serious public statements about women's lack of opportunity and unequal position in society. Strong notes of wit and virtue are evident in women's treatises, defenses, plans, letters, poems, proposals, and many other written genres of complaint and protest.

The third posture, *emotion,* historically has been gendered as a womanly appeal. Emotion encompasses not only feminine expressions of mood but also the fine feelings of discernment that we commonly call "taste," a cultivated, sensitive, and moral understanding of human nature, of beauty, and especially of the arts and letters. Desirable in both the masculine and feminine genders, the notion of taste in the eighteenth century required expertise and education, and so the highest level of taste was thought to be that of the educated man; however, the intuitive feelings associated with taste were gendered as feminine traits. The rising public valuation of emotion inspired, and was inspired by, the increasing popularity of sentimentalism in literary and artistic culture in the latter half of the eighteenth century. Thus emotionality fueled the related late eighteenth-century cultural trend of sensibility, which involved strong displays of sympathy, love, friendship, compassion, and sometimes even fear. One emotion that was not acceptable in the realm of sensibility was that of anger or any other form of aggressive feeling and behavior by women.

Wit, virtue, and emotion as the ordered postures of British women's Enlightenment rhetoric, furthermore, illustrate a gradual shift in rhetorical ecology wherein the inherited *deep rhetoric* of early modern culture naturally and necessarily adjusted to more accurately represent changing beliefs about gender, class, and other stereotypes of identity and sociability, which—fixed as these may appear in any given era—are always in a state of metamorphosis.[11] In Enlightenment rhetoric, as in every rhetorical ecology, exigencies for change put constant pressures on deep rhetoric. Transformations of deep rhetoric are wrought by what I call *ground truth,* by which I mean real events that are empirically observable in the present moment and also often preserved in writing and visual images. While ground truths often reflect deep rhetoric, the two forces can also be at odds with each other when subversive events, identities, and activities stray away from mainstream ideology. Divergent ground truths can exert transformative influence on mainstream material practices, as shall become evident with British women's Enlightenment rhetoric.

Impressed by the new ideas of the Enlightenment, women working in intellectual and professional networks began to see themselves as cohesive groups with shared aims and interests. Applying the language of feminist rhetoric, we might view their collective situation somewhat like "members" of a "border tribe" within their local and national cultures, and note that they began to use "the ecology of speaking situations . . . to shift values determined by dominant [masculine] publics" (Ryan, Myers, and Jones 7). As education and literacy increased for eighteenth-century British women, their identities and methods for gaining ethos became more developed. Thus, women's Enlightenment rhetoric paved the way for more egalitarian education of the sexes, which enabled progressive social movements that later became associated with and supported by nineteenth-century feminism.

As I have stated, the exclusion of women from universities and other public rhetorical venues and the lack of texts by women conforming to the paradigms that currently constitute Enlightenment rhetorical theory are two reasons why the eighteenth century remains a neglected area in the history of women's rhetoric. A third barrier that also warrants mentioning is that nineteenth-century myths of femininity—such as the angel in the house and the cult of true womanhood—formed a deep rhetoric that cast the image of eighteenth-century women into a restrictive domestic sphere. Until recently, the nineteenth-century idealization of the woman's domestic role has served to erect inaccurate idols of feminine homogeneity and to neglect the range of activities performed by real eighteenth-century women.

One more impediment to the investigation of eighteenth-century British women's rhetorical activities is the current and historical scholarly framework for describing Enlightenment rhetoric, a model that I refer to as the fivefold paradigm of Enlightenment rhetoric. The remainder of this introduction provides a working definition of the fivefold paradigm, discusses the limitations of this paradigm with respect to women's rhetorics, and proposes feminist ecology as a more effective model for studying women's contributions to Enlightenment rhetoric.

The Fivefold Paradigm of Enlightenment Rhetoric

In the late twentieth century, scholars of Enlightenment rhetoric divided works by seventeenth- and eighteenth-century Western European (male) academics into a fourfold paradigm consisting of the *neoclassical, belletristic, elocutionary,* and *philosophical epistemic* movements of rhetoric (Howell; Golden and Corbett; Horner; Bizzell and Herzberg; Kennedy; Moran; Sloan; Gaillet).[12] Both the second and third editions of Bizzell and Herzberg's *Rhetorical Tradition* contain chapters on Enlightenment rhetoric, describing it as consisting of these four overlapping movements—with the recent addition of *conversation* as a fifth feminine movement associated with women's rhetoric. Similar content appears in other anthologies under the category of eighteenth-century rhetoric with these same paradigmatic divisions. The original fourfold paradigm is especially useful for comparing the theoretical components of Enlightenment rhetoric to those of classical rhetoric, including similarities such as their close connection to philosophy; adherence to five canons (invention, arrangement, style, memory, and delivery); and view of rhetoric as a formal, civic, and masculine occupation.

However, in contrast to classical rhetoric, each movement of the fourfold paradigm of Enlightenment rhetoric tends, in its own way, to deemphasize lofty style and the profusion of rhetorical tropes and to advocate more for plain or perspicuous style and an individualized approach to crafting discourse for particular audiences and occasions. During the long eighteenth century, the purview of rhetoric broadened to include not just formal oratory but "all forms of discourse [as] rhetorical," and to encompass "the study of correct grammar and syntax, appropriate style and diction for types of discourse or occasions for speaking, taste or standards of literary and moral judgement, and the means of effective communication in general" (Bizzell and Herzberg 806). Toward these ends, the fourfold approach of studying Enlightenment rhetoric begins with the neoclassical foundation (based on classical rhetoric's models for speakers, audiences, appeals, and tropes) and then proceeds to view belletristic, elocutionary, and philosophical-epistemic developments, including new ideas about human understanding and will, and of virtue as the hallmark of good taste. Scholarship on the fourfold paradigm illustrates an increasing range of possible styles and occasions for rhetoric during the Enlightenment but still gives little attention to nontraditional genres, venues, and speakers.

British women's rhetorical practices during the age of Enlightenment most often fell well outside the generic and academic boundaries that define the fourfold categorical paradigm. The most significant revision to this paradigm is the *conversation* movement, which feminist scholars of the early twenty-first century identified as a fifth, predominantly feminine, movement. This addition has occurred in the past twenty years in the work of Jane Donawerth, Christina Mason Sutherland, and Tania Smith who have identified *cirmo* or *sermo* (Latin for *conversation*) as a separate and distinct form of Enlightenment rhetoric appropriated from the humanist tradition by seventeenth-century European women intellectuals and adapted to protofeminist forms of persuasion throughout the eighteenth century. With the addition of conversation, the canonical landscape of Enlightenment rhetoric has broadened from a fourfold into a fivefold paradigm, which is now more inclusive of women. However helpful, this categorical model inevitably imposes some inaccurate subdivisions. To help tease out some of the overlap, I offer a brief explanation of each movement.

First, the *neoclassical* movement, a tradition inherited from French rhetorical theory such as Fenelon's *Dialogues sur l' Eloquence* (1717), generally upholds the Aristotelian/Ciceronian focus on the public man as orator. British neoclassical theories of rhetoric adapt the five classical canons of invention, arrangement, style, memory, and delivery for usage in the English language and combine classical ideas with empiricism, rationalism, and a new branch of study known as natural philosophy (later psychology).[13] Eighteenth-century neoclassical treatises on rhetoric include John Holmes's *Art of Rhetoric* (1739), John Lawson's *Lectures concerning Oratory* (1752), and John Ward's *Systems of Oratory* (1759). Few eighteenth-century British women wrote academic treatises like these, and only two known works—the anonymously authored *The Lady's Rhetoric* and Mary Astell's *Serious Proposal to the Ladies, Part II*—are dedicated solely to theorizing the rhetorical practices of women.

The *belletristic* movement, which also developed from French neoclassical rhetoric, focuses on rhetorical theory's intersections with the criticism of the literary, liberal, and fine arts. Belletristic theory combines the study of rhetoric, poetics, and aesthetics with painting, architecture, drama, art, and history—all of the disciplines concerned with and requiring knowledge of taste, style, and criticism—under the umbrella of belles lettres.[14] Belletristic theory gained popularity in conjunction with early eighteenth-century British works on virtue and taste by Anthony Ashley Cooper, Third Earl of Shaftesbury, and Frances Hutcheson but reached its greatest scholarly expression in the latter half of the century when Scottish intellectuals, including Adam Smith, David Hume, Hugh Blair, and Lord Kames published philosophical treatises on rhetoric, taste, and belles lettres.[15] Bluestocking women were heavily involved in the discourse on belletristic theories and their applications to literature, art, and architecture. Montagu's *Dialogues of the Dead* (1760) and *An Essay on the Writings and Genius of Shakespeare* (1769) are two examples of bluestocking-authored works concerning belletristic topics. Critics of the belletristic approach, however, saw it devolve into the purview of amateur scholars, autodidacts, and "learned ladies."

The *elocutionary* movement presents a third paradigm, one that is focused on the principles, practices, and professional uses of oratory. Derived from the classical term *elocutio*, which stood for "style" in Roman rhetorical theory, the eighteenth-century term *elocution* came rather to mean "delivery or performance." Enlightenment elocution was largely gendered as masculine and tied to civic duty. Works of British elocutionary theory, including Thomas Sheridan's *Lectures on Elocution* (1763) and *Lectures on Reading* (1775), John Walker's *Elements of Elocution* (1781), and Gilbert Austin's *Chironomia or, Treatise on Rhetorical Delivery* (1806), focused on voice and body control to achieve the most persuasive and effective oratory. The elocution theorists drew their examples from the contemporary theatrical stage as well as from ancient descriptions of classical orators. Thus, the first English actresses are important, but little credited, contributors to this movement.

The fourth paradigm consists of what was then a new branch of rhetorical theory that emerged in late eighteenth-century Britain, which Golden and Corbett have identified as the *philosophical epistemic* movement. This heavily theoretical movement, also known as the *new rhetoric*, focused on moral reasoning and the will of the audience. Influenced by Bacon, Locke, and Hume, examples of this theoretical model include Adam Smith's *Theory of Moral Sentiments* (1759), Thomas Reid's *Inquiry into the Human Mind, on the Principles of Common Sense* (1764), and George Campbell's *Philosophy of Rhetoric* (1776). Exemplary of the *new rhetoric*, Campbell aligns rhetoric with the new discipline of psychology and its scientific analysis of the processes of the mind.[16] As the collections of their letters show, Bluestockings Elizabeth Montagu, Elizabeth Carter, and Catherine Talbot were highly informed readers and contemporaries of the Scottish Enlightenment philosophers who were the chief proponents of the new rhetoric. Montagu corresponded regularly with Lord Kames, and Talbot composed works of protofeminist Christian philosophy, which Carter published after Talbot's death.

The Bluestockings are also a central focus of the *conversation* movement that scholars now recognize as a fifth, and feminine, branch of Enlightenment rhetoric. Rooted in the humanist genres of the dialogue, the defense, and the philosophical letter, conversation became a socially acceptable form for women's participation in private intellectual debates and correspondence. Feminist scholars trace conversation, as a semiformal, private rhetorical practice back to the rhetorical theory of Mary Astell at the beginning of the eighteenth century and even further to seventeenth-century Parisian salons.[17] Salon conversation practices continued throughout the eighteenth century with Bluestockings such as Elizabeth Montagu, Elizabeth Talbot, Elizabeth Carter, Frances Burney, and Hannah More. The claiming of conversation as a rhetorical movement has opened a window into women's contributions to seventeenth- and eighteenth-century rhetoric. In *The Eloquence of Mary Astell*, Sutherland describes *sermo* as the feminine milieu of eighteenth-century rhetoric. Donawerth's most recent book, *Conversational Rhetoric: The Rise and Fall of a Women's Tradition, 1600–1900,* characterizes many forms of women's spoken and written interactions as conversation and examines "significant moments" in which seventeenth-, eighteenth-, and nineteenth-century women adapt conversation theory to informal, small-group rhetoric by "looking at details of each woman's life and each moment's era, registering the differences as well as the similarities" (9–10).

However, more recently David Randall's *Conversational Enlightenment: The Reconceptualization of Rhetoric in Eighteenth-Century Thought* argues that conversation, as a feminized and democratizing rhetorical form, became the most ubiquitous practice of Enlightenment rhetoric among both genders, eclipsing oratory and formal philosophical dialogue during the course of the eighteenth century. Randall's thesis on the centrality of conversation to Enlightenment rhetoric as a whole complicates its designation as a special category of Enlightenment rhetoric reserved for women and thereby exposes this notion as an oversimplification. While the deep rhetoric of the eighteenth century deemed conversation the only appropriate rhetorical milieu for women's speech, delineating conversation as a movement strictly of women's rhetoric implies an artificial boundary. The "conversation movement" effectively isolates women's body of work and their concerns from the larger culture and exacerbates the problems of overlap and exclusion inherent in the original fourfold paradigm.

Furthermore, although the divisions of the fivefold paradigm usefully organize major trends in Enlightenment rhetorical theory, this model strains to fit works, authors, and practitioners neatly into prescribed categories. Even without the addition of conversation theory, the original four divisions "do not serve well as fixed categories into which we can unambiguously place individual treatises" (H. L. Ulman 5). The ambiguity of this system of classification is apparent in works that theorize across the paradigms, such as works that cover literary tropes (a focus of neoclassical rhetoric) as well as literary aesthetics and taste (a focus of belles lettres). Thomas Miller adds that the four paradigms do not align with the eighteenth-century practice of oratory, noting that "the epistemological emphases of the 'new' rhetoric have tended to overshadow the civic relations of rhetoric and moral philosophy" and "how citizens translate received beliefs into practical action to address public needs" (228).[18] The current paradigms are more focused on rhetorical theory than rhetorical practice, which creates a methodological limitation by excluding nonacademic materials, such as ephemeral and performative examples of protofeminist Enlightenment rhetoric.

The overall inability of the fivefold paradigm to accurately describe women's Enlightenment rhetoric exposes the limitations of such categorizations and serves as an entrée to try differing approaches. Traditional tactics of recovering figures and movements through the close reading of treatises and essays, while still valid, should be accompanied by interdisciplinary methods that can help to identify historical materials related to progressive forms of women's communication and persuasion and to contextualize the social relationships, networks, and communities that promoted the expansion of women's roles, rights, and professional life within the societies that they inhabited, and for posterity.

New Methods for Studying Women's Rhetorics

New methodologies for exploring women's rhetorics, such as venue-based, cultural materialist, thematic, and reception research, are now available, and researchers have employed them successfully in many studies of nineteenth-, twentieth-, and twenty-first- century women's rhetorics. However, as Kate Ronald observes, with respect to new methods centering on rhetorical sites and strategies, "Nineteenth-century North American rhetoric predominates" (145). The comparative neglect of British eighteenth-century women by rhetoric and composition scholars may stem from the fact that researchers in the field have more access, experience, and interests related to the history of American rhetoric, but the existence of considerably more and lengthier studies of classical women's rhetoric (Jarratt, Swearingen, Graban) and Renaissance European women's rhetoric (Lunsford, Glenn, Donawerth, Wertheimer) seem to undercut this rationale. Over the past twenty years, new methodologies in feminist rhetorical historiography have made possible the rediscovery not just of female figures to add to the existing canon but previously unidentified realms and forms of women's rhetoric.

Several strong examples of venue-based and interdisciplinary scholarship on nineteenth-century women's rhetorics inform my approach. First, in her groundbreaking work on American women's rhetoric *Gender and Rhetorical Space in American Life: 1866–1910*, Nan Johnson focuses on the *cultural site* instead of concentrating on select figures (1). Johnson makes an important point: not all historic women's rhetoric is feminist liberation rhetoric; much of it involves particular groups of women finding voices and the means to speak within their cultural circumstances. Cultural context is also a major factor in Lindal Buchanan's *Regendering Delivery: The Fifth Canon and Antebellum Women Rhetors*, in which she recommends examination of six topoi:

education—the rhetor's training in delivery; *access* to public platforms; *space* between a rhetor and her audience(s) as a physical tool for managing audiences' perceptions; *genre* and its accessibility and taboos in relation to gender; *body* language and gendered physical attributes involved in delivery; and *rhetorical career* or the impact of public speaking skills and professions on women's lives (160–63).

Carolyn Skinner applies a similar heuristic focused on the rhetorical speaker in *Women Physicians and Professional Ethos in Nineteenth-Century America* in which she analyzes "education and professional affiliations, the professional's performance of expertise, authority, and status in rhetorical interactions with colleagues, patient/clients, and the public" (9). Like Buchanan, Skinner stresses the importance of considering situatedness and public perception in studying women's professional ethos. Skinner asserts that we can better understand professional women's "struggle to claim a persuasive ethos" by analyzing the accessibility of the communication medium to women, the attitudes about women in professions at that time, the negotiation of moral values between the woman speaker and the audience, and the power of the genre to grant rhetorical authority that supersedes the normal gender identity of the woman speaker (173–177). Skinner's and Buchanan's topoi are productive for understanding how cultural sites, professional institutions, and social mores impact a speaker's delivery. As Skinner notes, women as "marginalized speakers and writers have developed persuasive ethe despite the belief that they were not supposed to be effective or authoritative communicators" (Skinner 4). Success as a speaker, or a writer, begins with a belief in oneself, a concept that we take for granted today but that traces back to the Enlightenment philosophy of individualism.

In addition to methods focused on speakers and contexts of delivery, another type of feminist methodology that informs my research is the study of rhetoric's effects after initial delivery, in other words, how acts of persuasion extend beyond the immediate rhetorical situation. For example, Jessica Enoch's article "Releasing Hold: Feminist Historiography without the Tradition" explores remembering and gendering as two methods of analysis in the study of women's rhetoric. Enoch's first paradigm, remembering, is a material approach concerned with objects of public memory and the rhetorical purposes driving the historical preservation of women's stories. The second paradigm, gendering, as Enoch explains, "relies on discursive, material, and embodied articulations and performances that create and disturb gendered distinctions, social categories, and asymmetrical power relationships" and extends beyond the human body to "a host of historical subjects, spaces, and activities" (68–69). Enoch explicitly connects her notion of gendering to Judith Butler's theory of gender as performance, citing Butler's argument that masculinity and femininity are social constructions of identity that can and will change over time. The human body, as Butler argues, is "a surface whose permeability is politically regulated," and "the various acts of gender create the idea of gender" (2499–2500). As Royster and Kirsch also note, in recent decades gender studies has moved well "beyond female-male binaries" to consider a wide repertoire of "social, political, and cultural realities of gender" (44). Gender studies as a postmodern field recognizes that individual gendered performance and gender fluidity have always coexisted as factors of the rhetorical ecology, alongside hegemonic norms of gender, in all cultures and historical ages.[19] The study of gendering is highly pertinent to my project for examining repeated progressive acts, which slowly granted more rhetorical power for women within the Enlightenment rhetorical ecology.

The transference of rhetoric over time is yet another phenomenon that feminist researchers have studied. The concept of rhetorical accretion examines the effects and later appropriations of persuasive performances and displays. As Vicki Tolar Collins describes in "The Speaker Respoken: Material Rhetoric as Feminist Methodology," rhetorical accretion consists of the ripples of intended meanings that occur during reception and the appropriation and repackaging of a rhetorical performance by others, such as publishers and critics. The study of rhetorical accretion is particularly important when the speaker has no direct power. Women and other marginalized groups have made persuasive impressions by repeated linguistic and bodily displays, which then carry forward beyond the original audience to other groups. By expanding the focus of her study beyond the immediate rhetorical performance, Collins investigates larger rhetorical impacts. Collins's work, in fact, presages recent ecological methodologies, such as reading a rhetor's ethos as interruption, advocacy, and relation (Ryan, Myers, and Jones).

Keeping in mind these site-based, performative, and ecological analyses, my study follows other feminist historians of rhetoric in taking a context-driven approach. Using a combination of primary materials from the late seventeenth and the eighteenth centuries, along with current scholarly analyses from the fields of eighteenth-century historical, literary, and cultural studies, I conduct a rhetorical analysis of new and traditional British women's roles, and their written and embodied methods of persuasive communication, across the long eighteenth century. My undertaking has involved a decade-long journey in research, encompassing a broad array of venues, public and private, in search of, as Andrea Lunsford suggests, the "forms, strategies and goals used by women as rhetorical" (6). In order to situate women from diverse backgrounds, professions, and social statuses into the larger conversations of British Enlightenment rhetoric, my methodology involves working with their primary texts, as well as secondary analyses of their lives and work, to identify significant sites, occasions, delivery methods, and watershed moments of progressive protofeminist persuasion.

Like Johnson, my method of recovery centers on the *cultural sites* that created opportunities for women's rhetoric. By cultural sites, I mean the physical space of the rhetorical venue, be it a place of real-time live performance or the virtual performance enacted by a written document that a speaker produces at one point in time that is then later received by readers. My examination adapts Lindal Buchanan's methodology of studying rhetorical delivery as "a regendered fifth canon [that] . . . views rhetorical performance as the moment when dominant cultural values are enacted and, sometimes, are resisted and revised" (160). These performances may be oral or written, but, by keeping in mind the sites of delivery and reception, I attend to context and to audience as much as to text.

To consider the broader ecology in which protofeminist rhetorical sites operated, I use gendering as a method to examine the sociopolitical contexts and the deep rhetoric that regulated the sites. To show the ground truth and trajectories of women's rhetoric amid the larger ecology of the Enlightenment, my study interprets rhetorical accretions, which I see as not only the appropriation of rhetorical theory and performance by women rhetoricians but also as the audience's reception of women's rhetoric. By examining selected cultural artifacts, excerpts of primary texts, and anecdotes regarding speakers, audiences, and messages, my feminist methodology deconstructs rhetorical venues in which women operated and the accepted traditional feminine roles of queen, courtier, and mother, as well as innovative identities of actress, woman writer, and woman intellectual or learned lady. While broad and holistic coverage of British women's rhetoric in the age of Enlightenment is my mission, the sheer volume of spoken, written, and embodied discourse that is available for study requires some restriction of scope. My focus is on predominantly secular rather than religious rhetorical performances. Although Quaker and Methodist women did lead as rhetorical speakers in their communities, preaching and church venues are beyond the scope of this study. However, many eighteenth-century British women claimed spiritual ethos and their duty to God as a defense for speaking out in secular contexts to argue on topics that were not primarily theological, such as women's moral virtue, expansion of women's roles, and the societal need for education and professional opportunities for women. This study also does not examine the voices of Others that may have emerged from colonial counterflow, which brought women of color and other immigrants to the British Isles during the long eighteenth century. In selecting my examples for study, I have gravitated to those venues, speakers, acts, and artifacts that are striking and exemplary for their performance, argumentation, debate, dialogue, or deliberation of Enlightenment values by, to, or focused on British women.

While some of these women were successful in publishing arguments in the masculine genres of the treatise and other traditional rhetorical forms, many more adopted feminine forms of communication, such as conversation, letters, novels, journals, and other literary projects, for rhetorical and didactic purposes. Still others took a more performative approach to persuasion through acting, teaching, leading or speaking at salons and clubs, and even through fashion statements. However, the theoretical notions of equality that emerged in the discourse of the British Enlightenment did not guarantee that all people, and certainly not all women, were granted equal public access. The opportunities that women had to participate in venues for rhetoric were dependent on their social class, family, professional, religious, and political affiliations; their occupations, education, and pastimes; and even their physical appearance and personality traits.

Chapter Previews

My coverage of British women's Enlightenment rhetoric focuses predominantly on women and sites in England; however, I consider Irish and Scottish women's rhetorical practices and theoretical influences of the Scottish Enlightenment when they appear as factors in the British Enlightenment rhetorical ecology writ large. Hence, I use the designation "British" to describe the cultural breadth of my study.

In chapter 1, "A Revolution in Mood: Emblems, Embodiment, and Ephemera," I focus on the effects of the British social hierarchy on women's everyday lives and their possibilities to find public voices. I argue that political gendering of the monarchy and in party politics directly impacted traditional and evolving eighteenth-century feminine gender roles and embodied and ephemeral women's rhetoric, which occurred in common, everyday public activities.

In chapter 2, "On the Stage: Dramatized Women's Rhetoric," I analyze the Restoration theatre as a groundbreaking site of gendered rhetorical delivery and the first generation of British actresses as early deliverers of British women's Enlightenment rhetoric. In their collaborations with leading playwrights, the actresses embodied the complexity of women's issues, channeling critical attention toward their subservient and dependent status in patriarchal society. Following the immense popularity of the actresses, in the latter half of the eighteenth century, London's public debate forums opened up to include rhetorical performance by women debaters.

Chapter 3, "In Sociable Venues: Clubs, Salons, and Debating Societies," compares the rhetorical situations of women in the middle-class public debating societies to those of the highbrow, semiprivate Bluestocking salons. Debating societies as profit-driven, open commercial forums admitted all who could afford the price of entry and entertained subjects of concern to the middle class, including the topics of gendered manners, roles, professions, and legal rights. In contrast, the elite Bluestockings met in the private drawing rooms of wealthy hostesses for intellectual conversations chiefly focused on the aesthetics and stylistics of belles lettres and high culture.

In chapter 4, "On the Page: Written Rhetoric and Arguments about Education," I analyze how women authors and readerships developed into significant rhetorical elements of British society during the eighteenth century. Increased literacy, both in reading and writing, marks the most profound intellectual development for girls and women in the age of Enlightenment. To show how rising literacy allowed new venues of women's rhetoric, I present a case study of women authors' participation in Enlightenment arguments about education models and theories of rhetorical education.

Conclusion

Recent feminist re-visioning of eighteenth-century social and literary history has greatly expanded the historical assessment of women's roles in the British Enlightenment. The many recent discoveries about women and the Enlightenment have not, however, greatly impacted current histories of Enlightenment rhetoric. The most significant feminist revision has been the addition of conversation as a fifth movement that has expanded the traditional fourfold paradigm. While the conversation movement has helped to recover rhetorical theory by select figures, such as Mary Astell and Hannah More, there is more to women's Enlightenment rhetoric than conversation theory. Women's methods of speaking and writing, as well as the venues in which women drew gender to the forefront of public consciousness in Enlightenment Britain, shaped feminine identity and social standing during the long eighteenth century. New rhetorical venues, opportunities, and technologies available to women, as well as men, contributed to a surge in feminine voices.

With ideas of alternative protofeminist rhetorical performance in mind, *Wit, Virtue, and Emotion: British Women's Enlightenment Rhetoric* analyzes the unprecedented influence British women's communicative acts and theories had over the course of the long eighteenth century. The numerous socioeconomic changes in British society during this era, coupled with the simultaneous infusion of feminization into Enlightenment culture, in effect, opened many avenues for women's rhetorics even as dominant patriarchal institutions strove to strengthen and commercialize existing masculine power structures. Sites of eighteenth-century women's rhetoric were ubiquitous public, semipublic, and domestic spaces, including real-time performative venues (such as theaters, salons, clubs, and tea tables), as well as the recorded and distributed rhetorical space of print genres and publications.

In examining protofeminist Enlightenment rhetoric, I take the "feminist ecological approach" recommended by Ryan, Myers, and Jones, in which the researcher asks "what does it mean to act in the world as a woman, a feminist, an ecological thinker?" (viii). Applying this question to late seventeenth-century and early eighteenth-century British women rhetors invites analyses of stationary physical locations, such as performance spaces, salons, and debate halls, but also portable delivery platforms (such as books, treatises, and other print publications) as well as shared letters and unpublished manuscripts. Whether we describe it as ecological, site-based, or historiographic, feminist research in the history of rhetoric is often interdisciplinary, situated, and materially complex. As David Gold argues, "Rhetoric and composition historiography must not simply recover neglected writers, teachers, locations, and institutions, but must also demonstrate connections between these subjects and larger scholarly conversations" (17). Jessica Enoch further recommends, "Rather than working toward canonical revision, . . . envision a broader historiographic end: interrogating the dynamic relationships among rhetoric, gender, and history" (60). Applying feminist rhetorical research methods, I have found that women, as the largest subaltern group in late seventeenth- and eighteenth-century Britain, slowly and organically coalesced into a self-conscious, multilayered counterpublic and developed distinctive rhetorical identities and practices tied to the new ideals of the Enlightenment.

In contextualizing women's rhetorics within the major topics of Enlightenment debate, this book analyzes unique historical moments within the broader cultural landscapes, re-visioning what counts as Enlightenment rhetoric. *Wit, Virtue, and Emotion: British Women's Enlightenment Rhetoric* considers a broad range of source materials in order to illuminate the persuasive techniques of women in a complicated era of rising protofeminism countered by ongoing antifemale strictures and suppression of women's speech. This analysis informs our understanding of British women's rhetoric after the Renaissance and up to the nineteenth century. My work seeks to uncover and remember more about the evolution of protofeminist persuasion and to show that deep rhetoric, while firmly rooted in historic traditions, is constantly shaped by the ground truth of individual lives and the performative forces of gender, speech, writing, and education.

CHAPTER 1

A Revolution in Mood: Emblems, Embodiment, and Ephemera

As Nature teaches us Logic, so does it instruct us in Rhetoric.
—Mary Astell, *A Serious Proposal to the Ladies, Part II*, 1697

*A*STELL'S PITHY CLAIM—THAT the principles of rhetoric are inherent in our perception of nature—is beautiful in its simplicity. The straightforward logic of her statement exemplifies her style in *Serious Proposal,* in which she clearly and directly appeals to women readers to educate themselves and to put literacy and effective communication at the forefront of that education. Ruth Perry calls Astell "a true Enlightenment thinker" whose intellectual talents elevated her from her middle-class station and gained her "a kind of social equivalence" with the prominent aristocratic women of her day (358). Astell clearly advocated for women's intellectual capabilities, but she also rejected many tenets of mainstream Enlightenment thought, causing Perry, as her biographer, to conclude that Astell's "place in the Enlightenment is a complicated one" (367).

Hailing from the gentry class of Newcastle in northern England, Astell's family included guildsmen of the coal industry (as her father was) and Anglican clergymen, such as her uncle Peter who was also her tutor; however, both men died when Astell was a teenager, thereby leaving the women of the family well educated but impoverished, and Astell determined to "earn her living by her pen" (Sutherland xi-xiii). At the age of twenty-one, she traveled to London and successfully petitioned William Sancroft, Archbishop of Canterbury, for patronage; she then began to publish serious intellectual works and gained access to highly educated female members of London's nobility with whom she shared a great interest in Anglican piety (Perry 66; Sutherland xii-xiii). With her success as a professional writer and philosophical theorist, Astell provides a central starting place for the discussion of British women's Enlightenment rhetoric.

Yet as a politically conservative Tory Anglican, Astell's philosophical stance ran counter to that of many early eighteenth-century English Enlightenment thinkers, most prominently John Locke. At the turn of the eighteenth century, Locke was the most celebrated British intellectual and the leading proponent of new ideas about empirical reasoning. His *Essay Concerning Human*

Understanding (1689) rejects theories of innate human knowledge and instead proposes the mind as a *tabula rasa* at birth; based on methods of empirical observation and analysis, Locke's treatise makes radical claims (for his time) about natural human equality and cognitive learning, which he soon after extended to politics in his *Two Treatises on Government* (1690). In *Serious Proposal to the Ladies for the Advancement of Their True and Greatest Interest, Part I* (1694), Astell acknowledges the merits of Locke's egalitarian principles of moral reasoning; however, as a member of the Cambridge Neoplatonist intellectual circle and a devout Anglican, she found Locke's epistemological arguments incompatible with the unity of a perfect Christian God. In opposition to Astell, Damaris Cudworth Masham (1658–1708) and Catherine Trotter Cockburn (1679–1749) published treatises supporting Locke.[1] Masham's anonymously published *Discourse concerning the Love of God* (1696) directly responds to Astell while Trotter Cockburn's *Defence of the 'Essay of Human Understanding,' Written by Mr. Lock* (1702) responds to another critic of Locke's, Thomas Burnet, and makes an ethical argument for the compatibility of Locke's empirical theories of reason with existence of innate virtue (O'Brien 50). In these works, Astell, Masham, and Cockburn exemplify the dialogic nature of early eighteenth-century public intellectual discourse. Following Locke's lead, their works employ plain style, masculine wit, and rational argumentation, but they also maintain feminine propriety through commitment to virtue and piety.

As within the distinct circles of the Lockeans and the Neoplatonists, women's rhetoric developed along with the many diverse topics of British Enlightenment discourse, consistently appending the conversation with protofeminist arguments for women's moral worth, cognitive capabilities, and rights to education. Despite their voices and presence, however, even elite and educated women held a subservient place in the social order of eighteenth-century British patriarchy. Law and social decorum limited the public voice of all women by restricting them from access to traditional rhetorical sites. Thus, while Astell could publish a treatise challenging Locke, she could not join the Royal Society nor teach at Cambridge University. Nevertheless, over the course of the long eighteenth century, women's opportunities for engaging in rhetoric increased as ideas about gender were influenced by new Enlightenment models of government and economics, the emergence of a commercial literary marketplace, and the values of the growing middle-class.

The purpose of this chapter is to provide a historical foundation from which to explore the scope and forms of progressive protofeminist discourse of the British long eighteenth century as spoken, written, and embodied by real women of a variety of backgrounds. It is not my goal, nor would it be possible, to cover all venues, arguments, and discourse communities in which protofeminist rhetoric occurred. Rather, I examine trends in rhetorical gendering across the social hierarchy and analyze gendered symbolism, roles, sociability, and ephemera throughout the rhetorical landscape. In order to trace the progress of gendering and gendered symbolism, I apply Jessica Enoch's suggestion to "interrogate . . . the complicated imbrication of rhetoric, gender, and history" (72). I begin by showing that the demeanor and gender of the British monarchs offered an embodied rhetoric at the top tier of the social spectrum and set the tone for the political gendering of national identity. Widening my focus beyond court culture, I then consider how the feminizing trend that commenced at the top of the social hierarchy expanded gender roles for women across the British rhetorical ecology, including greater rhetorical agency for the established yet evolving role of the mother. Feminization within eighteenth-century British culture also gave rise to new professions for women and protofeminist rhetorical sites for spoken, written, and embodied women's rhetorics. To delineate my review, I use the common subperiod designations of the Restoration era (1660s to 1680s), the post-Glorious Revolution era (1688 to 1720s), and the Georgian period (1720s to 1800). While these periods overlap in many aspects of culture, this overall three-part division provides a general framework for discussing trends in gendering and feminization that shaped British women's Enlightenment rhetoric.

Political Gendering: From Sexuality to Politeness

Sex and politics (and sexual politics) drive the life of a community more than we often care to admit. The social construction of gender roles and their associations to cultural institutions and political hierarchies persist as natural forces in an ongoing cycle of sociability. Over the course of the British long eighteenth century, the trajectory of political gendering—the hierarchal associations of gendered bodies, behaviors, and ideologies—moved from a staunchly masculine political ethos to one infused with feminine metaphors and imagery. Scholars from across the humanities identify a symbolic feminizing trend in eighteenth-century English society (Staves 155–156; Hughes 8–9; Marsden 169–70; Orr 3–4; Randall 6, 8, 43–52). The transformation of political symbolism from an aggressively masculine to a politely feminine ethos stemmed, in part, from the personalities of the people in power, most prominently the British monarch, but also those who occupied positions in the royal family, the aristocratic court, and parliament.

During the long eighteenth century, women were present as members of all these socially prestigious categories, except that of parliament. British law restricted parliamentary positions by only allowing British citizens (which at that time meant only property-owning males who were born in England) to occupy seats. Roy Porter notes, the "post-Puritan ruling order" during the long eighteenth century reflected the trauma of the recent civil war, making "England both the most modern and . . . counterrevolutionary state in Europe" (32). Anxiously and consciously, the world's first two-party political system—the Tories and the Whigs—arose in England and, quite interestingly, adopted metaphorical patterns of gendering as part of their political identities. While the Tories identified with the masculinity and aristocratic traditions symbolized by the king, the Whig party increasingly embraced femininity as an emblem of civilized progress. The metaphorical gendered rhetoric of party politics, along with the embodied gender of the monarch, influenced popular perceptions and discourse about gender roles. However, the deep rhetoric around Britain's long-established social classes, which rigidly adhered to the concept of the great chain of being inherited from the Renaissance era, also remained an ingrained part of national culture. This included the well-known hierarchy of aristocratic titles and ranks. (For an ordered list of the titles and ranks of British aristocratic women, see appendix B: Table of Precedency among Ladies.)

At the very top tier of the social ladder, the monarch (queen or king) embodied a gendered persona that helped shape the ethos of the dominant culture, permeating the tenor and mood of the royal court and the English people at each level of the social class structure, from the aristocracy, down through the gentry, to the middle and lower classes. Dating back to the Renaissance, the monarch functioned as a gendered *emblem* and an embodiment of the hegemony of British society.[2] From 1660 to 1800, England was ruled by a total of eight successive monarchs (six men and two women) whose personas presented an emblematic and embodied rhetoric for the nation. In the Restoration era, the dominant persona was that of the witty libertine, a masculine type emblematic of Charles II and his court. However, a major cultural shift following the Glorious Revolution of 1688 resulted in the exaltation of polite manners and feminine emblems of virtue, a trend that persisted throughout the eighteenth century. Across the long eighteenth century, not only monarchs but also parliament cultivated ethos through gendered emblems, which often functioned as politically branded performances of morality.

In 1660, the restoration of the English monarchy, after the nation spent eleven years as a Puritan Protestant Commonwealth republic, stands as a landmark masculine emblem of England's traditional aristocratic patriarchy. The ascension of Charles II of the royal house of Stuart to the English throne returned England to a hereditary monarchy system of government and brought dramatic change, which was in some ways progressive but in others recidivate. During the Commonwealth era, which followed the English Civil War, English society lived under martial law and conformed to the strict religious principles of Puritanism—public theaters remained closed, and gambling and dancing were prohibited. Upon his restoration as monarch, Charles II reinstated Anglicanism as the official religion of England, reopened the theaters, and inaugurated a more socially permissive era, adopting a policy of religious toleration especially lenient on Catholicism. During Charles II's reign, England's cultural hegemony swung back in a secular direction, dominated by a model of aristocratic patriarchy, and London society assumed the libertine persona of Charles and his court. A promiscuous and aggressively heterosexual masculine ethos was in vogue with the social elite of Restoration society, both men and women. British culture was dominated by witty repartee, licentiousness, theatricality, fashion, and swagger.

Wit and sex appeal appeared to be among the highest forms of cultural capital. Within the Restoration court, politically minded court ladies appropriated the witty and overtly sexual libertine ethos to gain rhetorical and political influence. The aggressively sexual and secular tone of Restoration libertinism, however, raised public anxieties about promiscuity. Adding to this tension, Charles II, who was Anglican, and his royal consort, Queen Catherine of Braganza, a Portuguese Catholic who spoke little English, were unable to produce an heir (male or female)—even though Charles had many illegitimate children by mistresses such as Barbara Villiers Palmer who became Lady Castlemaine and later Duchess of Cleveland. As a long-time mistress of Charles II, Lady Castlemaine became notorious for her brazen sexuality and tremendous sway in English domestic politics.

As the king's powerful mistress, Castlemaine was said to rule an alternate cabinet of pleasure in which members from both the aristocratic Tory party and the Whig parliamentarians recognized the importance of maintaining her favor (Keeble 98–99). Her notoriety made her the object of numerous political poems and lampoons by Restoration writers, such as John Wilmot. Although she procured advancement for her male allies, she became, in effect, an emblem of the Restoration court's depravity. As N. H. Keeble points out, satirists in the 1660s portrayed "Castlemaine's inordinate sexual appetite [as] both symptom and cause of the court's political failures" (175). However, Castlemaine was no pawn; she used her sexuality as a power to promote the welfare of her family and her political allies. One of the earliest British women to achieve celebrity status, Castlemaine was the subject of gossip, admiration, and many official court portraits. Samuel Pepys's admiration of "my Lady Castlemaine" in his diary shows that her position as royal mistress did not significantly detract from her popularity in the public eye and is a testament to Castlemaine's ability to successfully appropriate the libertine ethos of her era. Libertinism encouraged misogyny and the commodification of women in Restoration culture; ironically, however, it also generated interest in the social roles and issues of women. The culture of libertinism extended beyond the royal court into London's artistic community. In 1662, Charles II decreed that actresses would replace male actors in performing women's parts in London's two new theater companies, an act that turned out to be a landmark decision for women's rhetoric, which I analyze in chapter 2. Competing with the era's penchant for libertine wit and virility, the fixation on actresses and feminine theatrical themes brought greater attention to the identity of "woman" and her most commonly accepted role as wife and mother. The profile of womanly virtue started to rise in response to the misogyny implicit in libertine masculinity. At the same time, the masculine image of the Restoration monarchy was suffering from critiques of immorality and the lack of a legitimate heir.

Without Charles's legitimate "issue," the line of succession to the English throne included his brother James as well as a number of his women relatives: his sister Henrietta Anne and his nieces, Princess Mary and Princess Anne. As potential future monarchs, the princesses received an Anglican education and were instructed from a young age to view their own actions as highly rhetorical. The princesses were trained in elocution along with Sarah Jennings (later Sarah Churchill, Duchess of Marlborough) by the famous actress Mary Saunderson Betterton (Highfill, Burnim, and Langhans 2:97). Both princesses, then, were immersed in the language of political rhetoric throughout the Restoration era, as courtiers and members of Parliament sought to form advisory relationships with them and to influence their religious and political views. After Charles's death in 1685, his brother James II (who was a Catholic) ruled only three years in an atmosphere of increasing political instability until Parliament deposed him and replaced him with his eldest daughter, Princess Mary, and her Dutch husband, William of Orange, in the Glorious Revolution of 1688.[3]

The reign of William and Mary simultaneously ushered in Whig power and introduced a new feminine ethos countering the previous Tory-dominated era of libertinism.[4] Ascending the throne at age 26, Mary co-ruled England with William for six years, until her death in 1694. While Mary prided herself on her chastity and virtue, her greatest interests as queen tended toward art and architecture, and she also supported the Societies for the Reformation of Manners and other benevolent organizations, which Clarissa Orr explains "inaugurated the British court's attempt to mix aristocratic style and bourgeois propriety" (Orr "Introduction" 31–32). Sarah Apetri states that the Glorious Revolution strengthened the "Manners" platform that William and Mary smartly undertook together and that Mary became a feminine "symbol of moral renewal," which she furthered in 1691 with her "proclamation against vice" (11–13). Although Mary's rhetorical power was somewhat diffused in sharing the throne with William, a Dutch monarch unpopular with the English people, her reign contributed to the creation of the feminine emblem of virtue and helped imbue British women with a new social responsibility.

In her public demonstration of domestic felicity, Mary was relatable to her female subjects, and her model of queenship inaugurated the English woman as the gendered arbitress of politeness. Mary as queen thus provided a fresh perspective and relief from libertinism. Jean Marsden argues that womanly virtue was adopted as a symbol of decorum by the Whig party as a counterpoint to several perceived cultural problems: the masculine absolutist corruption of the Tory party; Catholicism's perversion of femininity through the unnatural celibacy of nuns; and the immoral sexuality of prostitution, which Whigs warned was the fate of women who rejected Protestant moral reform (*Fatal Desire* 169–170). Whiggish womanhood, embodied by Mary as an emblem of feminine virtue, consisted of moral perfection, beauty, chastity, and silence—for Mary, a powerful set of traits—which, ironically, served both to minimize and to enhance the collective power of women.

After Mary's death in 1694 and William's in 1702, Anne's ascension to the throne at the mature age of 37 added a new national feminine emblem, that of pregnancy and motherhood. Married to George of Denmark at the age of eighteen, Anne was almost constantly pregnant. During her reign, her visibly pregnant body contributed to the growing recognition of a distinct maternal ethos in eighteenth-century Britain. Anne and George may have had a happy marriage; however, her luck with childbearing was not as great. She endured at least seventeen pregnancies, losing all her children but three in utero. Of the three children who went full term, two died in infancy, and one (a son) lived to the age of eleven. By the time of her accession to the throne, Anne was pregnant for the tenth time. Ruling from 1702 to 1714, Queen Anne was the first sole woman monarch in England since Elizabeth I.

Although Anne claimed Elizabeth as her role model, as queen Anne did not exude the masculine strength that Queen Elizabeth had seemed to possess. Anne was an invalid who unfortunately suffered from poor eyesight, lameness, obesity, and other chronic health issues. Her disabilities plagued her image and, for many years, have had a negative impact on the perception of her rule and legacy. However, Edward Gregg's seminal biography, *Queen Anne*, and Robert Bucholz's "Queen Anne: Victim of Her Virtues?" both reevaluate Anne's reign and leadership style. They conclude that, although earlier portrayals of Anne's shyness, reserve, limited education, and heavy reliance on advisors are correct, Anne was a more effective ruler than earlier accounts depict. As Gregg reports, from her early years, Anne was "shy and taciturn," as compared to her elder sister Mary, who was "voluble and self-assured" (75). Gregg and Bucholz argue that Anne's disabled body, her traditionally feminine persona, and the unflattering portrayal of Anne published by her former courtier, Sarah Churchill, Duchess of Marlborough, have dominated Anne's reputation in posterity to the extent that they erased from public memory other positive leadership qualities for which Anne was celebrated and beloved during her lifetime.

Anne was the first visibly pregnant woman monarch in England—the next would be Queen Victoria (1837–1901). Anne's often pregnant body symbolized fertility and prosperity. As Bucholz explains, Queen Anne's nickname of "the 'nursing mother' of her people" reflected her popularity (96). But, as pregnancy was against the norm for a head of state, her physical condition conveyed a serious weakness. As an example of the negative commentary, Bucholz cites a popular history, which sarcastically remarks of Anne: "her one hobby was eating" (95).[5] Sizing up public perception during her reign and historically, Bucholz states, "The view of Anne as a dull and overweight *hausfrau* may not fit the facts exactly, but it does fit quite nicely with a raft of longstanding prejudices about the public and private roles of women in general," but he also notes that Anne's admirers appreciated her leadership style and "frequently remarked on the Queen's reputation for gentleness, mercy, and clemency" (96–100). These recent revisions to Anne's history, based on archived correspondence between Anne and a host of courtiers and cabinet members, present a counter discourse to traditional portrayals of the queen as ignorant in state matters and show her, rather, as careful, decisive, and deliberate in her decisions.

Anne brought a knowledge of rhetorical performance, as well as feminine ethos, to political leadership. While she did not possess the comprehensive humanist education that Elizabeth I had, Anne received formal training in elocution from Mary Saunderson Betterton, a leading actress of the Restoration stage. While a young girl, Anne learned the elocutionary conventions of speech, movement, and gesture, and she was noted by contemporaries for her "regal bearing" and "mellifluous voice, which . . . charmed both Houses of Parliament at her first speech from the throne on 11 March 1702" (Bucholz 110). In this speech following her brother-in-law William III's death, Anne shows piety, confidence, and composure in a public pledge to serve her nation. She states,

> [T]he true Concern I have for our Religion, for the Laws and Liberties of England, for maintaining the Succession of the Crown in the Protestant Line, and the Government in Church and State, as by Law establish'd, encourages me in this great Undertaking, which I promise my self will be successful, by the Blessing of God, and the Continuance of that Fidelity and Affection of which you have given me so full Assurances. . . .
>
> My Lords and Gentlemen,
>
> It shall be my constant endeavor to make you the best Return for that Duty and Affection which you have express'd to me, . . . And as I know my own Heart to be entirely English, I can very sincerely assure you, There is not anything you can expect or desire from me, which I shall not be ready to do, for the Happiness and Prosperity of England. (3–4)

This first address of Anne's to Parliament announces the consistent themes of her reign: her loyalty to the Church of England; her allegiance to the kingdom of England; and pure and feminine Englishness as the basis of her identity as monarch. Anne's speeches throughout her reign keep to these three themes and exhibit clear, direct, and plain language to explain her reasoning for her political decisions. Topics of her speeches include acts of foreign policy (her rationale and defense for declarations of war against France and Spain, unification of England and Scotland, and British friendship with the Dutch) and domestic policy (staunch adherence to the Church of England, calls for the suppression of libelous pamphlets and critiques of the church, and laws against Papists and Jacobites).

In terms of bodily delivery, Anne's careful approach to public rhetoric is evident in her preparation for her coronation ceremony, which took place in April of 1702. In planning her coronation speech, Anne considered not just content, but also the venue's effects on her reception by her audience. As Gregg explains, Anne faced a number of challenges in preparing the speech, including the best location to deliver the speech (it was suggested that due to her lameness, Parliament should come to her at the palace, but she opted to give the speech to Parliament in Westminster); the need to make a graceful and commanding entrance despite her obvious "physical invalidism"; and the proper tone and content to please both parties, as she needed to make concessions to the Tories for their mistreatment by her predecessor without angering the Whig base (152). Her consideration of two possible locations for delivering the speech shows her knowledge of her audience and her concern for choosing a physical space that would afford her the greatest authority and mitigate the challenges of her impaired body.

Anne's preparations for her coronation speech also involved the careful construction of her ensemble to imbue it with the greatest possible level of authority and political symbolism. When Anne appeared before Parliament at her coronation, Gregg notes,

> It was obvious the new queen had taken great care in choosing what to wear. She dressed in a robe of red velvet lined with ermin and edged in gold galloon, she wore the crown and heavy gold chains with the badge of St. George, and bore the ribbon of the Garter on her left arm. Her costume was modeled on a portrait of Queen Elizabeth, whose motto, *Semper Eadem,* she was to adopt before the end of the year. (Gregg 152)

Anne's orchestration of her queenly persona through the appropriation of Elizabeth I's Latin motto, which means "always the same," and her choice of clothing and regalia (fig. 1.1) was an act of self-branding by which she meant to signify not only her consistency and stability but also her position in a sisterhood of political greatness. Anne used the precedent of Elizabeth I's successful reign as a platform for her own monarchy. In fact, a letter from one courtier and parliamentary spy states that Anne "often made a parallel between herself and Queen Elizabeth," both of whom followed in the wake of a sister monarch named Mary (Gregg 96). As a leader and a rhetorician, Anne did not possess Elizabeth's charisma, yet historical accounts describe Anne as a collaborative decision-maker who sought counsel from a close circle of advisors, like Elizabeth did.

Besides possessing the skill of listening, Queen Anne is also notable for her strategic use of silence. Bucholz observes that Anne transformed her shyness and reserve—qualities some might see as "defects"—into strengths by "becoming a keen listener and choosing her words carefully," making her silence "a necessary corollary of her regal dignity" and a means to "keep her position ambiguous or flexible" (112). Anne's rhetorical use of silence, which allowed her to maintain control among many divisive contingencies within her court and cabinet was, in fact, noted in her own time. *The Lady's Rhetorick: Containing Rules for Speaking and Writing Elegantly* (1707), a neoclassical handbook that feminizes classical rhetorical theory and figures, presents a detailed description of Anne's queenly persona as the primary example for the figure of silence. The handbook defines silence as a rhetorical device by using the metaphor of rowing a boat—a strategic activity in which people "turn their backs to the place where they purpose to land"—and then gives an extensive and laudatory example of Anne's quiet leadership style, noting

FIGURE 1.1. *Queen Anne.* Painting by John Closterman, oil on canvas, circa 1702. NPG 215 © National Portrait Gallery, London.

"the excellency of . . . her Genius, . . . Wit, . . . Judgement, . . . Sweetness of her Temper, . . . Goodness of her Disposition, . . . Patience and Humility, . . . her quiet Submission to the late Government" and concluding the description by remarking "with what Mildness and Wisdom she handles the Scepter, and governs three Nations: With what Discretion she moderates Passions and Factions of People of different Interests and Designs: How peacably and quietly we have liv'd at home under her Protection" (117). The verbal equation here taps into the age-old commonplace of peace and quiet. As Cheryl Glenn notes, "Silence can . . . indicate rhetorical agency and invention, a place to contemplate one's positionality" (*Unspoken* 82). In the case of Queen Anne, her strategic use of silence and listening allowed her to imbue the traditionally masculine authority of monarchial leadership with feminine rhetorical techniques, which facilitated her managing the political responsibilities of her rule.

Another rhetorical strategy that Anne adopted involved her purposeful presence and absence. Anne used her royal presence to indicate her show of support and lack of support. As Bucholz mentions, "She gave or withheld her presence to great political effect: attending . . . when she was in political sympathy . . . [and] withdrawing her presence when she was not" (111). Anne adopted this strategy of bodily rhetoric, attention, and withdrawal, in her dealings with her ladies in waiting, including Sarah Churchill, a beautiful and ambitious Whig courtier who, from the time that Anne was a young girl, had acted as her political and social mentor. Through the first few years of her reign, Churchill had enormous influence on Anne's policies and her cabinets. Churchill became the Duchess of Marlborough when Anne awarded her husband a dukedom for his military valor. In their correspondence, the two women used pen names for each other—not an uncommon practice at the time—with the queen going by "Mrs. Morley" and referring to Sarah and John Churchill as "Mrs. and Mr. Freeman."[6] As Churchill's biographer Frances Harris explains in *A Passion for Government,* Sarah became the most powerful woman in England. Eventually Anne became leery of Churchill's political maneuvering for Whig interests and banished the duchess from court and refused her audience. A thorough rhetorical analysis of the correspondence of Anne with Sarah Churchill, as well as with other ladies in waiting, such as Churchill's cousin Abigail Masham who rose in influence after Churchill's banishment, could make an interesting study of feminine conversational rhetoric in a political context.

Following Anne's death in 1715, the monarchy passed to the house of Hanover, launching the Georgian period, with the ascension of George I who was followed by George II, George III, and George IV, a continual line of male monarchs stretching into the nineteenth century. The British Enlightenment was inextricably linked with the "modern, stable harmonious, Christian polity," which from this point forward, as Porter argues, proclaimed "God and the Georges . . . the constitutional monarchs respectively of the universe and the nation"—although a wide variety of dissenting radical and conservative voices continually raised protests against the monarchy (32–33). The Georgian royals also offered to women's Enlightenment rhetoric four generations of queen consorts and princesses who displayed public feminine agency in ways that helped showcase the British monarchy as evolving with the development of Enlightenment values. The Georgian women built on the public image of motherhood as the house of Hanover succeeded in producing several generations of large royal families. As Clarissa Orr notes, the Georgian queens "figured as important exemplars of womanhood" in the age of Enlightenment by modeling feminine education, piety, and freedom of choice in matrimonial decisions and in their patronage of courtiers and scholars involved in literary, academic, and scientific endeavors (*Queenship* 5–6).

In the 1720s and 1730s, for example, Queen Caroline, royal consort to George II, stood at the apex of a deeply stratified, informal network of educated women that included courtiers, gentry, and scholars. At the top of the group in terms of social class were countesses Frances Seymour and Henrietta Fermor and socialite Mary Pendarves Delaney who, in turn, served as patrons to Anglo-Saxon grammarian Elizabeth Elston and pamphlet writer Sarah Kirkham Chapone, the latter of whom participated in early bluestocking circles (Orr *Sappho* 91–92). The public sociability of the royal Georgian women and their networks of prominent and educated women visibly stamped the feminine emblem of politeness into a cultural code, further eroding the previous acceptability of masculine libertinism.

The feminization of manners trickled down through the aristocracy and gentry to the educated middle class and into the deep rhetoric of eighteenth-century British cultural ideology. Politeness became a mandatory prerequisite to upward mobility and admission into educated and genteel society. As Paul Goring explains in *Rhetoric of Sensibility,* the code of politeness "allowed members of the middling classes to present a public image of civilised gentility" and "contributed a type of refined cultural cement that supported sociable relations by bringing people together within the framework of shared social practices" (22). By the mid-eighteenth century, politeness became a feminized hallmark of eighteenth-century British cultural ideology. Elite women, such as the Bluestockings, assumed the role of arbitresses of refined taste, and polite behavior became a teachable rhetorical practice.

Traditional Roles and New Identities

Undoubtedly, the deep rhetoric that dominated British Enlightenment culture leaned heavily against any form of feminine autonomy. Eighteenth-century conduct books such as John Gregory's *A Father's Legacy to His Daughters* (1761), James Fordyce's *Sermons for Young Women* (1766), and Hannah More's *Strictures on the Modern System of Female Education With a View of the Principles and Conduct Prevalent among Women of Rank and Fortune* (1799) prescribe limiting a young woman's rhetorical skills to practices that support her proficiency in reading aloud, polite conversation, and letter writing. The stereotypes of the virtuous wife and nurturing mother situated in the domestic household were clearly the hegemonic ideals. However, as Marilyn Francus reviews in *Monstrous Motherhood: Eighteenth-Century Culture and the Ideology of Domesticity*, recent scholarship in eighteenth-century studies has exposed the binary of the masculine/public and feminine/private spheres as an ideological "conflation of the domestic and feminine," which represents at least a partially inaccurate "spatial and social geography for women" that obscures their identities as "consumers," "practicing professionals," and "participants in national discussions on politics, education, and culture" (2–4). This is not to say that eighteenth-century British women possessed anything close to the freedoms and rights of men. As Eileen Hunt Bottin explains, "For the bulk of the eighteenth century, rights-bearing subjects were typically assumed, in theory and practice, to be adult white male landowners" (37). Yet, British women were not completely cloistered in their homes, and homes were not disconnected from society.

The dominance of separate spheres theory, which explains female domesticity in relation to patriarchal ideology, contributed to twentieth-century scholarly neglect of women's participation in the Enlightenment rhetorical ecology. These theorists rest their cases on eighteenth-century European political institutions, including the legal system, marriage customs, and economic and family models, that underwrote the notion of separate masculine public and feminine domestic spheres. Most prominently, Jurgen Habermas in *The Structural Transformation of the Public Sphere* (1962) analyzes the rise of the nuclear family in Europe as a socioeconomic change that began in England following the Glorious Revolution of 1688. Habermas argues that, at this time, economic praxis emerged from discreet aristocratic household hubs into a centralized public sphere and the family transformed from an extended kinship model to a nuclear unit, consisting only of parents and children, with the husband working in the public to provide income to the family while the wife focused on the private duty of maintaining the home but also gained an elevated status to partner and co-parent within the family (37).[7] Eighteenth-century women's roles also receive attention in *The History of Sexuality*, volume 1 (1976) by Michel Foucault who theorizes that the European Enlightenment was a coercive "discourse on modern sexual repression" within a Christian-dominated "bourgeois order" wherein leaders normalized sexuality within the confines of the conjugal family (5–7). According to Foucault, Western societies in the early eighteenth century commenced the "hysterization of women's bodies" and required women to be "regulated" into one sole role—motherhood—tied to the home and children "by virtue of a biologic-moral responsibility lasting through the entire period of the children's education" (104). In contrast, Lawrence Stone, in *Family, Sex, and Marriage* (1977) describes companionate marriage and the domestic nuclear family as two trends that diminished the strictures of domestic patriarchy and created greater autonomy for women of the middle and upper classes (325–343).

More recently, feminist literary critics have expanded upon and challenged twentieth-century theories of women's domesticity. Francus notes how feminist theory pays greater attention to the complex "narrative of female frustration, protofeminist in its outlook, as eighteenth-century women were confronted with an ideology in which they were bound to fail" (5). Furthermore, we know that a completely domestic life was not the reality for many eighteenth-century British women. Not all eighteenth-century women were mothers, and marriage did not preclude women from working outside the home. In fact, a sizable percentage of the English female population worked publicly. In *Women in Eighteenth-Century Europe,* Margaret Hunt states that at least 72 percent of women in early eighteenth-century London worked for pay—just as women worked throughout Europe (169). Most held low-paying farming and textile-related jobs, but professional opportunities for women as writers, performers, and visual artists increased throughout the century (Hunt 264–286).

Women pursued a variety of rhetorical activities according to their familial, social, and professional opportunities, which had everything to do with an individual's social class, religious affiliation, education, literacy, and physical location. While these intersections of women's identity most often (but not always) included their position within a family, protofeminist arguments regarding traditional and emerging women's roles in the British Enlightenment era challenge narratives of domesticity and patriarchal hegemony. With the growth in literacy came women's greater awareness of themselves as a collectively oppressed subaltern category. Whether occupying the traditional feminine gender roles of wife and mother, or in pursuit of the status of learned lady or public professional, eighteenth-century British women increasingly grew into a vocal counterpublic that sought and found alternative forms and sites for rhetoric.[8]

WIVES

The subordinate status of wives during the long eighteenth century in Britain was exacerbated, first, by the lack of marriage laws and, later by laws that favored the interests of men and lacked protections for women. Looking back to earlier in the seventeenth century, in 1653 precisely, during the period of the Puritan Commonwealth, the English Parliament had enacted laws defining marriage as a civil union, which gave married women an arguable legal status—but these laws were abolished by Charles II in 1660. After the Restoration, the legal status and rights of women in marriage remained ambiguous for many years. Even the new ideology of equality inscribed by the Lockean social contract at the outset of the eighteenth century did not support the same contractual relationship between man and wife as it advanced for political leaders and male citizens (Rosenthal 205–206). Daughters and wives were viewed as property of their families. Finally, after one hundred years of legal limbo, the Hardwicke Marriage Act of 1753 enacted new marriage laws, but these merely made explicit the rule that, in marriage, women gave up their rights to own property and rendered themselves legally subordinate to their husbands (Anderson, M. Collins, Staves).

By the latter half of the eighteenth century, women gained some level of autonomy in courtship, prior to marriage, when the idea that individuals, both male and female, should make their own choices of partners became the prevailing custom. That women should have the right of refusal in the selection of husbands marked a subtle yet significant move toward empowerment. But, once married, a woman legally became the dependent of her husband and, assumedly, the obedient wife. Throughout the long eighteenth century, as women's literacy increased, gender inequities in marriage and the subjugation and abuse of wives became major themes in women's rhetoric. The disempowered wife is reflected in British drama and literature throughout the entire period, which portrays courtship as an economic exchange and women as a commodity—the property of their fathers and guardians to be bartered for with prospective husbands.

Women writers also published serious treatises protesting the situation of wives. Mary Astell's *Some Reflections upon Marriage* (1700), one of the most famous of these pieces, employs neoclassical argumentation to critique the reasons that men and women marry. As a high Tory conservative, Astell's aim in her treatise is not to abolish the institution of marriage, nor to radically change marriage laws, but rather to delineate a moral philosophy of marriage. As Christina Mason Sutherland points out, Astell seeks to promote the "understanding" that men should be more honorable in courtship; that marriage should be sought based on love and natural compatibility—not for money, prestige, beauty, or wit; and that society should recognize the importance of education to enable women to better discern suitors' moral characters and to bring strong reasoning skills to the role of wife (87–88). After enumerating the many wrong reasons for marriage, Astell weighs in on the right reasons: "How must a Man chuse, and what Qualities must encline a Woman to accept . . . ?

43

This is no hard Question; let the Soul be principally consider'd, and regard had in the first Place to a good Understanding, a Vertuous Mind, and in all other respects let there be as much equality as may be" (*Some Reflections upon Marriage* 42). In this argument of policy, Astell appeals to common sense, a sense of justice, and natural virtue.

Astell writes in a direct and perspicuous essay style, without the use of ornate language or dialogic narrative devices, but she includes artful touches of sarcasm and wit, which serve to accentuate the dire treatment of wives, and she makes recommendations in a firm tone. Sutherland characterizes *Some Reflections upon Marriage* as a work of epideictic rhetoric, a refutation of flawed marriages, and a piece of writing that "uncompromisingly belongs to *contentio*, to the full public discourse of oratory" (80). Astell's rhetorical strategies include strong appeals to reason, parallels "between the political and the domestic," metaphors of slavery, witty invective, and sarcastic innuendo (Sutherland 89–92). The claims Astell makes about husbands' abuses of power over their wives share striking similarities to those made by John Stuart Mill's *Subjection of Women* (1869), published over 170 years later—a sad commentary on the lack of progress in gender equality in marriage from the early eighteenth to the late nineteenth century.

The stagnation of progress in the institution of marriage was not from lack of protofeminist arguments; several well-detailed appeals for the rights of wives appeared throughout the eighteenth century. The anonymously published treatise *Hardships of the English Laws in Relation to Wives* (1735), which was written by Sarah Kirkham Chapone, the daughter of a clergyman, directly addresses the matter to the attention of the King of England. Chapone petitions for new laws to protect England's wives who, she argues, by the current marriage laws and the immoral and secular influences of deism are "put in a worse Condition than Slavery itself" (2). Similar to Astell, Chapone likens wives to slaves—a comparison that Mill vigorously repeats later in *The Subjection of Women*. Chapone's development of this argument proceeds in a legalistic form by first enumerating three articles of complaint:

article 1) the wife's treatment as a slave
article 2) the lack of due process for article 1 violates the Habeas Corpus Act
article 3) the inability of wives to own property in any form, including not only money, but also their children and "their own Persons." (4–5)

Chapone proves these articles with facts, observations, and a series of extensively detailed case studies. Her first example argues that in marriage wives legally enter into a state of voluntary "captivity" in which they give up all rights and properties and receive no recompense of prior possessions or freedom even as widows (6). Chapone sites cases in which English husbands usurped their wives' premarital fortunes, prevented them from obtaining professional positions, and otherwise emotionally and physically abused them. Chapone states her points as factual "observations," like this: "*Observation,* Hence it appears, that Wives have no Property neither in their intellectual, or personal Abilities, nor in their Fortunes" (11). In her formalized complaints, she notes that the laws of England are harsher toward wives than Roman civil laws were in ancient times (28–29). Chapone also cites the difficulty of acting on existing legal protections for women. Prosecuting physically abusive husbands or suing for the upholding of jointures (financial trusts designed to ensure that women legally retain some of their wealth even after marriage) was impractical in the face of broad legal restrictions on women related to property.

Likewise in the usage of the legal case study, Lady Mary Wortley Montagu (1689–1762) dramatizes double standards for men and women in marriage in "Epistle from Mrs. Yonge to Her Husband" (1724). In this poem, based on the Yonges's real-life divorce court case, Montagu takes on the persona of the unfaithful wife who admits her infidelity but also explains that it came after years of infidelity by her husband. She writes,

> But this last privilege I still retain;
> Th' oppressed and injured always may complain.
> Too, too severely laws of honor bind
> The weak submissive sex of womankind.
> . . . .
> For wives ill used no remedy remains,
> To daily racks condemned, and to eternal chains.
> From whence is this unjust distinction grown?
> Are we not formed with passions like your own?

In the persona of the abused and accused wife, in the high style of neoclassical verse, the speaker protests with dignity against inequitable marriage laws that offered her no recourse nor protection of her privacy or economic standing while the same laws shield her husband from any wrongdoing. The question in the last two lines, "From whence is this unjust distinction grown?/ Are we not formed with passions like your own?," brings to mind Locke's assertion that all humans are equal cognitively and suggests strongly that gender roles are social constructions. This same theme appears in *Woman Not Inferior to Man: or, a Short and Modest Vindication of the Natural Right of the Fair-Sex to a Perfect Equality of Power, Dignity and Esteem with the Men* (1739).[9] Published under the pseudonym Sophia, this treatise is attributed to Lady Wortley Montagu or Lady Sophia Fermor (1724–1745). Bottin states that the author of this work argues from the "Enlightenment-era discourse of 'natural rights,' arising from seventeenth-century treatises by Frenchman François Poulain de la Barre and Englishman John Locke" to demand equal rights for women (30).

The lack of natural and legal rights for women, and wives specifically, is also an embedded theme of works arguing for education for women. For example, in *Letters on Education with Observations on Religious and Metaphysical Subjects* (1790), Catherine Macaulay notes that "married women . . . have hardly a civil right to save them from the grossest injuries" (210). At the century's end, Macaulay's criticism of civil inequity for wives is echoed in works of fiction as well, such as in the character of Mrs. Dashwood in Jane Austen's *Sense and Sensibility* (1811), which Austen revised from her earlier unpublished novel, *Elinor and Marianne* (1796). Thus, we can surmise that eighteenth-century protofeminist public arguments, although they did not empower the role of wife with new civil rights, did bring attention to the inequities of gender that the eighteenth-century marriage laws allowed. Using a variety of subtle, direct, and sometimes even angry language, eighteenth-century arguments for the rights of wives complicate nineteenth- and twentieth-century narratives about the widespread acceptance of feminine domesticity in eighteenth-century British culture.

MOTHERS

Compared to the stagnant and fairly powerless status of the wife, the identity of mother gained greater rhetorical significance during the Enlightenment due to a new emphasis on maternal responsibility in the education of children. While mothers had held an essential procreative position as childbearers in the aristocratic family model of the early modern era, childcare had often fallen to servants, the education of children to tutors, and children's character formation to other relatives as much as to the mother. However, with the rise of the conjugal family in the new ideological model of bourgeois patriarchy during the eighteenth century, mothers attained a higher level of ethos in the public imagination as compared to their status in early modern aristocratic patriarchy. This was an important cultural change for women in the British Enlightenment: the responsibility for nurturing and teaching children shifted definitively from the extended family to the parents, and the rhetorical role of the mother in British domestic life increased significantly.

The emphasis on parents as the primary teachers of children was a major point of Locke's influential essay, *Some Thoughts Concerning Education* (1693). Reflecting best educational practices of the early eighteenth century, Locke describes both parents as the ideal instructors for young children. However, with the familial division of the father's professional role and the mother's domestic role, the mother often assumed the job of primary home school instructor for young children, and in many families, she supervised the entire education of girls into womanhood. Because of this newly acknowledged responsibility for the mother's role, motherly ethos intensified in the eighteenth century, and the mother figure became an emblem of domestic virtue that persists to this day.

In *Rhetorics of Motherhood,* Buchanan identifies the identity of Mother as a gendered cultural code imbued with the "persuasive force ... to stir emotion and inspire trust, ... to encourage acquiescence and mute critique and reflection" (7). Citing Foucault's argument on the increasingly restrictive constructs of feminine gender from the seventeenth to the nineteenth century, Buchanan notes the usage of contrasting terms, *mother* and *woman,* as two opposing cultural codes within a "rhetorical continuum" in which *mother,* as a positive term, describes a female at the "apex" of moral virtue and "firmly associated with the private sphere" whereas the term *woman* connotes a female devoid of maternal domestic attributes, especially those females who "address civic or political topics in 'masculine' public spaces" and are "pursuing their own ambitions, by focusing on a career, by entering the public sphere" (15–18). In her analysis, Buchanan supports Foucault's claim of eighteenth-century culture's misogynist attitudes toward women working outside the home. Although this continuum excoriated women who tried to professionalize themselves, it did award the eighteenth-century mother greater rhetorical power over her children than British society had heretofore admitted.

The influence of the mother as educator became more pronounced in the eighteenth century, in part, because an increasing percentage of women, including mothers, were literate. As the number of mothers who possessed the skills necessary to teach reading and writing grew, mothers became a target market for pedagogical materials in the new literary marketplace. Carol Percy explains that many textbooks particularly addressed "future mothers" who held an important rhetorical role as promulgators of practical literacy among the educated classes (42). Besides their economic standing as consumers of primers and other books on education practices, mothers were also composers of their own pedagogical materials. Faced with "competing guidelines" for teaching, mothers had the need and the power to customize the teaching methods to reflect their own personal interests, skills, and the cultural influences important in their own families (Hannan 38).

Evidence of mothers' rhetorical roles as teachers resides in the large but scattered body of unpublished letters by eighteenth-century British women accessible in numerous archives of family correspondence from the period. In her meticulous study of ten women letter writers, Leonie Hannan in *Women of Letters: Gender, Writing, and the Life of the Mind in Early Modern England* analyzes several eighteenth-century correspondences of mothers. Hannan states that "the letter of advice from parent to child is a common find, both in the archive and in print" (98). Letter writing between parents and children during the long eighteenth century became both a pedagogical and a rhetorical tool for developing literacy and etiquette. For example, a letter from Frances Taylor to her daughter in 1744 corrects the girl for "putting a little i where you should put a great I" and instructs that "you or your sister will write once a week, write every little thing that comes into your head, it will keep your hands in writing & it will give pleasure to your pappa & mamma" (Hannan 101). This mother's advice letter—albeit through private correspondence to a small audience—focuses on habits of mind, moral duty, and the finer points of grammar. With their everyday duties of childrearing, as Hannan points out, mothers' "lives rarely fitted a model of consistent intellectual output" (43). However, in teaching reading and writing, and instilling the rules of social behavior and etiquette—I would argue that eighteenth-century British mothers, especially those who were literate, constantly practiced and modeled the skills of rhetoric in their everyday tasks.

Numerous demonstrations of rhetorical motherhood are apparent in the papers of Jane Johnson (1706–1759), wife of Woolsey Johnson, Vicar of Olney. An Anglican clergyman's wife and mother of four, Johnson was an educated, upper middle-class woman who lived her entire life in the county of Buckinghamshire. During the eighteenth century, Olney was an artisan town of lacemakers, as Susan Whyman explains, "noted for its bone lace and impoverished workers," which included a substantial pool of distressed and wretched child laborers; the town was also known as a center of fervent religious dissent (586–589). While raising her own children in a comfortable and pious Anglican home, Johnson was keenly aware that poverty and protests were rampant in Olney. In addition to her religious faith, knowledge of economic danger colors Johnson's maternal ethos and her multifaceted textual compositions, which include an array of written and visual materials, many of them pedagogical.

The centerpiece of Johnson's maternal rhetoric consists of an exemplary nursery library (a specialized genre of children's literature). Recently rediscovered in the 1990s—in a hatbox in Muncie, Indiana—Johnson's nursery library contains over 470 homemade pieces of pedagogical material that she created and used in the education of her children (a daughter and three sons).[10] Andrea Immel and Lissa Paul describe Johnson's nursery library as a rare "manuscript teaching aide," which "offer[s] dramatic and unprecedented evidence" that Locke's *Some Thoughts Concerning Education* actually describes the domestic pedagogy used by "engaged homeschooling parents" of the eighteenth-century; further, they note Johnson's personalized lessons incorporate instruction on the material conditions of Olney's social classes: "The street verse in Johnson's 'Nursery Library' points to a world that lay a stone's throw from the secure, orderly family circle . . . a world Johnson also wanted her children to know, a world where life was hard" (95–96). Johnson's appropriation of "street verse," common tidbits from songs and sayings, not only aided memorization; it focused her children's attention on the realities of their time and their world. Complementing her astute use of language, her nursery library pieces also include visual appeals that capture the attention and imagination of her primary audience, her children.

In their fascinating archival study of Johnson, *Reading Lessons from the Eighteenth Century: Mothers, Children, and Texts,* Evelyn Arizpe, Morgan Styles, and Shirley Brice Heath state that Johnson's nursery library exhibits "multimodal originality so ahead of her time" (vi). Johnson's collection of pedagogical material graphically exemplifies eighteenth-century maternal rhetoric and shows how "educated women played an active role in the education of their children, turning their talents to the creation of material . . . and not just relying on . . . published primers. . . . These mothers valued this ephemera which . . . took account of children's experiences and drew on the material of their everyday lives" (Arizpe, Styles, and Heath 1). Johnson's customized pedagogical materials include alphabet blocks, flashcards, lists of word groupings, little handmade books, and other loose materials—all designed to teach reading. Written in beautiful penmanship and illustrated with original drawings, these ephemeral documents depict the profound effort that Johnson made to educate and direct the minds of her children. Figure 1.2 shows the opening page of the little book Johnson created for her oldest son, George. The book for George totals thirty-seven leaves (pages) of handwritten text, a few with pasted-in engravings and colored illustrations. The contents consist of three types of pages: short pithy passages on goodness and God, such as "A fool will / be wicked / but he that / is wise will / be good"; lists of words with similar vowel sounds, such as "Curl furl churl / burn turn churn"; and bits of basic knowledge, such as "Parts of /the body/ head heart/ face eye eyes" (Johnson *Lilly Library* Leaf 24 verso, Leaf 20 recto, Leaf 29 recto). The book, and other loose materials in the archive, illustrate Johnson's homeschool curriculum. While not all mothers were as accomplished in creative writing and document design as Johnson, her work illustrates the types of academic activities an educated woman in eighteenth-century Britain could do at home with and for her family.

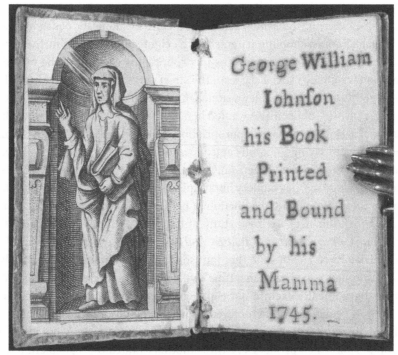

FIGURE 1.2. Frontispiece and title page from Jane Johnson's little book for her son. Set 11. *George William Johnson his Book*, Johnson, J. mss., ca. 1740–59, Lilly Library, Indiana University, Bloomington.

The teaching role that mothers fulfilled in eighteenth-century domestic settings also included the rhetorical education of children. The lessons of the maternal speaker conveyed ethos through her reliability and consistency, logos through the educational content that imparted moral and academic literacy, and pathos through love and gentle threats. These principles, including allusions to tangible rewards and punishments, energize Johnson's correspondence with her sons who went off to public boarding school between the ages of eight and ten. Johnson's letters to her sons show her attempts to maintain her influence on them outside the home. In a 1753 letter to her eight-year-old son Robert, Johnson writes:

> Dear Robert,
>
> It gave me great pleasure to hear . . . that you are very well, but I am
> . . . fearful you neglect your book & if you forget how to read, it will
> give you a vast deal of trouble to learn again, so pray be so good
> to yourself as to read twice a day to pretty miss Pruey every day.
> (Johnson, Two letters to her son Robert, 1753–55)

Even though Robert is away at school, his mother sends him logical and emotional appeals to reinforce his need to study. To convince her son that practice is needed to master reading, she suggests pleasurable images of him successfully reading aloud to her and "pretty miss Pruey," contrasting these with an appeal to fear—"a vast deal of trouble"—if he does not read. Johnson's letters operate on the motivational power of a mother's praise and love. Arizpe, Styles, and Heath observe that, in making her "moral priorities clear to her children," Johnson teaches them that "the worst consequence of not being 'good' was God's anger," but she also implies the "withdrawal of maternal love" as another potential effect (97). Not just love but also fear of losing love are inherent in her rhetorical appeals.

Simultaneously gentle and firm in her techniques, Johnson strives to teach her son leadership and socialization skills, as well as to encourage literacy practices. Johnson uses the technique of presenting positive imagery again, in 1755, when she writes:

> Pray my Dear Robert,
>
> Remember God Almighty in everything you do & where ever you go, & pray continually to him to make you wise and good. Remember this was King Solomon's prayer that his mother taught him when he was a little Boy . . . because he pray'd to God to make him wise, God was so well pleased with him, that he not only made him wiser than all the men in the Earth, but likewise gave him more riches than anybody ever had either before or since. I would have you teach Little Benny to be very good, & tell him he should pray to God a great many times a day as you, & . . . I have him & you a few more nuts and raisins, I have nothing else to send you, or I would send it, for I Love you Dearly, & think you one of the most sensible children of your age in the world . . . so I wish you good night. (Johnson, Two letters to her son Robert, 1753–55)

Johnson's advice to pray, and to teach Little Benny to do the same, illustrates the importance of religious faith in her pedagogy and also implies her understanding that teaching someone else is one of the best ways to learn. She demonstrates high standards when she challenges her son to live up to the exemplary behavior of a king and to the expectations of God. She also sends the reward of food—a very motherly move—as immediate reinforcement.

Maternal rhetoric has always been rewards-based and performative. For many eighteenth-century mothers, the craft skills they possessed could be employed for everyday rhetorical purposes. While writing was central to Johnson's maternal ethos, she also continued to employ the symbolic power of visual media, such as in a set of cut papers shown in figure 1.3, which now reside in her archived materials at the Bodleian Library. Johnson's cutout work illustrates how eighteenth-century mothers used printed designs as iconography specifically directed to their children. Holloway describes this maternal scissor work as "a wholly new way of communicating individual emotions"; flowers symbolized the bloom of childhood; birds and butterflies represented a mother's hope for her child to have a carefree future; snowflakes embodied "a mother's desire to safeguard the purity of her infants, and protect them against corruption and sin"; and paper hearts provided a "token" of the mother's "undying love" while the interior cutouts within the heart, often in the shape of crosses, convey further maternal and Protestant messages (166–68). (Holloway contrasts these pristine white paper hearts to the visceral Catholic iconography of the bloody heart.) Concerning Johnson's specific samples in figure 1.3, the heart contains a downward pointing sharp arrow, perhaps suggesting that love endures amid earthly pain. Her use of flowers and birds, however, implies

FIGURE 1.3. Paper cutouts made by Jane Johnson for her son George, undated. *Correspondence and papers of Jane Johnson, 1732–1759.* Oxford, Bodleian Libraries MS. Don. c. 190 fol. 5.

natural joy. Johnson probably intended the sun cutout as a symbolic play on its homonym, son, to represent the importance of her sons to her.

In fact, she specifically designated the sun cutout and the rightmost floral cutout shown in figure 1.3 as gifts for her eldest son George, and as a remembrance for posterity. These two cutouts are currently in a folder at the Bodleian Library along with the small sheet of paper shown in figure 1.4. The cutouts lay folded beside Johnson's note, which states, "For my son George William Johnson when I am dead," and at the bottom, the handwriting of another person notes, "Died 1759." At the time of her death, Johnson was fifty-three and George was nineteen. The specific personal meaning attached to these cutouts cannot be known, but the sun would seem to symbolize her wishes of her own son to shine in life, and the blooms growing out of the vase likely convey the message that she wants her son to thrive and cultivate himself. As Arizpe, Styles, and Heath explain, "Jane's careful housekeeping (her instructions to keep documents for posterity are handwritten on many notes and letters) ensured the survival of a remarkable set of family papers spanning several generations" (xx). Johnson's work exemplifies the influence of maternal domesticity in establishing and preserving family ethos, thereby creating a personal and feminine rhetorical legacy. Carrying on the Johnson family's tradition of multimodal writing, Johnson's daughter, Barbara Johnson, authored "a large handsome book entitled, A Lady of Fashion, . . . an album of fashion and fabrics," which is now housed in the Victoria and Albert Museum (Arizpe, Styles, and Heath vii).

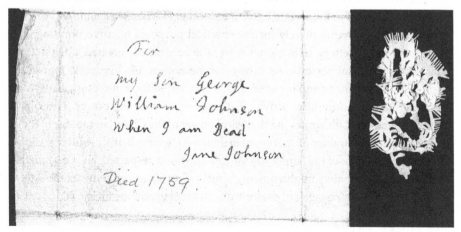

FIGURE 1.4. Note from Jane Johnson to her son George, undated. Correspondence and papers of Jane Johnson, 1732–1759. Oxford, Bodleian Libraries MS. Don. c. 190 fol. 6.

Johnson's multimedia visual and verbal legacy, once pieced together from the various archives where it resides, presents a woman and mother who demonstrates confidence in maternal rhetoric. An earlier letter by Johnson, written to her aunt, Mrs. Brompton, in 1749, provides further proof of her beliefs about feminine creative power. In commenting to Mrs. Brompton about the pregnancy of another cousin, Mrs. Garth, Johnson states:

> I don't know any body so fit to people the earth as she, . . . & then sure it must be esteem'd a Blessedness to be the immediate instrument in the hand of God to give Life to Immortal Spirits! To Beings that can never die! To meet our own Sons & Daughters in Heaven, must add great joy to the Happiness of that glorious place, when we reflect that had it not been for us, such had never been . . .

Essentially, Johnson honors women by according to them the ultimate creative act on earth. Johnson insists that, without mothers to bear, nourish, teach, love, and sustain children, life would be impossible!

Later in the same letter to Mrs. Brompton, Johnson theorizes her own writing process. As she attempts to write a story to entertain her reader, she declares, "I want Rhetorick & Eloquence to put my sentiments in a proper light." This self-conscious commentary on her own style as she is writing her letter resembles Samuel Richardson's narrative fiction technique of writing in the moment. Arizpe, Styles, and Heath assert that Jane Johnson "almost certainly" read Samuel Richardson's *Pamela; or Virtue Rewarded* (1740), the most popular novel of the 1740s, as evidenced by her knowledge of education philosophy, which Richardson comments on in the second book of *Pamela in Her Exalted Condition* (6–8). Johnson did not write merely for the practical purposes of corresponding or teaching; in her letters, as in all her work, she consciously created a distinctly Christian maternal persona. As a thematic message across her work, Johnson implicitly argues for feminine creativity as a specialized form of rhetorical invention, a gift from God, and an activity that gave her purpose and power. Johnson's multifaceted work illustrates the rhetorical power of the Christian mother in the nurturing and character formation of eighteenth-century British youth. In fact, the domestic realm of the family was the most justified, respected, and condoned site of British woman's Enlightenment rhetoric—but it was certainly not the only site. Many women engaged in rhetorical activities beyond motherhood.

LEARNED LADIES

Prior to the eighteenth century, a small number of middle- and upper-class British women authored written works of rhetoric, mostly in the form of treatises, essays, and miscellaneous works of nonfiction. Women intellectuals came from a variety of middle- and upper-class backgrounds, and their numbers increased as literacy rose in Britain during the eighteenth century. By the latter half of the century, learned ladies—or bluestockings, as they came to be called—became one of the most important groups contributing to women's Enlightenment rhetoric. The bluestockings, as Elizabeth Eger describes, were a multigenerational and predominantly female "network of intellectuals . . . involved in a diverse range of cultural activities, from writing poetry, political pamphlets, educational and moral philosophy, legal essays, novels, plays, and Shakespeare criticism to performing arias and exhibiting paintings" (1). The leaders were upper-class women; however, the bluestockings also included educated women of the middle class. Gary Kelly describes the diversity of bluestockings as members of the "landed and professional middle classes" who "struggled with and rejected women's expected roles in the political, social, and sexual-emotional economy of the social elites" ("Bluestocking Work" 183). These women sought more intellectually stimulating social lives. In the 1750s, bluestocking groups met in private "salon" gatherings, usually in the drawing rooms of opulent homes. The groups included affluent and educated women, elite male clergymen, members of the literati, and academic professionals; their discussions focused mostly on literature, art, aesthetics, and moral philosophy.[11]

Certainly, bluestocking women supported educational reforms, but for many of them, their social and economic status allowed them to live a somewhat rarified existence removed from the concerns of earning a living. Kelly argues that the bluestockings had a complex relation to "modernity" and "different kinds of knowledge and work" (176). Through family fortune and established social connections, many of the leading Bluestockings were able to devote themselves to a life of the mind. As Kelly states, these elite educated women pursued their interests "unfettered by material interest or exploitation" and were able to define their own "self-reflexive subjective identity" during a time of rapid social progress and change (186). Bluestocking circles of learned ladies contributed to intellectual and philosophical discourse in the age of Enlightenment. Although, they eschewed public celebrity and distanced themselves from politics and public debate, bluestocking women participated as readers, commentators, and writers of Enlightenment rhetorical theory. In their written correspondences and publications, bluestockings helped shape and adapt the Scottish Enlightenment philosophy of progress, and its economic underpinnings, to considerations of gender (Thale 4–6, O'Brien, DeLucia).

The multifarious ideas and accomplishments of the bluestockings as participants in the British Enlightenment are now well documented in numerous books and articles. Works such as Elizabeth Eger's *Bluestockings: Women of Reason from Enlightenment to Romanticism,* Karen O'Brien's *Women and Enlightenment in Eighteenth-Century Britain,* and Deborah Heller's collection *Bluestockings Now!: The Evolution of a Social Role* detail intellectual, scholarly, and civic contributions of dozens of educated eighteenth-century women. These studies link bluestocking culture back to the first and second generation of early eighteenth-century British intellectuals, and even to the seventeenth-century Parisian salons. As Deborah Heller notes, the bluestocking label and the salon tradition "rapidly spread to other 'learned ladies' and other social configurations" (1).

Only a few studies, however, cover bluestocking contributions to the history of women's rhetoric. Those that I have found focus almost exclusively on women's rhetoric as conversation, including, for example, Jane Donaworth's analysis of Hannah More in *Conversational Rhetoric* and Tania Smith's "Learning Conversational Rhetoric in Eighteenth-Century Britain: Hester Thrale Piozzi and Her Mentors Collier and Johnson." The contributions of several generations of bluestocking women to the history of rhetoric, however, includes not only conversation theory and practice, which I cover in my discussion of sociable venues and clubs in chapter 3, but also belletristic theory, rhetorical education, mentoring women authors, and participation in social reform rhetoric, which I discuss in relation to women's written rhetorical theory and arguments about education in chapter 4.

PROFESSIONAL WOMEN

While upper-class women formed social groups for intellectual exchange, middle-class women were more likely to parlay demonstrations of wit, virtue, and emotion into rhetorical activities related to paid work. The concept of women partaking in public professions did not conform to the prevailing deep rhetoric of Enlightenment patriarchy, but the ground truth for women was that many needed to work outside the home to support themselves and their dependents. Even without legal status as citizens, women contributed to the workforce in a variety of professions, including those calling for rhetorical skills, such as teachers, governesses, actresses, and writers. The main professions that provided rhetorical opportunities for women were those involving public theatrical performance and writing for publication. The jobs of actress and author offered the most obvious and common professional paths associated with these skills, but neither profession was completely socially acceptable.

As professionals, actresses received traditional training in rhetorical delivery, as I detail in chapter 2, but their profession fell outside the norms of respectability. Other than on the dramatic stage, custom and law prohibited women's participation in public oratory; they were barred from speaking in the traditional public venues of Parliament, the law courts, universities, and the pulpits of the (conforming) Anglican Church of England. However, female orators began to take the stage in debating societies starting in the mid-century, and women preachers like Margaret Fell, Sarah Crosby, and Mary Bosanquet found public voice on the dissenting pulpits of the Quakers and Methodists. However, opportunities for oratory and public speaking for women outside of the theater were uncommon.

In comparison, the burgeoning literary public marketplace of eighteenth-century Britain presented a wider and more bountiful professional arena for women writers, providing them genres, sites, and opportunities for publishing and sharing many types of texts. In nonfiction, literary, and dramatic genres, women writers embedded proto-feminist theories and expounded on topics such as education, gender roles, and women's involvement in society and culture. In the early part of the century, as Apetri notes, polemical women writers began integrating the strategies of the humanist *querelle des femmes* (or "women question") with "the overriding concerns of the Reformation of Manners" and claimed for women "the side of virtue and piety in the struggle for England's moral identity" (60–61).[12] As the century progressed, the rapidly growing commercial literary marketplace continued to offer an arena for women writers to publish treatises, proposals, plans, and tracts using arguments of feminine and protofeminist morality to address social injustices from many political perspectives.

The field included opportunities for women periodicalists, such as Eliza Haywood and Lady Mary Wortley Montagu, who proffered women's Enlightenment rhetoric through satirically covert protofeminist points of view. Even female hawkers—women who sold pamphlets and other cheap publications in coffee houses—held rhetorical roles in marketing and sales for the Grub Street publishers. Brian Cowan argues that hawkers, in effect, acted as "powerful agents in shaping the modes and forms of political discourse of the time through their keen understanding of the tastes and desires for news and printed ephemera"; yet he also states that these women, who were poor and likely illiterate "can hardly be considered to have been full-fledged participants in the masculine public sphere" (228, 251). In response to Cowan's second remark, we might observe that, regardless of their lack of education, subordinate gender, and lower-class status, the rhetorical presence—and economic labor—of the women hawkers facilitated the growing success of periodical print ephemera in eighteenth-century Britain. Their critical function in the marketing of periodicals and newspapers adds to the evidence that women of many back-grounds and social classes were involved in launching new genres and venues of rhetoric.

Behind the public scenes of the literary marketplace, women writers found patronage and opportunities for serious intellectual conversation in more gentile venues through networks of literati, which included bluestocking women who facilitated the exchange of peer feedback and acted as mentors for fledgling women writers. For example, Elizabeth Montagu encouraged Hester Chapone to publish her writings on education as *Letters on Improvement of the Mind* (1773); Hester Thrale encouraged novelist Frances Burney; and Montagu and Hannah More together discovered and promoted working-class poet Ann Yearsley.

ACTIVIST WOMEN

The century's end also saw the emergence of activist voices of protofeminist Enlightenment rhetoric in the surge of British political debate, which emerged in the wake of the French Revolution. These debates, which increasingly in-volved the British middle class, included progressive appeals for social class and gender parity. Protofeminist political protest emerged in Britain within radical mixed-gender circles of fervent political dissent in the 1780s and 1790s. Progressive women writers, including Mary Wollstonecraft, Mary Hays, and Helen Maria Williams, aligned themselves with the British Jacobin movement in supporting the Jacobin leaders of the French Revolution and viewing aris-tocracies as oppressive and tyrannical social evils. Taylor and Knott cite the group that included Wollstonecraft and publisher Joseph Johnson as the "most intransigent" and "the most revisionary in their attitudes toward women" (xix). Williams, Wollstonecraft, and Hays were deeply committed to social progress and voiced their egalitarian views in a wide range of literary and polemical genres, including poetry, novels, treatises, and published letters. As Miriam Brody notes, Wollstonecraft, who frequented the "intellectually generative community of political radicals and religious Dissenters" of Newington Green in the 1780s, also embraced the "new rhetoric" of the Scottish Enlightenment for its plain and direct style and healthy rejection of excessive ornamentation (Brody 109, 111). While scholarship exists on Wollstonecraft as a rhetorical theorist and a political rhetor, all three of these important women need greater attention in their contributions to women's Enlightenment rhetoric.[13]

Ultimately, radical protofeminist rhetoric was suppressed in a wave of cen-sorship and seditious libel acts in the 1790s and early 1800s, which I touch on in my discussion of the debating societies in chapter 3. However, the accretive rhetorical influence of Wollstonecraft's radical progressive views on gender, along with the sustained focus on women's issues through the end of the century, caused the emblem of woman to evolve politically. A new "figure of womanhood" arose in postrevolutionary Britain, as Kelly explains, representing a middle-class national identity and deposing the "narrow interests of rank and region" (4). Moving into the nineteenth century, the British government, in their reaction to the French revolution and the Irish rebellion, squelched much of the radical discourse, but both progressive and conservative women continued to participate in various reform groups to address specific areas of social concern, such as education, abolition, and child labor.

Sociability and Ephemeral Women's Rhetoric

Social networking, conversation, and ephemeral rhetoric proliferated across Britain throughout the long eighteenth century as entertainment, travel, and leisure activities became more accessible pastimes of not just the upper but also the middle class. Researchers note that mixed-gender sociability increased as a practical aspect of everyday eighteenth-century life. As the century progressed, Goring argues that the rise of a "new bourgeois identity" instigated "the growth of new social spaces and discursive situations" increasingly concerned with the feminine trait of politeness (21–22). Eighteenth-century intellectuals advocated for the "historical investigation of human sociability" in their own time, and sociability as an area of research persists as current scholars from a variety of disciplines revisit sites of eighteenth-century sociability and sociality as a means to study the interrelations of emotion and gender in conversation and community practices (Broomhill 2). The study of sociable sites, and the ephemeral media contributing to and consumed in those sites, also needs to be examined from the perspective of women's rhetorics.

Sociability functioned as a rhetorical exigency that increased the availability and variety of periodical publications in tandem with the rise of the literary public marketplace. Mirroring practices of sociability, the conversational style found in eighteenth-century British periodicals models a particularly feminine form of rhetoric designed for interactive audience consumption in public settings. These ephemeral publications and informal spaces of sociability interacted together progressively transforming the gendered rhetorical ecology, addressing multitasking and transient audiences whose attentions were divided between talk and text. The rhetoric of sociable spaces, including coffeehouses and tea tables, intersected with that of ephemeral print genres, including the periodical essay and the lady's pocketbook. These spaces and genres, and their relationship to each other, illustrate developments in rhetorical sociability that also follow the trajectory of wit, virtue, and emotion as rhetorical appeals over the course of the century.

SOCIABLE SPACES, CONVERSATION, AND GOSSIP

As the British eighteenth-century economy transformed into to an increasingly consumer-driven model, masculinity and femininity evolved as rhetorical modes of expression tied to commerce and sociability. Recent scholarship on sociability analyzes eighteenth-century tea tables and coffeehouses as gendered spaces for conversation and gossip. Susan Broomhill calls attention to "coffee houses, salons, and polite society" as important conceptual and physical hubs wherein attendees partook in "affective practices" within "specific communities" (1). Cowan describes the London coffeehouse as the "primary social space" in which "news was both produced and consumed," and he contrasts the "male preserve" of the coffeehouse with the tea table, its feminine counterpart, which was "properly located within the 'private' domestic household" (Cowan 170–72, 246).[14] Amanda Vickery describes the tea table as a practical and "socially inclusive" place for entertaining visitors, sometimes of both genders and sometimes only women (207–08). Despite a substantial degree of gender fluidity in both sites, eighteenth-century coffee houses held the image of public masculine spaces and centers of substantive conversation about current topics of cultural importance whereas tea tables held the connotation of private spaces where conversation focused on feminine topics of little consequence.

As feminized sites, tea tables represented both politeness and idleness. Conduct-book principles of decorum would require attendees of the tea table to aspire to genteel ladylike behaviors. However, in popular culture, the tea table stood as an emblem for superficial chit-chat, a space associated with "the antisocial energies in female taste and manners, especially luxury consumption and gossip" (Ellis, Coulton, Dew, and Mauger xxii.). The common association of tea tables with gossip has persisted for centuries as a negative stereotype of women's conversation as superficial, lacking in substance, rigor, and logical reasoning. However, gossip merits reexamination as a rhetorical practice, especially as a gendered descriptor of eighteenth-century conversational rhetoric.

Historically, *gossip* as a term derives from the Old English masculine noun *godsib,* and originally referred to "one who has contracted spiritual affinity with another by acting as a sponsor at a baptism"; by the eighteenth century, gossip had come to mean "a familiar acquaintance, friend, chum, . . . A person, mostly a woman, of light and trifling character . . . who delights in idle talk; a newsmonger, a tattler" as well as "the conversation of such a person; idle talk;

trifling or groundless rumour; tittle-tattle. Also, in a more favourable sense: Easy, unrestrained talk or writing . . . about persons or social incidents" (gossip).[15] Thus, *gossip* had many connotations in the eighteenth century, mostly negative but some positive. Furthermore, there is no doubt that both men and women practiced gossip frequently in sociable situations, much like they do today. As an engaging form of sophistic rhetoric, gossip served to introduce a variety of opinions and perspectives into the discourse of eighteenth-century sociable sites.

The commonplace that only women engaged in gossip reflects their relegation to the domestic site of the tea table and the taboo against upper-class women appearing in public. The eighteenth-century coffeehouse, gendered as a masculine public site for discussing matters of public importance, would therefore seem to be off limits to gossiping women. Historical evidence shows, however, that these gendered prescriptions do not entirely match the rhetorical ecology of the times. Although coffeehouses proliferated as generally masculine spaces in London, at least some English coffeehouses were mixed-gender venues. In the 1690s, over 20 percent of coffeehouse proprietors were women (Cowan 251). Women who regularly frequented the coffeehouses included the coffeehouse keepers, workers, servers, hawkers, and prostitutes. Cowan argues that upper-class women were least likely to be present except at coffeehouses that were hosting art auctions (137). While it appears that women across the class structure did frequent coffeehouses for a variety of reasons, Cowan and Ellis suggest that their presence was peripheral.

However, early eighteenth-century periodicals display an ambivalence about gendered associations within London coffeehouses. Rather, they advise both men and women to frequent coffeehouses but provide gendered instructions for socializing and reading. An advertisement in *Ladies Mercury* (1693), a short-lived spin-off of *Athenian Mercury* (1690) and one of the earliest magazines to target women readers, directs that questions about love be sent to the attention of the Ladies Society at the Latine Coffee House on Ave Mary-Lane, suggesting that at least some of the magazine's women readers regularly visited the coffeehouse and perhaps even used it as a meeting place (*Ladies Mercury* 1:3.2).[16] Publishers explicitly roped off serious masculine subjects from the feminine sphere of questioning, but the existence of the *Lady's Mercury* and its inclusion of targeted advertising demonstrates a public move to appeal to the interests of British women readers. The magazine directly addresses women and encourages their legal questions and participation in the public venue of the coffeehouse, but the seriousness of these directions is unclear. Conjecture that advertisements soliciting input from women readers were staged—a form of fake news—would indicate that the magazine's purpose was satiric, and the tone of the advertisements could be taken as playful.

The gendered associations of coffeehouses in early British periodicals may have functioned more as points of conversation and gossip than as prescriptions for attendance. The major sections of Richard Steele's popular magazine the *Tatler* (1709–1711) use various coffeehouses of London to symbolize categories of cultural activity—entertainment (White's Coffee House), poetry (Will's Coffee House), learning (the Grecian), and news (Saint James's). While these topical locales suggest masculine tastes, the *Female Tatler* (1709–1710) playfully muddies gender assignments when it identifies its venues as "White's, Will's, the Grecian, Garraway's in Exchange Alley, and all the India Houses" where "Grave Statesmen, Airy Beaus, Lawyers, . . . Poets, and Parsons, and Ladies of all Degrees assemble" to converse on books, happenings in the royal court, legal cases, stock prices, fashion, and "general Tittle-tatle" (*Female Tatler* no. 1). Notably, the term "tatler" in the title of both magazines promotes the pastime of tattling or gossiping as a pleasurable activity. These everyday conversational practices fall far beneath the lofty rhetoric of neoclassical oratory; nevertheless, the popularity of tittle-tattle (gossip) among people of many intersecting identities and socioeconomic classes indicates its power as a strong shaper of culture. The advertisement of coffeehouses as public sites of gossip also defies the stereotype of this form of conversation as something in which only women engage.

PROTOFEMINIST EPHEMERA

The rhetorical power of gossip fueled the popularity of ephemeral print periodicals, including over fifty new periodicals primarily targeting women from 1700 and 1800.[17] Manushag N. Powell notes in *Performing Authorship in Eighteenth Century Periodicals* that "though attached rhetorically to the masculine aura of the coffee-house, periodicals were frankly very interested in women as both subjects and readers" (133). The earliest periodicals constituted "a reinvigorated form of political essay sheet with a humorous edge" offering cultural critiques, as well as "advice and guidance on taste, fashion, and behavior" in "tightly argued, accessible prose" (Conboy 6). The appeal of the periodical lay in its friendliness, entertainment affect, and accessibility at sociable venues, such as booksellers and coffeehouses, for purchase, borrowing, reading, and discussing. The playful and humorous slant of early periodical essay magazines interjected feminine voices, often ironically, creating a genre of rhetorical complexity in its mixture of opinion, news, advice, and gossip.

Many magazines, such as the *Athenian Mercury, Tatler,* and *Spectator* targeted a mixed-gender audience. Those that primarily targeted women, such as the *Female Tatler, Ladies Magazine,* and *Female Spectator,* focused their subject matter on philosophy, love, romance, literature, fashion, and current events. Almanacs and puzzle books were also popular periodical forms whose interactive features attracted women readers. The catering of publishers to women readers presents striking evidence of how literacy granted women clout as an important and sizable demographic in Britain's growing capitalist structure. The success of the feminine-focused periodical in the eighteenth-century British literary public marketplace demonstrates the effect that women had as consumers of news media and also emphasizes the power of large target audiences to shape the content of discourse in a complex rhetorical ecology. The informational and entertainment needs of women as consumers influenced the format and the content of early periodicals even though these ephemeral texts conformed (mostly) to the didactic purpose of prescribing traditional stereotypes of gender. As Carol Percy suggests, through their titles, advertising, engaging tone, and discussions of poetry, rhetoric, and literature, as well as the sciences, British periodical publications throughout the eighteenth century purposely cultivated a sizable readership of women who were "in need of education and aspiringly polite" in their interests and tastes (40–41). Magazine publishers strove to develop accessible, interactive materials that would entertain women readers. Thus, women's collective identity as a massive commercial audience helped to elevate them from subaltern status.

While women were a major and influential demographic in the periodical market, not all magazines for women were protofeminist in their messages. However, because of the strong association of periodical reading with women readers, many periodicals adopted what Tedra Osell calls "rhetorical femininity." In "Tatling Women in the Public Sphere: Rhetorical Femininity and the Periodical Essay," Osell analyzes the central rhetorical role in the earliest English periodicals of "rhetorical femininity"—by which she means "a version of the author, characterizing a text as being by and for women"—noting that periodical writers of both genders employed this device to write from the stance of a feminine persona and to "represent women as a class" (283). We can see rhetorical femininity at work in the *Ladies Library* (1714), a periodical of three volumes published by Richard Steele, which on its title page states that it was written by a lady. Possibly compiled by Lady Mary Harrison Wray, granddaughter of Anglican theologian and author Jeremy Taylor, the *Ladies Library* announces that its female compiler organized and edited the volumes as a guide for her own conduct, and recommends it will "improve the Readers, as Daughters, Wives, Mothers, and Widows" (preface). The *Ladies Library* advocates women's reading, especially history, as necessary to cultivating conversation skills, proper pronunciation and smooth delivery, and the ability to write English with "a good Hand," correct spelling and grammar, and with "Clearness and Brevity" (Steele *Ladies Library* 11–15). Whether Steele or Wray was its primary editor, the *Ladies Library* advocates a conservative perspective and favors the extremely polite style and narrow sphere of feminine activity endorsed by the hegemonic genre of conduct literature.

However, the most popular early periodical, the *Tatler,* and its imitators, such as the *Female Tatler,* entertained a more worldly and colorful picture of women as a group. These early periodicals personified progressive views of gender in a tongue-in-cheek tone through the use of *eidolons,* the powerful device of fabricated fictional editors. As Powell describes, eidolons are "fictional personas" that allowed periodicalists to satirize the social class structures and the questionable boundaries of public and private "to police the audience into behaving as an ideal English society, usually by adopting the mores of the middle class" (3). Using satiric pennames, eidolons sometimes posed as editors of a periodical, as in Mrs. Crackenthorpe, the alleged editor of the *Female Tatler* (1709–1710), who was the counterpart to the *Tatler*'s Isaac Bickerstaff, Esq. The eidolon as editor engaged in a one-sided show of witty repartee, which provided news as it satirized contemporary social constructs.

Osell notes that female eidolons of early periodicals were "instrumental" in the literary construction of the public sphere because, in their concern for "social reputation" and "public opinion," they united the feminine with the public, thereby causing women to become "both the subjects and the objects of public discourse: talked about as well as talking about others" (286). (Probably the most radical eidolon of all was Haywood's talking parrot who was the editor of the magazine called the *Parrot.*)

All the early eidolons, even the female ones, relied heavily on the masculine rhetorical appeal of wit. Powell observes that wit was a "category of literary commodity" that periodical authors used to establish credibility and to "make the private public . . . because of the pleasure readers derive from taking part in public-private transgression" (28, 37). The *Female Tatler,* as a gossip magazine, is a prime example of the periodical's use of gendered wit in appealing to a general audience. The editor of the magazine, Mrs. Crackenthorpe, addresses her readers as "Ladies of all Degrees," ironically emphasizing women of the middle and lower classes. The identity and gender of the real author behind Mrs. Crackenthorpe are unknown, but rumors that the author was Delarivier Manley are thought to be false, mainly because the magazine supported Whig values, yet Manley was a Tory writer. In her in-depth analysis of the *Female Tatler,* Powell notes that the Mrs. Crackenthorpe eidolon was likely the work of multiple writers of undetermined gender and that "feminized modes of discourse were useful in the periodical genre" for many reasons, including their rhetorical positioning as nonthreatening voices and their ability to attract readers (59–72).

In the first volume of the *Female Tatler,* the eidolon announces that her intent is not to "invade" Bickerstaff's domain, "rival his performance," nor "prejudice the Reputation he has deservedly gained" (1). Her saucy tone implies that those really are her goals, and she argues that "tatling" is the talent of her own sex. She further states her purpose is primarily to gossip, as she states, "to prate a little to the Town, and try what Diversion my Intelligence can give'em," but also to avoid personal attacks (1). Crackenthorpe is a feisty female eidolon who cajoles her audience. In her teasing posture, she notes, "My Acquaintance . . . is a very great part of the Town . . . from her Grace my Lady Dutchess, to the Sea Captain's Wife. . . . half the Nation visits me" (Steele 1). By this, we might assume that the *Female Tatler's* readership spans class distinctions. All women readers who aspire to jovial society are welcome, and she encourages readers to engage with the text on the grounds that everybody else does.

Although the Crackenthorpe eidolon is clearly a humorous gendered device, she uses wit to invite rational discourse, for example, when she states:

> The Society I aim at, are those . . . that not only talk good Common Sense, but can state an Argument in any Art or Science, and dispute with Learning, Judgement, and Force of Reason. Wit is entertaining, but People are not oblig'd always to be upon the Grin. (*Female Tatler* no. 3)

The Crackenthorpe eidolon advocates for common sense, but her conversational style is marked by perpetual joking. The effect of this satiric tone is to make the reader smile, laugh, and reflect on society's absurdities.

Likewise, when Crackenthorpe encourages the fair sex to desist from gossip and turn to morally improving subject matter, she does so with playful irony:

> I would have the Ladies too relish somewhat above mere Tittle-Tattle, and . . . conversing with ingenious Persons, would so far improve their Natural Parts, as to give em a more noble Idea of Things and create in em at least a Value for Matters serious and instructive, which would stifle a World of Scandal and Detraction. (no. 3)

Affecting mock haughtiness and lofty language, the eidolon argues that ladies should train themselves away from trivial pursuits. Underneath her humorous style, Mrs. Crackenthorpe delivers a similar message and theme to that offered in Mary Astell's *Serious Proposal to the Ladies, Part I* (1694). While most readers would agree that "Mrs. Crackenthorpe is no Bluestocking" and that "*The Female Tatler* grounds its power in gossip rather than morality," it is also clear that "Mrs. Crackenthorpe emphasizes women's central role in social discourse" (Osell 293). Notably, this common call to raise the intellectual level and broaden the scope of women's sociable activities appears in both highbrow "serious proposals" and lowbrow "tattling" periodical essays, marking a shared protofeminist understanding of changes already under way in women's communicative practices and foreshadowing later developments in women's education and sociability.

It is also important to realize, no matter the sarcasm and trivialization of this subject matter, that discourse on feminine-focused topics such as courtship, marriage, women's rights, and girls' education was not frivolous. Women needed practical advice on how to handle social situations, such as engaging with the tactical maneuvers of male suitors. Mrs. Crackenthorpe provided courtship advice while also, ironically, maintaining her own single status. In number 47, she writes of her numerous suitors, "One of almost every class has done me the honour of a visit. . . . , which still gives me penetration into mankind, for courtship does certainly discover people's sense and education more than any other undertaking" (Morgan 108). Crackenthorpe goes on to enumerate many different types of suitors in an Aristotelian catalog of behavior and emotion. Notably, the *Female Tatler* also presents variations on the eidolon identity. Starting in number 52, Mrs. Crackenthorpe takes her leave from the magazine, and the female contingency of Emilia, Arabella, Rosella, Lucinda, Artesia, and Sophronia join in as co-eidolons for numbers 53 through 111.

The model of a female contingency of co-eidolons speaking on subjects of courtship, gender identity, and femininity further develops in the *Female Spectator* (1744–1746), a less cheeky but still witty protofeminist essay periodical designed specifically for women. Written and edited by Eliza Haywood, one of the most prolific women writers of the eighteenth century, the *Female Spectator*, as Patricia Meyers Spacks claims, "was in fact the first periodical for women actually written by a woman" (xii).[18] This remark undoubtedly points to the inconclusive authorship of the *Female Tatler*, as well as Haywood's preeminence as an author and her unabashedly feminine perspective, which differs from the male-gendered persona of Lady Wortley Montagu's *Nonsense of Common Sense* (1737–1738), a political periodical ostensibly written to support the Walpole administration. As Powell notes, both Montagu and Haywood developed their periodicals in the shadow of the immensely popular *Spectator* but with very different stances: Montagu's male eidolon openly competes with the *Spectator* while Haywood capitalizes on the titular association of the *Female Spectator* to both complement the original and interject overtly feminine voices into public conversations on a wide range of social, philosophical, and political subjects (149–50). Haywood's unapologetically feminine writing style ranging over the periodical subject matter marks a protofeminist rhetorical innovation in women's print ephemera.

In the first issue of the *Female Spectator,* Haywood responds to Addison's male eidolon, Mr. Spectator, by introducing her unnamed female eidolon. The persona of "the female spectator" is a worldly middle-aged woman who claims to have useful experience in a wide range of social situations. Far from pompous, she portrays herself as an average woman who was no beauty in her youth. To provide her readers with a great store of insights, she states that she will be assisted in her narratives by three other female characters: the "excellent" wife of a worthy gentleman; an independent "widow of quality"; and the sweet "daughter of a wealthy merchant" (Haywood 9–10). Through these personas, Haywood develops a committee of female eidolons, each one with her own area of expertise in sociability. In each issue, Haywood narrates dialogues through these eidolons and the contributions of letters from fictitious readers in order to illustrate the pitfalls and social traps that eighteenth-century women faced. The text deals with real women's issues—from the trivial to the serious. Its lofty hyperbolic language, ancient character names (such as Europhresine and Alcibiades), and the neoclassical dialogic format give the *Female Spectator* a mockingly highbrow tone, which conforms to the mid-eighteenth-century style. The magazine functions rhetorically as an early form of an advice column, such as *Ann Landers* or *Dear Abby* did in the twentieth century.

Although Haywood dedicates each volume of her periodical to members of the nobility, she targets a general female readership to whom she delivers practical advice. As Spacks notes, the *Female Spectator's* controlling theme was "the urgency of experience for middle-class women" (xii–xiii). In keeping with the rise of bourgeois culture, the *Female Spectator* models the eighteenth-century woman as an emblem of virtue and also relies heavily on the device of the woman's cautionary tale or vignette emphasizing both experience and passion. Aleksondra Hultquist's appraisal of Haywood's fiction—it demonstrates that "experience with passion is crucial to keeping the individual balanced"—also applies to her periodical writings (xx). In Haywood's rhetoric, passion always coexists with logic; the rhetorical scale between logos and pathos must equal out.

Haywood uses a query and response format in which her eidolons council fictional readers on managing problems in their lives. In their letters, the invented readers ask questions and share their own experiences on topics ranging from love and courtship to parental respect while the eidolons dole out advice, such as on how to avoid malicious gossip, guard against prejudice, and seek education and opportunities for real-world experience. Over the course of the periodical's 111 issues, Haywood's writing becomes more direct; in the later issues, she downplays the use of allegorical fictional narrative in favor of direct polemics, in what Powell characterizes as an "evolution from coquette to stern-but-fair mother" (153). Moving through many elaborate examples and stories toward the development of a protofeminist rhetorical theory, the *Female Spectator* advocates for "virtue and wisdom [as] the only two pursuits where Ardency is reconciled with Reason" and calls for women to have an active place in the world and "not be stifled by a wrong Education" (Haywood 312, 132).

The scenarios that Haywood presents are wide-ranging, encompassing many difficult and realistic situations that women may encounter. On some points of discussion, the *Female Spectator* seems to align with hegemonic conduct book literature, but on others it veers into a subversive anticonduct book with content that verges on shocking. Haywood maintains politeness while taking radical poetic license to oppose the abuses of patriarchy. For example, in book 14 the eidolon starts by stating that her goal is to improve society through stories of wit and virtue:

> Whether these monthly essays answer the great End . . . of conducing in some Measure . . . [the] rectification of Manners which this Age stands in so much need of, we cannot yet be able to determine, but of this we are certain, by the letters we receive, that Wit and the Love of Virtue are not altogether banish'd [from] the Realm. (155)

She then immediately introduces a letter from a reader named Elismonda. The letter from this fictional reader introduces a "little narrative" called "The Lady's Revenge," which she claims is a truthful account in which a lady called Barsina carries out an elaborate ruse to take revenge on a man who breaks off their courtship and marries another woman. In their last meeting, Barsina confronts her ex-lover with her knowledge of his marriage and makes him believe she has poisoned him and herself. The man then goes to much expense and endures painful and excruciating cures to rid himself of the alleged poison, almost dying in the process. At the conclusion of this narrative, the editors of the *Female Spectator* voice their approval of the story because it represents a true account of justice being served, stating of the fooled man "wherever there is *Guilt* there will be *Fear:*—We naturally *expect* what we consciously *deserve*" (Haywood 174). Clearly readers can see that Haywood is not advocating that spurned women should take the extreme measure of staging a fake poisoning;

rather, it is obvious that Haywood uses the fictional example to moralize about the gendered double standards of courtship.

Haywood's use of conversation and letters between multiple speakers to convey moral philosophy reflects the influence of the Platonic humanist dialogue, but it also allows her to adopt a sophistic approach to her analysis of sociability. The editorial commentary that Haywood laces throughout the *Female Spectator* at times reinforces mainstream patriarchal views, such as the necessity of a lady's virtue and obedience to parents, but she also shows how women and parents sometimes need to oppose the status quo to do what is morally right and just. As Powell comments, Haywood's *Female Spectator* "broke some serious ground" for women writers who would follow her by constructing "a clever feminine voice to negotiate social boundaries and hold forth publicly even while the female body was supposed to be more domestically confined" (149–50). Haywood not only forged a path for future women writers; she also articulated the desires of contemporary readers for social justice for women.

In the *Female Spectator,* Haywood constructs a protofeminist moral philosophy, which includes elements of rhetorical theory. In book 15, Haywood meditates on the subject of taste, an ongoing topic of belletristic rhetoric, which garnered attention from early eighteenth-century British philosophical writers, such as Shaftesbury and Hutcheson, and poets, most prominently Alexander Pope.[19] Weighing in on this intellectual discourse, Haywood echoes the notion of taste as an internal capacity to judge complex sensory experiences and sense what is right and good.[20] She writes, "An early knowledge of ourselves and of the World, will prevent any ill Humours from getting the better of us; and, as we rise towards Maturity, produce that distinguishing Power in us which we express by the name of *true Taste*" (179). In accordance with Lockean empiricism as well, Haywood affirms that experience is what builds one's capacity for "Reason and Reflection" and forms the basis for true taste, which requires careful, polite, discerning, detailed, and charitable judgments (177–184). Adding her own protofeminist pitch for women's education, Haywood argues that any person—of either gender—whose experience is confined or undeveloped cannot possess or develop truly good taste. Book 15 of the *Female Spectator* amplifies this thread on the importance of education by introducing a supporting anecdote in the form of a letter from a fictionalized male reader, Philo-Nature, who advocates that ladies can and do gain experience in natural philosophy (natural science) through close observations of nature. The *Female Spectator*'s eidolons concur with Philo-Nature's observation and also add their opinions: that wide reading and a deep knowledge of world history are necessary for ladies to develop a capacity for true taste. Providing evidence of womanly wit, as well as taste, the *Female Spectator* discusses selected quotations and excerpts from acclaimed canonical authors such as Dryden, Milton, Cowley, and Shakespeare.

The subject of taste and the frequent use of literary allusion in women's periodicals is a feature in keeping with the style and content of the leading essay periodicals of the century, such as the *Spectator* and the *Rambler*. The popular and widely read periodical genre demonstrates a major public channel through which women, as readers, experienced developments in rhetorical theory connected to taste. As Thomas Gilmore notes, in the mid-eighteenth century, the concept of taste became increasingly analytical, less focused on an internal sense of beauty produced through experience and more focused on acquired knowledge of "standards of taste" (xvii). In *The Temporality of Taste in Eighteenth-Century British Writing,* James Noggle analyzes these two eighteenth-century views of taste as a faculty of immediate perception and the historicized application of communally accepted standards developed over time (1–5). The latter idea was strongly informed by David Hume's "On Standards of Taste" (1757), which advocated for expert critics to establish standards, or touchstones, of taste (a general proposition that aligns with Haywood's earlier argument in the *Female Spectator,* which specifically advocates for education to improve women's critical abilities). Noggle's study devotes a chapter specifically to analyzing how women writers partook in this discourse, noting that "feminine taste uses its status as an object to discover a unique subject position. The condition of being judged always already informs feminine judgement" (127). Adding women's perspectives to the discourse on taste was a preoccupation of the bluestockings, as well as a major thread of discussion in the essay periodical from the 1740s through the 1780s. By the latter half of the eighteenth century, taste had become a central focus of belletristic rhetoric.

By the end of the eighteenth century, however, discourse on taste and the belles lettres, although still popular among literary critics, was waning in the periodical essay genre. Accordingly, Scottish author, intellectual, and saloniste Elizabeth Hamilton states that she and her women colleagues thought about publishing "a periodical paper" focused on discussion of literature and culture but then decided that "this species of composition was obsolete in England" (Benger 291). To this end, Hamilton drafted but did not publish a collection of essays, entitled *The Breakfast Table*. Several issues of this unpublished periodical are noteworthy specimens of women's belletristic rhetoric for their articulation of a feminine literary critique of the masculine-style of the most successful essay periodicalists: Joseph Addison and Richard Steele, co-editors of the *Spectator,* and Samuel Johnson, author of the *Rambler*.

In *The Breakfast Table* no. 2, Hamilton critiques the styles of Johnson, Addison, and Steele in terms of standards of taste and skill in composition. Hamilton finds Addison's style tolerable but not impressive. Speaking of his style, she notes, "His is not coarse; he is not harsh; he is not vapid; but expression eminently beautiful, language modulated to positive harmony, thoughts pointed and energetic, have seldom proceeded from his pen" (312). She rates the strength of Addison's compositions not at the sentence level but in "the correctness of the whole. His mind was elegant, his observation acute, and his ear rejected whatever was harsh in composition; yet . . . he had nothing which was peculiarly his own" (312). She further comments that "neatness of elucidation, rather than splendor of ornament, was what . . . he attained. His style may be called truly Attic" (316). By Attic, Hamilton means manly in the Greek sense: logical, coherent, and backed by evidence. She finds Johnson's style less regular but maybe more memorable and inspiring. Hamilton describes Johnson as "far beyond negative: his conceptions are forcible, . . . and his phraseology has a fertility and precision, which have rarely been equalled, and never excelled"; and his "style is marked and peculiar" (311–12). She also notes that "whatever was his subject . . . he clothed it with dignity and importance; and he could detail the composition of a pudding with more force than another could picture the horrors of a battle" (316–17). While Hamilton finds Johnson's writing vivid, nuanced, and emotionally compelling, she discounts Steele's prose as "vulgar, loose, and slovenly" (312).

Hamilton's status as an acclaimed novelist and an expert scholar of Orientalism lends ethos to her critique of the Attic masculinity of male literary critics. As a woman and an Orientalist, she brings the perspective of nonmasculine and non-Western otherness to her assessment. Her criticism shows keen awareness of and attention to gendered stylistics both from classical theory and by eighteenth-century periodical writers. Hamilton's rhetorical moves in this unpublished periodical demonstrate the application of educated taste based on standards—with a clearly feminine critical eye and without apology for making a critique. This unpublished work of literary criticism likely reflects the kind of verbal belletristic rhetoric that took place among bluestocking women and literati in salon conversations during the latter half of the eighteenth century.

POCKET BOOKS

By the end of the century, more utilitarian ephemera also developed to serve the growing audience of middle-class women who were increasingly active consumers, creating a demand for tools to support everyday practical rhetoric. Pocket books, as Jennie Batchelor explains, reflect "paradoxal responses" to women's power to have and spend their own "pin money"—at once attempting to attract women as buyers and to "police and control" their spending (2). The pocket book provided a journal and notebook of sorts for women to record their purchases and other notes. It also served a didactic function through the inclusion of short essays on topics such as the glorification of marriage and codes of politeness and answered women's needs for reference information by providing useful lists and tables. *The Ladies Pocket Journal; Or Toilet Assistant: For the Year 1791*, shown in figure 1.5, is an example held at the Bodleian Library of a pocket book catering to the middle-class British woman. This pocketbook, according to Elizabeth Crawford, belonged to Mrs. Mary Crespigny of Champion Lodge, the wife of a military captain and a close friend of travel writer Mrs. Mariana Starke.[21] The title page shows that the journal contains many items of reference information, including useful lists, recipes (called receipts), and short essays. While these items function hegemonically to teach women acceptable feminine activities, they also encourage sociability and illustrate public awareness of women's collective identity as a commercial demographic with buying power. The lists include "Days and Hours for Transferring Stock," "Table of Precedence," and "An Index of Remarkable Days." Within the list of "remarkable days," March 25 is noted as "Lady-day." The list of country dances, includes the "Ching Chit Quaw," "The Haunted Tower," the "Ding Dong Bell," the "Whim of the Moment," and the "New Highland Reel" (143). These vivid dance titles convey some feeling of the everyday rhetorics of 1790s British popular culture (in a similar way that a list of popular music today conveys current tastes and styles). As evident from Frances Burney's *Evelina* and many Jane Austen novels, dancing was an important mode of performative bodily rhetoric for women, and men, in eighteenth-century England. To dance well evidenced social grace and a properly composed presence among one's peers. The inclusion of this information on feminine pastimes, interspersed with diary pages for writing and recording financial transactions, illustrates the commercial attributes of women's identities, as they shaped and were shaped by the publishing industry.

As such, print ephemera also depicted women's fashions in the age of Enlightenment. Despite numerous arguments in eighteenth-century poetry and other literature about the superficiality of fashion, advertisements such as the following page from the *Ladies Toilet Assistant,* delivered visual rhetorical messages that inspired new levels of feminine sociability. Figure 1.6 shows two women in a parlor. With her shawl, high hat, and umbrella in hand, the woman standing is dressed to go out while the sitting woman is dressed to stay in, wearing a white cap and holding a basket. The women appear to be busy,

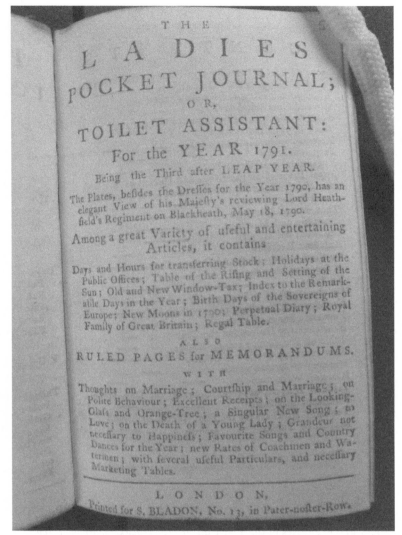

FIGURE 1.5. *The Ladies Pocket Journal; or, Toilet Assistant: For the Year 1791* (London, S. Bladon). Diary of Mary Crespigny née Clark, of Champion Lodge, Camberwell. Oxford, Bodleian Libraries MS. Eng. e. 3767, fol. 1.

socializing and making plans together. Their image is fashionable yet wholesome, suggesting that they are respectable and well off, but not extravagant. As Batchelor notes, "Pocketbooks . . . judiciously attempted to steer a middle course between the polar models of unrestrained consumption and a failure to consume at all" and "encourage[d] women to regulate their consumption in order that they may be better equipped to fulfill the duties of wife and

FIGURE 1.6. Dresses of the Year 1790. *The Ladies Pocket Journal; or, Toilet Assistant: For the Year 1791* (London, S. Bladon). Diary of Mary Crespigny née Clark, of Champion Lodge, Camberwell. Oxford, Bodleian Libraries MS. Eng. e. 3767, fol. 2.

mother" (8). Ostensibly hegemonic in their purpose, pocket books constitute a sign of rising middle class prosperity and bear further examination as an ephemeral text genre, which functioned rhetorically to encourage the economic participation of women in eighteenth-century daily public life. The country dances, fashion advertisements, and recipes they contain might be studied as documentation of the embodied rhetoric of women's sociability.

Conclusion

Over the course of the long eighteenth century, political and economic forces enacted slow yet liminal changes to the deep rhetoric of social class and gender, which translated into new gendered symbolism and roles, as well as new ephemeral rhetorical sites. Among many significant cultural transformations, the age of Enlightenment was marked by women's growing literacy and identity as a commercial demographic. As Arizpe, Morgan, and Heath note, "Women's and girl's literate practices were intrinsically related to their multiple roles (present or future), as wives, mothers, teachers, household managers and social beings" (1).

The increased authority of the mother figure as moral exemplar and director of domestic education is one of the strongest examples of rhetorical feminization in eighteenth-century England. While the new responsibilities of the mother aligned noncontroversially with the transformation of the family in bourgeois patriarchy, other more public and controversial roles arose for women. From 1660 to 1800, British women found available means to address many social and political issues through rhetorical performances customized to a variety of audiences and spectators for a variety of purposes. The fashions, styles, and pastimes of the upper classes became more accessible to those in the middle, and venues for developing rhetorical theory opened up for educated women. The wider accessibility of education, rhetorical venues, and new professional opportunities also aided in the development of women's' rhetoric among the growing middle class.[22]

One hundred years after John Locke published his *Two Treatises on Government* (1690), England had progressed to more egalitarian ideas about citizenship and individual rights, yet direct political power was still in the hands of the elite males in Parliament. British Enlightenment philosophy had not gone so far as to invite, or even permit, the average woman of any social class to directly participate in the political process, nor did the traditional rhetorical venues of podium and pulpit open up to women. Nevertheless, the feminized code of politeness had impacted the cultural hegemony and rhetorical practices of England significantly. This rippling of developments in many levels and venues of British society together instigated a sea change, what Royster and Kirsch have described as "tectonic shifts" allowing new sites of women's rhetorics to emerge.

The patriarchal conjugal family and the feminine reformation of manners were two of the most important ideological trends to shape the fabric of eighteenth-century British life and culture (Marsden, Lowenthal, Apetri, Staves). Replacing the extended kinship model of the aristocratic family, the conjugal or nuclear family still conformed to a patriarchal model, but the partnership of the husband and wife became a more prominent feature of the family. Politeness was quickly becoming an important performative quality and requirement for success among the rising middle class. Changes to the scope of the family, gender roles, and gendered sociability profoundly affected women's participation in rhetoric in eighteenth-century Britain—even as political hegemony and conduct literature continued to repress women's voices and to maintain the façade of essentialized gender roles based on separate spheres.

Many precedents exist for analyzing women's roles and venues in the rhetorical ecology of British Enlightenment culture, as well as the long-term accretive effects of eighteenth-century women's nontraditional rhetorics. This chapter has suggested how new public opportunities for women affected and changed the dominant public discourse of Enlightenment Britain. Applying feminist rhetorical ecology as a research strategy (more open than the traditional five-fold paradigm) reveals the development of British eighteenth-century women's ethe in the relationships between "individuals, audiences, values, written texts, and physical locations" (Ryan, Myers, and Jones 6). In the next chapter, we will return to the earlier years of the long eighteenth century, to the Restoration and the several decades following it, in order to trace the specific influence of the theater on British women's rhetorical performance.

CHAPTER 2

On the Stage: Dramatized Women's Rhetoric

Forasmuch as . . . the women's parts . . . have been acted by men
in the habits of women, at which some have taken offence, . . .
we do . . . permit and give leave that all the women's parts to be
acted in either of the . . . two companies from this time to come
may be performed by women.
                                    —Royal patent of Charles II, 1662

HE THEATRICAL STAGE has long been a site of both rhetorical performance and gender fluidity. From the theaters of ancient Greece and Rome
through those of the Renaissance, the Western tradition of drama consisted
largely of tragedy and comedy performed by all-male casts, including cross-
dressed male actors in women's roles. In England, this theatrical tradition
suffered an interruption, from 1642 to 1660, with the closure of public theaters
during the eighteen years of the Puritan-ruled Commonwealth era. Soon after
the restoration of the monarchy in 1660, Charles II reopened London's public
theaters and approved the formation of two new public theater companies:
the King's company, managed by Thomas Killigrew, and the Duke's company,
managed by William Davenant.[1] As the epigraph of this chapter shows, Charles
also regendered the rules of theatrical performance in England. In 1660, the
first professional woman actor (hereafter referred to as actress) appeared on the
London stage, possibly in *Othello* in the role of Desdemona (Howe 19).[2] Prior
to this, in the golden age of Renaissance drama, all women's parts performed
in England's public playhouses had been played by men or boys.

Charles's 1662 decree that women's roles be played henceforth by actresses,
rather than male actors, implicitly begs the question: Was the sight of female
players speaking on a public stage a less outrageous violation of gender norms
than male players appearing "made-up" as women in dresses and skirts?[3] Both
acts—male cross-dressing and female public speech—subverted the patriarchal
heteronormativity of early modern England, but it is debatable which of the
two was more objectionable to theater audiences and to the wider populace.
Although public theater and acting in any form was unacceptable to Puritans,
the wider audience of early modern English society was accustomed to theatrical drag performances by male actors. In contrast, female public speech was

a cultural taboo. The deep rhetoric inherited from Renaissance culture was that "excessive speech [in women] was an indication of unchastity. By speech, women seduced men" (King and Rabil xxviii). The earliest British actresses were disdained in the public eye and collectively denounced as prostitutes, but, ironically, they also enjoyed instant popularity with Restoration theater audiences.

Restoration actresses regendered the London public stage and helped introduce protofeminist rhetoric to the British public eye. Although they fell outside the margins of respectability, Restoration actresses comprised an official government-mandated female contingent, which, by its very existence, challenged the notion that the public sphere was available only to men. The popularity of actresses was not a short-lived fad of London theater but a milestone that wrought profound change for the identity and professional status of women in British culture. Beginning with the first generation of women players on the Restoration stage, Britain's actresses evoked a realistic feminine theatrical mode, which expanded the neoclassical style of delivery while illuminating the myriad complexities of women's experience and the social inequities they faced in Western patriarchal society.

The contribution of actresses to Restoration theater has held an undisputed place in theater historiography for centuries and recently has received attention from feminist scholars of eighteenth-century theater and performance studies.[4] Ongoing, authoritative theater histories, such as the *London Stage 1660–1800: Part 1:1660–1700* (Van Lennep) and *A Biographical Dictionary of Actors, Actresses, Musicians, Dancers, Managers and Other Stage Personnel in London, 1660–1800* (Highfill, Burnim, and Langhans) have long acknowledged the careers and accomplishments of the early English actresses. Starting in the late twentieth century, the actresses' impact on early Enlightenment culture gained attention in feminist literary histories of the theater, such as Susan Staves's *Players' Scepters: Fictions of Authority in the Restoration,* which studies actresses as well as actors.[5] Exclusively focused on the actresses, Elizabeth Howe's *First English Actresses: Women and Drama 1660–1700* is the most comprehensive work to date and an essential starting point for learning about Restoration actresses. Howe collates a wide array of sources to detail the personalities, backgrounds, training, stage personas, roles, delivery style, performance effects, and financial situations of fifteen Restoration actresses, especially focusing on the legacies of the two top earners of the first generation, Elizabeth Barry (1658–1713) and Ann Bracegirdle (1671–1748).

Several studies suggest the rhetorical agency of Restoration and early eighteenth-century actresses, especially Cynthia Lowenthal's *Performing Identities on the Restoration Stage,* Jean Marsden's *Fatal Desire: Women, Sexuality, and the English Stage, 1660–1720,* Gilli Bush-Bailey's *Treading the Bawds: Actresses and Playwrights on the Late Stuart Stage,* and Helen E. M. Brooks, *Actresses, Gender, and the Eighteenth-Century Stage: Playing Women.* Some also continue the analysis of the early actresses to include the next several generations. In *It,* Joseph Roach theorizes how the early British actresses, from the late seventeenth to early nineteenth century, captivated audiences on the stage and beyond through an age-old form of charisma. Felicity Nussbaum, in *Rival Queens: Actresses, Performance, and the Eighteenth-Century British Theater,* extends the cultural analysis of early English actresses to the second and third generation of star actresses and identifies the eighteenth century as "the age of *women* in the theater and especially the age of the *actress*" (6). Nussbaum argues that, as the top eighteenth-century British actresses gained celebrity, their onstage performances increased the public's understanding of the middle-class woman as a force of civic virtue even while critics maligned actresses personally for the immorality of their public profession (22–26). These studies provide excellent contextualization and analyses of the early British actresses in cultural, literary, and theater history. They do not, however, explicitly theorize the actresses' place in the history of rhetoric.

A few publications focused on the elocutionary and belletristic trends within eighteenth-century rhetoric have attended to the innovations in delivery by early British actresses. In *Rhetoric of Sensibility,* Paul Goring argues that actors and actresses were instrumental in the combined rise of elocution, sentimentalism, and the aesthetic of sensibility, all of which he states began in the theaters in the 1720s (several decades before sensibility's appearance in the novel). Goring states that "the bodies of orators and actors were important to the growth of politeness because they occupied supremely public positions in eighteenth-century life, and thus were ripe for dispersing this quality through a broader public" (25). Lindal Buchanan's two articles: "Sarah Siddons and Her Place in Rhetorical History" and "Angels in the Theatrical House: Pregnancy, Rhetorical Access, and the London Stage" examine late eighteenth- and early nineteenth-century actresses' contributions to the canon of delivery and to maternal rhetorics. Both Goring and Buchanan focus on imbrications of acting and rhetoric with feminizing themes—politeness and maternal virtue—that were trending in British culture in the latter half of the eighteenth century. But the rhetorical impact of British actresses commenced a century earlier, as I explain in my article, "Before Garrick: Elizabeth Barry, Mistress of Emotion on the Restoration Stage." As the first generation of professional women in English history to command a popular and highly persuasive public voice, Restoration actresses warrant further study from the perspective of feminist historical rhetoric.

This chapter adds to the scholarly conversation on actresses of the Restoration era by claiming them not only as innovators of modern feminine rhetorical delivery but as a foundational contingency within the history of British women's Enlightenment rhetoric. Using feminist rhetorical analysis methodology, I extend Howe's exploration of the "general dramatic consequences" of Restoration actresses and their "individual influences . . . on the plays that were written for them" (x). Collectively, these women hold a pivotal role in the rhetorical landscape of Restoration London where, I argue, they became the first widely acclaimed and highly successful group of British women orators. I begin my analysis by contextualizing the relationship between theater and oratory within the Western rhetorical tradition, specifically elaborating on how first-generation British actresses appropriated the feminine theatrical mode of neoclassical delivery and how their performances affected theater audiences. Secondly, I analyze Restoration actresses as professional public speakers who honed and transmitted their craft through a mentor/mentee training model encompassing a shared repertoire of performative techniques and skills augmented by individuals' unique specializations and personas. Of course, as dramatic performers, actresses did not deliver their own written compositions, but rather they assumed roles created by playwrights, and so the third major section of this chapter examines several examples of Restoration actresses and playwrights collaborating as doublespeakers to produce customized roles and new female types as embodiments of feminine and womanly gender issues inherent in early modern British society.

Restoration Theater as Rhetorical Site

Oratory and drama as performative practices have shared in methods of delivery for thousands of years. Dating back to ancient Rome, classical theories of rhetoric describe two basic delivery styles: the masculine Attic style, ideal for serious public oratory, and the feminine Asiatic style associated with acting and theatrical performance. As Amy Richlin explains, the prescribed, clean, and trusted Attic delivery style conveyed authority, objectivity, and masculine reasoning skills, whereas the descried, sexy, and distrusted Asiatic (or Asianist) delivery style, conveyed signs of emotional femininity, such as a high or faltering voice, uneven use of literary figures, erratic gesturing, and immodest or flamboyant dress, all of which were associated with acting, a profession that was considered effeminate and "suffered a diminished civil status" (100). Nevertheless, classical theory also acknowledges that both oratory and acting require similar skill sets. Cicero and Quintilian frequently compared orators with actors—stressing the importance of the voice and bodily gestures in the art of persuasion. In *The Ideal Orator*, Cicero describes delivery as the ultimate test of effective oratory, and he stresses that proper training of the voice, face, eyes, and body is necessary for both orators and actors (3.213). In *The Orator's Education*, Quintilian draws upon examples of emotionally powerful stage performances in his analysis of delivery as consisting of two main parts: voice and gesture (11.3.15–18).

In keeping with the classical tradition, in the neoclassical dramatic productions of Restoration theater, both male and female roles took on lofty tones and exaggerated gestures, often involving gender-bending bodily displays in accordance with the Asiatic style. At the same time, the popularity of libertinism on and off the stage, coupled with the dominance of men in early modern patriarchal culture, infused misogyny into many plays and otherwise created anxiety and confusion about gender roles. Doubling back on the gender prescriptions inherent in the classical delivery model, theatrical portrayals of masculinity continued to stand for physical and mental power while femininity tended to connote physical and moral weakness, coquetry, and sexuality. In their stagecraft, the first British actresses copied and appropriated masculine, as well as feminine, practices of classical delivery. In their portrayals of wit—a masculine device—actresses broke gender stereotypes by showing that women could be clever. In their shocking bodily spectacles and the witty nuances of their delivery, Restoration actresses provide a historical link from the exclusively masculine classical rhetorical tradition of oratory to the modern appreciation of feminine style and of women as public speakers and performers.

The classical connection between drama and rhetoric held strong influence offstage as well in British Enlightenment rhetorical theory. The classical Latin term *elocutio*, referring to the rhetorical canon of style (and figures of speech), transformed into the modern English term *elocution*, and changed its referent from the canon of style to that of delivery. Eighteenth-century British proponents of elocution embraced the canon of delivery as the main pursuit of rhetoric and advised that, to achieve the most persuasive and effective oratory, rhetoricians should be trained as actors in voice and body control. Charles Gildon's *Life of Mr. Thomas Betterton* (1710), for example, provides an extensive conjoining of acting and rhetoric, detailing how speakers—whether preparing for the stage, bar, or pulpit—require training in gesture, expression, and speech to achieve their shared goal of persuading an audience.[6] Gildon's manual identifies the virtues of effective speech as purity, perspicuity, ornament, and hability (or aptitude) (93). In describing the various speech acts, movements, gestures, and facial expressions in portraying human passion, he includes examples of Restoration actresses along with actors and celebrated orators.[7]

Despite the noted professional excellencies of Restoration actresses—and the immense popularity of the London theater scene as a whole—in comparison to the masculine practice of oratory, the acting profession held a lower social status and carried a negatively feminized connotation throughout the long eighteenth century. As feminine spectacle, the sight of actresses performing in public, although wildly popular, amounted to a violation of deep rhetoric and an intrusion into the ideologically male public sphere. The actresses were doubly devalued in respectability—by gender and profession—as women and as actors. As Cynthia Lowenthal states, "Bodies were valorized when they were aristocratic, male, and Protestant, while the most intensely performative, aggressively veiled, and oft 'discovered' bodies were always those of women" (19). The female authenticity of actresses and their presence on stage destabilized established early modern notions of gender. As Butler notes, gender "as in other ritual social dramas . . . requires a performance that is repeated" (2499–500). Actresses' ritualized theatrical performances disturbed the status quo by repeatedly subverting the patriarchal norms for feminine silence.

ACTRESS AND AUDIENCE INTERACTION

Actresses embodied public proclamations of female experience. Yet, as Howe points out, this new public profession for women made them "in one sense merely playthings for a small male elite" (front piece). The objectification of the Restoration actress as a "working girl" who existed outside the prescribed social order might have eased the audience's gaze into the mirror of its own society. If the audience viewed the actress as an exotic, fantastical, yet lowly creature then it could watch her as a glamorized object far distanced from real women. But, as the audience gazed in judgment on an actress, she gazed back. One of the interesting subversions of Restoration theater, with its well-lit and relatively small space, is the reverse gaze from actor to audience. On average, the audience attending a performance at one of the two Restoration theaters consisted of about five hundred people (Holland 16–17). This community of spectators was intimate. As Douglas Canfield explains, Restoration actresses "were not just objectified by the gaze of the audience . . . ; in their reciting of prologues and epilogues, in their asides, and merely in their making eye contact with the audience, they conveyed their personalities and enacted their own gaze" in "roles of significant agency, from queens to more private women of powerful passion and intelligence" (xix). The gaze of the actress was attractive to men, but it also created a bond between the female speaker and the female spectator.

The implicit bond between women performers and their counterparts in the audience was something new in London society. As Paul Goring notes, "Flesh can bestow authority through the persuasive rhetoric of 'nature'" (19). The Restoration actress conveyed agency to the women in the audience and to feminine gender identities within their society. Her immediate visual impact is explained by Jean Marsden:

> The actress was recognizably female, with her breasts, loosened hair, and frequently revealed legs, all signs of womanhood emphasized in the roles she played. These physical signs not only established the actress's sex, but also linked her to other women, especially those sitting in the theater. (4)

In this communal space, the audience interacted with the actresses on stage, who became vehicles for exploring questions about femininity and women, such as: What did society think about the purpose, status, and condition of women? Should the female voice be heard? Could women be rhetorically effective? Was dramatic performance by women dangerous to spectators?[8]

Dangerous or not, Restoration actresses drew a loyal body of spectators. Londoners eagerly flocked to see actresses perform in the two new theater companies, which, as eighteenth-century actor, playwright, and critic Colley Cibber states, "were both in high Estimation with the Publick, and so much the Delight and Concern of the Court" (54). These public audiences were of varied composition, leaning toward the aristocratic, fashionable set but also including London's middle-class citizenry, as well as the lower classes who accompanied the aristocrats as servants or were able to purchase discount tickets midway through a show (McAfee 278–85). In this mixed society, genteel ladies who attended theater had to guard their reputations. In the earlier decades of the Restoration, ladies in the audience kept their faces covered with masks, which, as Cibber states, were "daily worn, and admitted, in the Pit, the Side-Boxes, and Gallery" (155). Many prologues and epilogues use the term *vizard mask* to connote the female contingency in the audience. As Rosenthal explains, "Appearing at the theater in a mask became so widespread a custom that the device that covered the face and the identity became a synecdoche for the whole person" (206). Although women theatergoers wore masks to shield their identities, they did not take such strong offense to the plays and players as to stay away from the theater, nor did theater companies discourage their attendance. Women audience members represented a sizable consumer demographic contributing to the rhetorical ecology of Restoration theater.

PUBLIC IDENTITY AND CELEBRITY

With the mixed-gender composition of its audiences and the debut of the actresses on stage, the rhetorical situation of Restoration theater created a popular site for public imagination, which lead to multiple cultural transformations in the latter part of the seventeenth century. Howe suggests that, due to the advent of the first generation of actresses, "a profound change in contemporary attitudes to women [and] female sexuality" occurred in England and included the recognition of women as private individuals (21–22). Although actresses dramatized unfortunate (and not uncommon) situations faced by women as individuals, the plots, themes, and symbolism they portrayed also held broader connotations of political gendering. Staves describes the public's acceptance of actresses and women-focused themes in the theater as resulting from the combination of the Protestant insistence on equality for all humans, the growing view of marriage as a contract between two individuals, and an increasingly bourgeois bent within the system of patriarchy, which created a disdain for traditional masculine aristocratic values and sought to appropriate symbols and behaviors of nonviolence from femininity (155–56). If Staves is correct—and I think she is—then Restoration actresses contributed strongly to the pronounced literary and political feminization of eighteenth-century British culture.

However, the profession of the actress certainly had its downside. As celebrities, actresses cultivated personas that belonged to the public. By extension, actresses' private lives also became the source of public scrutiny, a fact that theater companies began to capitalize on as part of actresses' economic value and rhetorical appeal. Many Restoration actresses were popular, in part, for their openly wanton public personas. Nell Gwyn, Elizabeth Barry, Rebecca Marshall, Elizabeth Boutell, and Charlotte Butler were all promoted on their apparently accurate reputations of promiscuity. On the other hand, a few Restoration actresses, such as Mary Saunderson Betterton and Anne Bracegirdle, were known for their high morals and chastity. (This ideal of the chaste actress as the rare epitome of feminine performativity would continue into the eighteenth century with Anne Oldfield and Sarah Siddons.) Questions of actresses' chasteness and promiscuity were never far from the audiences' minds. However, actresses on the Restoration stage always offered audiences more than just sexualized spectacle; they publicly symbolized women as feeling individuals confronted with the misogyny, legal obstacles, and financial difficulties that were inherent for women within patriarchal society.

The Actress as Professional Rhetor

Collectively, actresses formed a group of professional craftswomen who worked together, rehearsing and performing in the mixed-gender business of the theater company. To analyze actresses as professional rhetors, I apply Buchanan's and Skinner's topoi to assess their background and training, performative contexts, key roles, and individual styles of speech and material bodily delivery. The profession required individuals who could speak and move well, sing, dance, and portray genteel and refined characters. Thus, the job of actress not only required a retinue of performative skills but also a cultivated demeanor. In the Restoration era, finding new actresses was difficult for theater companies because "no woman with serious pretensions to respectability would countenance a stage career, and yet the profession demanded more than women of the brothel class" (Howe 8). Good candidates for actresses included girls of impoverished aristocratic families, bastard daughters of the gentry, and daughters of tradesmen.

Actresses usually had fewer roles available to them than actors, who outnumbered them in most seasons, and, except for the most successful actresses, they were paid significantly less than the actors—although they worked just as hard (Howe 27–28). Howe states that each theater would produce from forty to sixty different plays a season and that leading actors and actresses might play up to thirty different parts (9). Working with their fellow actors and playwrights, the actresses taught each other and developed their own professional networks. For example, leading actress Elizabeth Barry was both a friend and a business partner of her frequent costar, Anne Bracegirdle, who was the adopted daughter of Mary Saunderson Betterton, another renowned actress. As a network of professional performers, they rehearsed together and likely discussed and theorized their delivery methods with each other.

Actresses and orators undertook similar training in delivery. While they did not attend formalized academies or schools for their craft, actresses did indeed receive formal training in which they practiced, honed, and received critiques for their delivery skills. Of course, no video, film, or photographic recordings exist of the earliest British actresses, but ubiquitous and meticulously curated theater records provide details on their roles, personas, and theatrical performances, including descriptions of their delivery techniques. In her detailed collation of materials on second-generation British actresses, Nussbaum reviews the variety of methods by which actresses were most likely to have received their acting training. These included apprenticeships with acting tutors; acting schools for the young (called nurseries); private lessons with family members, husbands, and lovers who were established in the profession; training from playwrights; and trial periods with theater companies (34–35).

Many actresses were daughters or adopted daughters of theatrical families, but some women initially unattached to the theater found their way in through related trades. Some fell into the profession by chance and for financial needs. The rest of this section looks at the rhetorical training and careers of five successful Restoration actresses: Mary Saunderson Betterton, Nell Gwyn, Susannah Mountfort Verbruggen, Elizabeth Barry, and Ann Bracegirdle. The stories of these women serve as case studies of Restoration actresses' rhetorical training and illustrate their impact on feminine delivery and the new types of women's roles that began to appear on the British stage.

THE ACTRESS/MENTOR

Mary Saunderson Betterton (1637–1712) gained fame as a highly emotive tragic actress, who developed a wide repertoire of at least fifty-seven roles, from virtuous girls to villainesses, over an acting career that spanned from the 1660s to the early 1690s (Howe 180–181). One of the first critically acclaimed English actresses, she received her theatrical training from Thomas Betterton, the premiere actor of the Restoration era, whom she married. Colley Cibber notes that Mrs. Betterton "was so great a Mistress of Nature that even Mrs. Barry, who acted Lady Macbeth after her, could not in that Part, with all her superior Strength and melody of Voice, throw out those quick and careless strokes of Terror from the Disorder of a guilty Mind" as well as Mrs. Betterton did (Highfill, Burnim, and Langhans 2:98). Of the earliest professional English actresses, Mary Saunderson Betterton was a standout for her range, longevity, and as a role model to other women in the theatrical world.

The *London Stage* documents that Betterton worked behind the scenes as an acting coach, mentor, and teacher of elocution, providing support and training to younger actresses up through 1710, during and after her own acting career. She and her husband served as foster parents to fledgling actresses, including Ann Bracegirdle, who became one of the top actresses of the early eighteenth century, and Elizabeth Watson, who married actor John Boman (Highfill, Burnim, and Langhans 2:97). Mrs. Betterton also trained Princess Anne, daughter of James II, in elocution; and for this "kindness" was remembered by the future queen who rewarded her with a royal stipend in her old age (Highfill, Burnim, and Langhans 2:97). Bush-Bailey notes that Mary Betterton's "gifts as a teacher are remarked on in most reference to her work" and that she was also influential in the early career of playwright Aphra Behn

(34–35). Mrs. Betterton's career exemplifies the mentor/mentee model of rhetorical training, following the precedents of ancient Greek and Roman rhetoric wherein the experienced rhetor/teacher worked in an established private setting in instructing novices and apprentices in the skills of voice, expression, and gesture.

THE ORANGE GIRL TURNED ACTRESS

As a counterpoint to actresses who were born into theatrical families and raised in the acting business, Nell Gwyn (1650–87) worked her way into the profession. Yet Gwyn—perhaps better than any other woman—embodied the libertine image of a Restoration actress. She was known as a witty, beautiful, sexually available, happy-go-lucky whore, who wore her promiscuity proudly, like a libertine badge. According to Highfill, Burnim, and Langhans, in 1663, Gwyn began working in the theater as an "orange girl"—selling fruit and sexual favors to theater patrons—sometime in her teens or very early twenties, but within a year and a half turned from vending to acting in minor roles (6:458). Coming of age amid the libertine culture of London's Restoration theater at its sharpest, Gwyn witnessed and adopted a rakishly playful, cavalier attitude toward sexuality, authority, and money. A flamboyant beauty with spark and sauciness, Gwyn parlayed her performative gifts into professional and monetary success by first becoming one of the most popular comediennes of the Restoration theater and then assuming the role of royal mistress (one of many, but also a favorite) to Charles II.

Gwyn's legendary rise includes many entertaining anecdotes and conjecture about the sources of her training as an actress, which are impossible to verify completely, but her talents of comedic delivery are beyond doubt. The *London Stage* reports that Gwyn was nearly illiterate and that she must have had the assistance of a reader to help her learn her lines, as well as "a remarkable ear and memory" (Highfill, Burnim, and Langhans 6:460). By 1666, Gwyn was promoted to major roles and quickly rose to popularity. An extremely charismatic performer, Gwyn, shown in figure 2.1, captured and captivated the attention of theater audiences, playwrights, and even the king himself. The caption of the engraving states of Gwyn, "No Arte can shew her Will." However, the artifacts and records of history can aid in describing her legacy; one indicator of Gwyn's popularity is her frequent delivery of prologues and epilogues—the short speeches preceding and following a play, which function like appetizer and dessert, designed to whet the audiences' palates and send them away satisfied. The honor of delivering these speeches only went to the most popular players.

FIGURE 2.1. Portrait of Nell Gwyn as a shepherdess, with a lamb under her arm. *Nell Gwyn* by Gerard Valck, after Sir Peter Lely, line engraving, circa 1673, NPG D10959, © National Portrait Gallery, London.

Aphra Behn's dedication of her play *The Feign'd Curtizans* to Nell Gwyn— the first play that Behn ever dedicated to anyone—affirms Gwyn's innate charisma and describes the effect of Gwyn's appearance and speech on audiences:

> She was infinitely fair, witty, and deserving, but to what Vast degrees in all, they can only Judge who liv'd to Gaze and Listen; so Natural and so fitted are all your Charms and Excellencies . . . , you never appear but you glad

the hearts of all that have the happy fortune to see you, as if you were made on purpose to put the whole world into good Humour, . . . when you speak, men crowd to listen . . . and bear away the precious words to home to all the attentive family . . . *but oh she spoke with such an Ayr, so gay, that half the beauty's lost in the repetition.* 'Tis this that ought to make your Sex . . . despise the malicious world that will allow a woman no wit, and bless our selves for living in an Age that can produce so wondrous an argument as your undeniable self. (Todd, *The Works* of *Aphra Behn* 6:86)

Writing to and about Gwyn, Behn proposes the actress's presence as no less than an exemplum of female wit, an indisputable embodied "argument" for women's public performance. In her dedication to Gwyn, Behn creates a profile so laudatory that Samuel Johnson, in his biography of Dryden, remarks that it even exceeded the "servility of hyperbolic adulation" displayed in Dryden's excessively styled dedications (Todd 85). This tribute by one professional woman for another's work may seem unremarkable today, but in the Restoration era, these public displays of women's speech by Behn (in writing) and Gwyn (on stage) were highly controversial and constituted radical protofeminist statements of feminine power.

Gwyn's celebrity status itself became a rhetorical commonplace. Numerous pamphlets and bawdy works of verse derided Gwyn, particularly attacking her for becoming a mistress of Charles II. Yet letters of correspondence and legal documents of the period show Gwyn to be well liked by the people, politically neutral, generous, and charitable to the poor (Highfill, Burnim, and Langhans 6:463–69). Over the centuries, Gwyn has been remembered in over a half-dozen biographies. Although the facts of her life are often mixed with legend, theater historians credit her as an outstanding and memorable public female figure of the rising British middle class. Gwyn's persona is a major piece of Restoration theatrical history; as Highfill, Burnim, and Langhans note, "It surely would have pleased Nell, who came from common stock, to know that common folk today who might look blank at the names of Burbage, Betterton, Garrick, Kemble, or Siddons might well recognize the name of Nell Gwyn—and recognize her not just as a famous whore, but a famous actress" (6:470). Gwyn's place in the public memory attests to the rhetorical power of the theater and specifically of comedy. Her combination of wit, humor, and femininity combined to produce a stage persona that facilitated the development of the witty couple as a performative trope (which I discuss later in this chapter) and laid the groundwork for future women comedians as rhetorical speakers.

THE COMEDIENNE

Another comic genius of the Restoration stage, Susannah Percival Mountfort Verbruggen (1667–1703) represents versatility in delivery and the bravery to defy feminine standards of beauty. Mountfort Vebruggen was born Susannah Percival and raised in a theatrical family; her father was a minor actor in the Duke's company.[9] Trained by her family, as part of the family business, she acted her first small role in the Duke's company in 1681 at the age of fourteen, and her first starring role as "the robust Nell" in *The Devil of a Wife* in 1686 at the age of nineteen (Howe 82). Following Susannah Percival's first marriage to leading Restoration actor William Mountfort in 1686, the couple had at least four children, and the actress was pregnant at the time of her husband's murder in December of 1692 (Highfill, Burnim, and Langhans 15:137).[10] Soon after, between February and April of 1693, the widowed Susannah Mountfort is listed in the *London Stage* as playing at least three roles when she would have been in the last trimester of her pregnancy. As Highfill, Burnim and Langhans note, the dating of these performances seems questionable, but possible, as Restoration and eighteenth-century actresses often continued performing late in their pregnancies (15:137).[11] The actress married for a second time in 1694 to another actor, John Verbruggen. Over the period from 1694 until her death in 1703, Susannah Mountfort Verbruggen gave her most popular and finest performances. Howe's research from the *London Stage* shows that the actress played a total of sixty-one named parts over the period from 1681 to 1703 (187–88).

Over the course of her career, Mountfort Verbruggen became famous for her skill in creating visual comedy in a wide variety of roles—from witty heroines, to coquettes, to character parts. Mountfort Verbruggen possessed the talent to breathe life into dull roles and make them interesting through the nuances of her delivery; as Cibber states, "Nothing, tho' ever so barren . . . could be flat in her Hands. She gave many heightened Touches to Characters but coldly written, and often made an Author vain of his Work, that in it self had but little merit" (98). As the leading comedienne of the London stage for a number of years, Mountfort Verbruggen was renowned for both "witty breeches roles" in which she wore pants and was disguised as a man and for "grotesque characters" with comically exaggerated appearances and demeanors (Howe 82).[12] Her comedy relied heavily on the physicality of her delivery, and she was not averse to playing unglamorous parts. According to Cibber, "She was so fond of Humour, in what low Part soever to be found, that she would make no scruple of defacing her fair Form, to come heartily into it" (99). In the title role of *The Western Lass*,[13] "Mrs. Montfort transform'd her whole Being, Body,

Shape, Voice, Language, Look and Features, into almost another Animal; with a strong Devonshire Dialect, a broad laughing Voice, a poking Head, round Shoulders, an unconceiving Eye, and the most be-diz'ning, dowdy Dress, that ever covered the untrain'd Limbs of Joan Trot"[14] (Cibber 98). And, as Mary the Buxom in *History of Don Quixote,* Mountfort Verbruggen became a "a young tadpole dowdy, as freckled as a raven's egg, with matted hair, snotty nose, and a pair of hands as black as the skin of a tortoise, with nails as long as a kite's talons upon every finger" (Cibber qtd. in Styan 127). Mountfort Verbruggen's astounding vocal and bodily transformations transgressed the patriarchal expectations of beauty and silence in women.

Amazing as she was in her delivery of grotesque character parts, Mountfort Verbruggen possessed the versatility to portray the attractive coquette as well. In her most celebrated role, Melantha in Cibber's *Comical Lovers* (1707), Verbruggen's portrayal of Melantha fluidly translated her character's flirtatious nature into ridiculous affectations that appeared quite natural, thus keeping the comedy believable (Gildon 53). For the role of Melantha, Verbruggen created a "compleat System of Female Foppery," which included "Language, Dress, Motion, Manners, Soul, and Body" (Cibber 99). Cibber's description of her famous curtsey sounds like a slow-motion action-movie clip, noting her

> whole Artillery of Airs, Eyes, and Motion; down goes her dainty, diving Body, to the Ground, as if she were sinking under the conscious Load of her own Attractions; then launches into a Flood of Fine Language, and Compliment, still playing her Chest forward in fifty Falls and Risings, like a Swan upon waving Water. (Cibber 99–100)

Such a description begs for a visual artifact; as Cibber attempts to convey, the full impact of Melantha is not realized simply within the play script. The lines came fully to life only through flamboyant bodily performance. Captivating her audience through powerful visual arguments, Mountfort Verbruggen's delivery defied the early modern commonplace that women lacked the ability for public performance. Her repertoire of uniquely unconventional characters exploited the comic potential of the Asiatic delivery style to produce laughter and excitement in her audiences.

THE MISTRESS OF EMOTION

Flamboyant and persuasive feminine emoting reached new heights in the acting of Elizabeth Barry (1658–1713). In terms of moving audiences to tears, Barry surpassed all the other actresses of the Restoration era. Elizabeth Howe notes that, for over thirty-six years, "from 1673 to 1709 the brilliant Elizabeth Barry is known to have played 142 named parts"—the most of any actress in her era—including comic ingénues, adulterous wives, female libertines, prostitutes and fallen women, mothers, and, her specialty, the tragic heroine (9, 81). In addition to her undisputed status as the Restoration's supreme tragedienne, Barry's skill as a comedienne and a businesswoman attest to her multifaceted delivery skill and her astuteness as a speaker. Channeling public attention toward many injustices that women faced within the Restoration era system of aristocratic patriarchy, Barry's performances contribute significantly to women's Enlightenment rhetoric.

Many stories circulate about Barry's acting and the source of her training in elocution and delivery. As I have discussed in "Before Garrick: Elizabeth Barry, Mistress of Emotion on the Restoration Stage," theater histories have credited notorious court libertine John Wilmot, Earl of Rochester, with coaching Barry, who was his mistress, and aiding her transformation from a mediocre actress with "no ear for line-reading" to an emotionally riveting performer with the power to mesmerize audiences. The narrative of Barry's origin story reports that Wilmot trained her how to "enter into the Nature of each Sentiment; perfectly changing herself . . . into the Person, not merely by the proper Stress or Sounding of the Voice, but feeling really, and being in the Humour, the Person represented, was supposed to be in" (Highfill, Burnim, and Langhans 2:314; Howe 114).[15] However, Nussbaum argues that Barry more likely acquired her skills in the acting nursery of Lady Davenant who, along with her husband, theater manager William Davenant, was Barry's guardian (37). Either way, comments from colleagues later in Barry's career support the supposition that Barry maintained a *method approach* to acting. As multiple sources indicate, Barry acted as a conduit of emotion: she could feel as her character would and make the audience feel that way too. Her fellow actress, Mrs. Bradshaw, stated that "Mrs. Barry" taught her to "make herself Mistress of her Part, and leave the Figure and Action to Nature" (Highfill, Burnim, and Langhans 2:324). Barry brought a new style of performance to the stage, in which the actor personalized classical emotional expression (in addition to commanding the prescribed classical delivery poses) to create a stronger pathetic appeal to the audience.

In fact, Barry's powerful delivery served as a textbook example of Restoration elocutionary standards for creating pathos through movement, gesture, expression, and speech. In *The Life of Mr. Thomas Betterton* (1710), Charles Gildon uses Barry's acting to illustrate many of his points on exemplary elocution. Praising "the incomparable Mrs. Barry" as outstanding among her peers, Gildon describes her acting as always "just" and notes her ability to completely embody "the Sentiments of the part, which she acts" (39). Cibber describes how Barry used her body and voice to convey pathos:

> A Presence of elevated Dignity, her Mein and Motion superb and gracefully majestick; her Voice full, clear, and strong, so that no Violence of Passion could be too much for her; And when Distress or Tenderness possess'd her, she subsided into the most affecting Melody and Softness. In the Art of exciting Pity she had a Power beyond all the Actresses I have yet seen. (95)

Barry captivated audiences with her nuanced portrayals of mood. Her technique included a pattern of succession in which her facial expression spoke first, before gestures and words. As Jocelyn Powell notes, Barry was the creator of "a new acting style designed to 'stir rather than penetrate human nature' and . . . tragic actors like Betterton then followed her lead" (quoted in Howe 108). By today's standards, Barry's acting might seem extremely melodramatic, but her contemporaries saw it as "just or judicious" (Highfill, Burnim, and Langhan 2:324). Barry's emotive acting style offered a compelling vehicle for representing women's problems and prefigures later eighteenth-century trends in sentimentalism and sensibility. Even as she portrayed feminine emotions and characters, she also demonstrated a level of control and strength in her stage presence heretofore possessed only by male actors and orators.

Barry's innovative acting style garnered a level of public acclaim unprecedented for a theatrical performer during the Restoration. Through the power of their wallets, audiences demanded her stage presence. In the 1680s, she became the first actor (male or female) to be granted a benefit performance in which she alone received all of the night's profits, a perk that no other performer received before 1695 and one that made her annual salary exceed even the top paid actor, Thomas Betterton. The career of Elizabeth Barry, from the 1670s until her retirement in 1710, is one of the greatest professional success stories of the early British actresses. Barry's reputation for realistic and riveting delivery style prefigures David Garrick and Sarah Siddons, renowned British actors of the mid- and late-eighteenth century (Tasker 212; Buchanan "Sarah Siddons" 413–14). In fact, reports of Barry's achievements in delivery seem to challenge claims that, in the 1740s, David Garrick was the first actor to introduce a more naturalized style of acting to the English stage, providing welcome relief from the overly mannered Restoration style of delivery. While it is possible that what seemed natural to theatergoers may have changed by the mid-eighteenth century, it is also possible, as Goring suggests, that Charles Gildon's Restoration-era elocution manual exaggerated the similarities of style between Restoration stage elocution and classical oratory and declamation (121–25). And the claim for naturalness in Barry's acting may have had to do with her unique qualities of delivery. Regardless, Barry's innovations in elocution made a strong impression both on the audiences and on theatrical delivery techniques of her own era.

As for Barry's legacy in comparison to that of Sarah Siddons's, both were famed tragic actresses who achieved longevity on the stage and reached the top of their field in their own time. Both were lauded for their innovative, emotionally riveting portrayals of strong women characters. That they even played the same roles—such as Siddons's portrayal of Isabella in Southerne's *A Fatal Marriage*, a role originally written for Barry—indicates a feminine theatrical tradition of rhetorical magnetism. Like Barry, Siddons was one of the very few actresses whose delivery techniques became documented textbook examples. As Buchanan claims, Siddons's "appearance in landmark treatises on delivery," as well as her "negotiations of feminine norms and display of pregnancy on stage" as a maternal rhetor argue for her place in the history of women's rhetoric ("Sarah Siddons" 416). Those qualifications, which apply to Elizabeth Barry as well, were also leveled as critiques. Just as critics and satirists in Elizabeth Barry's time often disparaged her financial success as a sign of sexual insatiability, Siddons was also criticized for "having an inordinate interest in money." In Siddons's case, her sexual virtue was not in question but rather the public saw her as putting her career and salary before the care of her children (Buchanan "Sarah Siddons" 432–33). Both women are significant in their protofeminist performances, which helped transform the image of women in Western society. Whereas Barry's risqué persona, historically situated within the Restoration era of libertinism, fell outside conventions of respectability, Siddons's persona exemplified the valorization of maternal virtue in late eighteenth-century culture. Along with other figures of Restoration libertinism, Barry's name lost respectability and fell out of elocutionary theory in the latter half of the eighteenth century. Her impact on the history of rhetoric was lost.

THE CHASTE BEAUTY

Purity was possible in Restoration theater, and it resided in the persona of Anne Bracegirdle (1671–1748). In contrast to Barry's identity as the fallen woman, Bracegirdle exuded the image of a chaste but sexually desirable woman, an image that she often parlayed into stage roles of aristocratic and virtuous heroines. Starting around 1688, Bracegirdle began charming audiences and admirers with her persona of beauty and refinement. Little is known about Bracegirdle's early life, but, according to early eighteenth-century publisher Edmund Curll, she was raised from infancy by the famous acting couple, Thomas and Mary

Betterton (Highfill, Burnim, and Langhans 2:271). If this story is true, it further corroborates conjecture that Mary Saunderson Betterton, herself a renowned actress and woman of reputed wifely virtue, served as Bracegirdle's acting teacher, mentor, and role model. From Mrs. Betterton, Bracegirdle would have received instruction in elocution and proper moral conduct, and the connection for entering into the acting profession at a young age. The *Biographical Dictionary* notes that Bracegirdle may have played several unnamed parts as a young girl although the evidence is not strong enough to be sure; however, theater records show that Bracegirdle was a paid member of the United Company by 1688, when she was seventeen, and acted several roles in 1688 and 1689. By the 1690s, Bracegirdle, in her early twenties, was in high demand for acting "pathetic roles in tragedies and sophisticated heroines in comedies," as well as for speaking prologues and epilogues (Highfill, Burnim and Langhans 2:271). Howe states that "among the actors and actresses of her day, Bracegirdle "seems to have been the greatest favourite with spectators" and "the mass of examples shows that every dramatist, more or less, had the public's view of Bracegirdle in mind when he or she produced roles for her" (98, 100–101). By virtue of her popularity with audiences, Bracegirdle's persona influenced the content of plays, epilogues, and prologues by Dryden, Congreve, Motteux, Durfey, Manley, Rowe, Pix, and others.

Bracegirdle's chaste public image perpetuated her as a crossover figure during the early eighteenth century when masculine libertinism (as the dominant English cultural ideology) gave way to the ascendancy of feminized decorum and politeness. The pivotal position of London actresses like Bracegirdle—those who rose above the slurs of indecency by embodying virtue—deserves greater consideration as an early example of the rhetoric of moral reform. At the turn of the century, when the morality of the players became a growing concern, defenders of the stage often cited Bracegirdle as an example of a woman's ability to succeed in the acting profession without compromising her feminine duties. Colley Cibber mentions Bracegirdle as possessing the moral character befitting the highest and most genteel echelons of society (52), and he further states:

> Never was any Woman in such general Favour of her spectators, which . . . she maintain'd, by not being unguarded in her private Character . . . And tho' she might be said to have been the Universal Passion, and under the highest Temptations; her Constancy in resisting them, serv'd but to increase the number of her Admirers. (Cibber 101)

Of course, as a close friend of Bracegirdle, and as a critic given to hyperbole, Cibber might have been biased in his high praise. Cibber's claims about

Bracegirdle's popularity with audiences, however, point to a new form of public feminine power that arose during the early eighteenth century. The idea that a woman could be chaste while inspiring sexual passion had immense rhetorical appeal by both permitting male lust and preserving female virtue. This development was not entirely a case of patriarchy commodifying the image of women (although that was part of the rhetoric). Bracegirdle's success also shows that, through performance, early British actresses were able to cultivate personas that pushed against prevailing stereotypes, such as the innate immorality of women players—at least to a point.

The chaste Bracegirdle persona, as it worked out, inspired a cult following that was only partially in her control. As Highfill, Burnim, and Langhans describe, Bracegirdle had an entourage of suitors and admirers, from playwrights (such as Congreve and Nicholas Rowe) to noblemen (such as the Earl of Scarsdale and Lord Lovelace), but she was never proven to be romantically involved with any man (2:276–79). According to theater lore, Bracegirdle, in her life, was very much like the characters she played, unattainable and virtuous. She never married, nor openly entered into a romantic relationship as a mistress. She crafted her combination of beauty, chastity, and refinement into a powerful appeal for womanly virtue, but as a celebrity, she could not control the public imagination.[16] Cibber states that, in the early 1690s, "it was even a Fashion among the Gay, and Young, to have a Taste or Tendre for Mrs. Bracegirdle" (Cibber 101). While Bracegirdle's chaste demeanor aligned with the changing ethos at the turn of the century, her portrayal of virtuous women characters who were often in sexual danger had scary real-life repercussions.

The mass infatuation of young beaus for Anne Bracegirdle led to one of the earliest examples in popular culture of fandom gone awry. In December of 1692, the fashion for being enamored with Bracegirdle led to unfortunate consequences when Captain Richard Hill and Lord Mohun, during a botched attempt to abduct the actress, stabbed and murdered actor William Mountfort whom they believed to be Bracegirdle's lover (although their suspicion is not supported by any known evidence). These events temporarily soured Bracegirdle's popularity with the public, as shown by her absence from the stage for a month followed by a decline in box office receipts for the first few months of 1693 (Highfill, Burnim, and Langhans 2:272–73). This frightening tale is an early example of how performative bodies can perpetuate sometimes uncontrollable emotional reactions in spectators, and, further, illustrates the rhetorical accretion of a familiar speaker's persona over time and the unpredictable spontaneous agency of audiences within the rhetorical ecology.

Bracegirdle's persona allowed her to overcome this early scandal of her career quickly. Ironically, the role that redeemed her reputation was that of a heroine who "emerges victorious after a series of abduction attempts" in *The Richmond Heiress* (1693), a role that required her to perform as "perhaps the first singing actress of her period" (Highfill, Burnim, and Langhans 2:272–73). She broke new ground as the first leading lady on the English stage to add singing, an auditory skill with strong pathetic appeal, to her rhetorical delivery. Once again, Bracegirdle endeared herself and persuaded the public that she was still pure despite the recent scandal surrounding her. Bracegirdle accomplished her recovery of public esteem by using rhetoric as a tool for recuperation and professional growth.

By the mid 1690s, Bracegirdle was one of the top actresses in London. Her popularity with audiences is apparent from her delivery of epilogues and prologues for at least twenty plays that decade (Highfill, Burnim, and Langhans 2:271). In 1695, she joined Thomas Betterton and Elizabeth Barry in forming their own theater company. Although often cast as opposites or rivals on stage, Barry and Bracegirdle were not only friends but also financially successful business partners. By 1705, Bracegirdle's salary was equal to Barry's, as well as to the top-paid male actors, including Thomas Betterton (Highfill, Burnim, and Langhans 2:274). Bush-Bailey emphasizes the importance of this joint venture in the feminization of theater, noting that "the company also premiered at least seventeen new plays written by five female playwrights, representing approximately one quarter of all new dramatic works produced in London between 1695 and 1705" (19). By the end of the first decade of the eighteenth century, both Barry and Bracegirdle had retired. Bracegirdle retired early, in 1707, while still in her prime at the age of forty-four. A variety of accounts detail the events that led up to Bracegirdle's retirement, but it is generally agreed that competition from up-and-coming actress Anne Oldfield had much to do with it.

While actresses ever since the Restoration era have continued to make strong persuasive appeals in many artistic venues of popular culture, in the early decades of the eighteenth century, in an era of increasingly polite theater, Bracegirdle and the rest of the Restoration actresses practically faded from public memory. Luckily, details about their lives and specialties as public performers were preserved in the annals of theater history. In the next section, I bring their rhetorical performances back into the spotlight by examining some of their key roles and their collaborations with cutting-edge Restoration playwrights, which established new precedents in the development and evolution of feminine gender identities.

Dramatic Collaborations and the Double Speaker

In its collaborative nature, drama as rhetorical situation is always marked by a *double speaker;* in essence, at any given point in the performance, the speaker is the combination of the player of the role and the author of the text. As Peter Holland notes, "The actor's intervention becomes not simply an available vehicle to be combined with the dramatist's purpose but the essence of that purpose" and "in themselves the actors can constitute a new possibility of form" (81). Play scripts guide theatrical performances, but in addition to the verbal rhetoric originating in the script, the acting half of the dramatic speaker also adds visual rhetoric to the message, through expressions, gestures, and movements. Thus, the relationship between playwright and player is accretive: this collaboration between first-generation British actresses and playwrights produced a new embodied form of protofeminist rhetoric. Scholars have argued the presence of the actress facilitated the emergence of professional women playwrights, who wrote sympathetically about women's issues (Hughes, Pearson, Todd, Gallagher). Many have also noted that, in response to the talent and depth of realism brought to the stage by the Restoration actresses, a fair number of male playwrights began creating sympathetic women's roles and themes in their plays (Hughes, Howe).

In Restoration theater, women's roles were most often constituted of a male+ female speaker, that is, the male playwright and the female player or actress. Women playwrights also produced plays in this period, thereby creating in their women's roles the double female speaker, female+female. The biological sex and gender identity of playwrights held significance in several ways: first, playwrights' personal life experiences colored their perspectives in the creation of various gendered roles, and secondly, the playwrights' sex and gender identities often factored into their relationships with particular actresses for whom they created unique parts. The relationship of playwright to actress could range from colleague, to close friend, to lover, to unrequited lover. These collaborative relationships constituted unique instances of double speakers that shaped the creation of women's roles. Through a combination of scripted words, choreographed actions, and improvised delivery, the performances of male+female and female+female dramatic double speakers in the Restoration era and throughout the eighteenth century sharply critiqued gender problems within aristocratic patriarchy, including forced marriage, the rule of primogeniture, and the lack of provisions for younger brothers and unmarried women—issues that would continue to be dramatized well into the Georgian era of bourgeois patriarchy.[17]

Especially important in any discussion of Restoration protofeminist rhetoric and the dramatic double speaker is the work of Aphra Behn, the first professional woman dramatist in England, who collaborated with many actresses and wrote roles specifically for them. As Behn's dedication of *The Lucky Chance* states, she viewed plays as "secret Instructions to the People, in things that 'tis impossible to insinuate into them any other Way" (Todd *Works* 183). From 1670 to 1689, Behn is credited with authoring at least twenty-nine plays, all of which used the stage as a rhetorical medium to explore gender issues from the woman's perspective. The record of Behn's collaboration with actresses is vital to the study of women's rhetoric because she stands at the forefront of publicly upholding feminine agency against the masculine vigor of the libertine (or "rake") character type.

Working with the first generation of British actresses, Behn and other innovative playwrights developed new feminine gender types (including the witty woman, the female libertine, the victimized woman, and the sentimental heroine) based on the talents of the actresses who could realistically portray the challenges women faced in Restoration patriarchal culture. Restoration audiences were affected by these pathetic types and craved information about and contact with the performers who embodied them. Joseph Roach calls this kind of performative appeal "It," which he describes as a form of rhetorical ethos characterized by the opposing forces of "magnetism" and "radiance" (7). Felicity Nussbaum terms this appeal "interiority effect," which she explains happened through "the blending of the actresses' putative personality with the assigned character's emotions and thoughts," to create private personas for public display in which the actress becomes "a commoditized version of the self" (20, 21). These new performative stereotypes of the feminine self were indicative of Britain's transformation into a capitalist patriarchal culture and its coming to terms with the fact that half of the consumers were women. Adapting classical delivery models to actresses' authentic female bodies, the collaborative work of actress and playwright viscerally shaped feminine desire and developed a new brand of realism on the stage. In the creation of realistic witty, libertine, victimized, and sentimental women characters, the dramatic double speaker rhetorically represented the effects of patriarchy on women as individuals. Plays with ensemble casts of women even held up a mirror to women as a societal group. The repetition of these roles and ensembles established a collection of rhetorically influential types of women on the Restoration stage, each of which appropriated the appeals of wit, virtue, and emotion to varying degrees and effects.

WITTY WOMEN

In the first decade of the Restoration, the debut of actresses contributed to a major innovation in comedy and a new pair of dominant character types: the witty lovers. In the mid-twentieth century, theater historian John Harrington Smith dubbed this pair from the Restoration "the gay couple" and described them as "two young people who express the mood of their time" (47). John Dryden's *Secret Love or The Maiden-Queen* (1667), which paired actress Nell Gwyn with actor Charles Hart, first propelled the gay couple into the spotlight (Howe 70–71; Holland 81–86; Loftis 332). Loftis states that "Dryden and his fellow dramatists, searching for a new style in comedy in that first decade of the professional actress, found in Nell a living model for their quick-witted and saucy heroines, those anti-Platonic coquettes who influence if they do not establish the tone of the plays" (332). Gwyn's talent for witty repartee answered the demand for women players who could engage in the stylized libertine mode with energy and humor. Feminine appropriations of masculine wit became the earliest hallmark of the first generation of actresses on the English stage and contributed to the success of the Restoration comedy of manners.

The specific chemistry between Gwyn and Hart truly defined the formula of the gay couple on stage and cemented its success. In the early years of the Restoration, the gay couple interacted as a pair of equals sparring in contests of witty repartee. John Harrington Smith states that the gay couple were almost always portrayed as "two well-matched players—neither under a handicap, neither given a special advantage" (41). As Holland asserts, so great was Gwyn's comedic ethos in her pairing with Charles Hart that she publicly proved herself "a woman who could credibly rival male wit" (86). However, the female wit's confidence and individuality also produced public anxiety. Underlying the seeming equality of the gay couple existed a double standard for sexual virtue, a trait not required of the hero but always required of the heroine. Nevertheless, the gay couple as a dramatic form gave women a public voice, allowing them to become more than a silent partner. But the perceived equality of the gay couple was debatable or, at least, only temporary.

By the mid-1670s, women characters in new plays suffered a loss of equality brought about by increasingly libertine storylines that depicted the mistreatment of women. By 1675–76, in most comedies, the woman's advantages are "lost and the gallant takes the lead"—a trend that begins with the brilliantly witty but misogynist rake character Dorimant in Etheridge's *The Man of Mode* (Smith 84). The libertine rake tests the moral strength of women, specifically the gendered prescription for female chastity within the fabric of patriarchy, which

requires fidelity for wives (but not for husbands) and virginity for unmarried ladies (but not for bachelors). Ironically, this trend of disciplining the behavior of women in Restoration drama created opportunities for protofeminist rhetorical performance. To enable women characters, especially heroines, to withstand libertine advances, playwrights often endowed women's roles with intelligence and the capacity for reason and learning—in the parlance of the era—with masculine wit. The possession of financial fortune is another way that playwrights gave women characters power over the rakes (Weber 145–46). Empowering women characters with brains and money, the dramas of the late seventeenth century provided them defense against male rakes, thereby easing the vicarious anxiety of theater spectators. However, audiences enjoyed watching libertinism as well, and so playwrights feminized this trait too.

FEMALE LIBERTINES

The female rake or libertine, a twist on the male rake hero, provided Restoration theater a feminine trope of equality to neutralize the activities of the male libertine. Probably first seen in the character of Hellena in Aphra Behn's comedy *The Rover* (1677), the female libertine shares many of the characteristics of the male libertine. Elizabeth Barry's portrayal of Hellena, a young rebellious aristocrat, effectively launched Barry's career and initiated her reign as the leading actress of the duke's company for the next ten years (Howe 80–81).[18] In the first scene of *The Rover*, the audience learns that Hellena, having been raised in a convent and designated by her family for a life of enforced chastity as a nun, has very different plans for herself. Hellena assumes the disguise of a gypsy in order to roam freely through the streets of Naples during carnival. She flirts around and encounters the roving English libertine Willmore who becomes her rake-hero love interest. When pressed by Willmore to reveal her identity, she exclaims to him, "I am called Hellena the Inconstant" (Behn 643).[19] Throughout the play, Hellena emanates a light-hearted and witty style of repartee, showing herself confidently and comfortably equal to any man. As an intelligent, outspoken, and lusty female rake (who also manages to be virtuous), Hellena presents a radical challenge to prescribed feminine gender stereotypes. However, she is "difficult to domesticate . . . [because] her sexual vitality and defiance of male authority create fears that remain unresolved" (Weber 153). The female libertine, much more so than the male libertine, subverts patriarchal ideology, which may account for her popularity with theatergoers.

It is easy to imagine why Barry flourished in the role of Hellena, a most savvy, manipulative, and intelligent character, triply-endowed with fortune, wit, and sex appeal—arguably qualities Barry possessed as well. Like Barry,

the character Hellena also resists marriage. Hellena's position as a female libertine symbolizes an aberration of gender norms, which might have entertained audiences but also defied the deep rhetoric of mainstream gender roles. What could a female libertine do to survive in seventeenth-century society? Nothing. In the opening scene of Behn's *The Rover*, part 2 (first performed in 1681), the audience learns that Hellena has died—but not Barry. She came back in another part. In the opening season for this sequel to *The Rover*, Barry played the role of a courtesan, the beautiful La Nuche who, like Hellena, falls in love with the rake Willmore. This time the female libertine, La Nuche, tames Willmore's libertinism, abandons her profession as prostitute, and lives with him happily ever after in shockingly unwedded bliss.

Despite growing public resistance to licentious theatrical displays, the female libertine in light comedic roles remained popular with audiences into the late seventeenth century, thanks in part to continued innovations by author/actress collaborators. The female libertine trope provided pleasant shock value, which could be enhanced when combined with a breeches role. Many female libertine roles included risqué breeches scenes; from 1660 to 1700, eighty-nine plays—one quarter—of the 375 plays shown on the London stage contained a breeches part (Styan 134; Howe 57). Breeches roles are found in plays from the 1660s (such as Nell Gwyn as Florimel in Dryden's *Secret Love*) to the 1670s (such as Hellena masquerading as a boy for a few scenes in *The Rover*) through to the early eighteenth century (such as Anne Oldfield in Farquhar's *Recruiting Officer*). Women comedians in breeches roles served to titillate audiences with the sight of female legs and to shine a spotlight on customs of gender norms. The performative gender fluidity of the breeches role was a long-standing theatrical practice dating back to ancient times when male actors played all the parts of a plays. The gender bending tradition continued on the Renaissance stage in plays in which plot twists called for women characters (who were played by young male actors dressed as women) to disguise themselves as men, thereby enacting double cross-dressing (such as with Viola/Cesario in *Twelfth Night* and Rosalind/Ganymede in *As You Like It*). With the advent of actresses in women's roles, Restoration theater turned the tables by allowing actresses in breeches parts to take on multigendered identities, presenting a new form of sexualized gender spectacle and testing the range of women's performative capabilities and the limits of public decorum.

The titular character of Thomas Southerne's *Sir Anthony Love* (1690) provides an outstanding example of a female libertine breeches role challenging gender norms. Originating the role of this female libertine hero, Susannah Mountfort Verbruggen appears cross-dressed throughout the entire play. The

combination of Mountfort Verbruggen's acting and Southerne's script took the breeches device to new psychological depths to produce the wild, cunning, and doubly gendered character of Sir Anthony. As Howe notes, Mountfort Verbruggen specialized in playing women as the "pursuers rather than the pursued" (88). These traits made her the perfect actress to play the swaggering mock libertine. As Southerne states explicitly in his dedication, he wrote *Sir Anthony Love* specifically for Mountfort Verbruggen: "I made every Line for her, she has mended every Word for me; and by a Gaity and Air, particular to her Acting, turn'd every thing into the Genius of the Character" (quoted in Weber 163). As collaborators, Southerne and Mountfort Verbruggen supremely exaggerated and satirized the rake hero as a libertine mastermind who displays hermaphroditic traits and the social dilemmas of both genders.

The character of Sir Anthony is quintessentially gender bending. From the outset, the audience is aware that Sir Anthony is a woman, but his extremely masculine attitude defies his/her true identity. He/she confounds all expectations of gender, as another character tells him/her, "Thou art everything with everybody, a man among the women, and a woman among the men" (Southerne 1229). The character of Sir Anthony has the advantage of dual-gender subjectivity, yet the radical twist is that the audience watches these socially constructed gendered experiences empower a player who is biologically female. Howe notes that "Southerne's lively heroine . . . proves that a woman can do everything a man can do in society and do it better" (83). Weber states that Sir Anthony "so enjoys the freedom which her male attire provides that her disguise has come to dominate her personality" (166). Sir Anthony thoroughly subverts not only the identity of the libertine but also the prescribed personality of the early eighteenth-century woman. Mountfort as Sir Anthony swaggered, joked, and caroused with men, chased and spurned women, hoodwinked con artists, and generally fooled everybody as "the arrantest rakehell of them all" (Southerne 1216). On seducing women, Sir Anthony says, "When I can't convince 'em I conform" to whatever their political or religious views might be (Southerne 1220). This statement alludes to woman's culturally enforced submission to patriarchy, and the dictate that she should not voice her own opinions.

Through comedy, Southerne and Mountfort playfully mock the social situations that existed between men and women at the outset of the eighteenth century in England. Rather than offering a serious solution to the problem of forced marriage, Sir Anthony weighs in with the comic solution of consensual cuckolding and living separate lives as acceptable workarounds and means for incompatible spouses to find happiness. In some ways, all of the women, including Sir Anthony, are fighting to escape from patriarchal prescriptions, but Sir Anthony has developed an if-you-can't-beat-'em-join-'em attitude. At the conclusion of the play, Sir Anthony unmasks, revealing his/her biological sex as female, but does not choose marriage—the usually inevitable outcome for happy endings in comedy. Instead, he/she decides to remain single, to retain his/her freedom, and in doing so subverts the traditional ending of the breeches comedy. The devices of mockery, in the double-speaking writer/actress team of Southerne and Mountfort Verbruggen, include appeals to laughter and a hermaphroditic woman hero who interrogates the gendered double standards of late seventeenth-century English society.

WOMEN AS VICTIMS

The most pathetic women's roles in Restoration theater include those of tragically tormented and victimized heroines. Story lines of rape and attempted rape in many Restoration and post-Restoration plays graphically convey the age-old problem of the sexual victimization of women. In "Rape, Voyeurism, and the Restoration Stage," Jean Marsden reviews the spectacle or insinuation of rape in plays, especially tragedies of the 1680s and 1690s, as a misogynist display of male power in Restoration culture, which fed a voyeuristic need in spectators and upheld the deep rhetoric about women as powerless objects of the masculine gaze. Marsden describes the semiotics of Restoration stage rapes, citing quite a few examples, including a play by Nicholas Brady titled *The Rape; or, The Innocent Imposters* (1692), which starred the chaste and desirable Anne Bracegirdle as the victimized heroine Eurione (191).

Critics have also argued that depictions of rape, especially in the hands of women playwrights and leading actresses such as Bracegirdle or the emotionally riveting Elizabeth Barry, served a feminist purpose of revealing the threat of sexual violence that unprotected women faced in late seventeenth- and early eighteenth-century society. In fact, Barry's inspiration in the establishment of the "she-tragedy" genre in the 1680s and 1690s and her codevelopment of its hallmark character type, the suffering woman, may be one of the greatest contributions to women's Enlightenment rhetoric. She-tragedy constitutes an important eighteenth-century protofeminist rhetorical site by exposing power imbalances in patriarchy, which were affecting women at that time. At the forefront of this dramatic genre, Barry created a new model of feminine psychological realism on the stage, thereby scrutinizing the reductive labels of virgin, wife, and whore that described the three possible gender identities of adult females during their years of fertility. These labels categorized individual women according to biological (virgin/nonvirgin) and legal (married/unmarried) binaries, mapping them to restrictive socially constructed identities and imposing assumptions about their sexuality and moral character. Barry's tragic heroines, however, offered enthymemes of society's complicity in the failures of women.

In her tragic roles, Barry posed an argument for empathizing with women, particularly suffering women, in a society dominated by men. With her pathetic style, Barry became renowned for playing fallen women as sympathetic characters often thrust into unjust situations in both comedy and tragedy. As pointed out by Howe, Barry's work gave focus to the sexual double standard in English society:

> It was only when Barry's mesmeric talents were employed in the portrayal of prostitutes and mistresses that their problematic situation was given detailed consideration and their sufferings vividly realized . . . Thanks to Barry, the prostitute and the mistress became a source of conflict and debate in the theater and so contributed to the fresh upsurge of interest in women and women's problems at the end of the [seventeenth] century. (130)

Barry's portrayals of women outside the margins of respectability showed them as victims of social circumstance. Through Barry, audiences could see that the transgressions of fallen women were often the result of patriarchal corruption. Her dramatic depictions of social injustice enacted serious persuasive appeals, but she did so in an artistic context, less directly than the appeals of the orator, the preacher, or even the treatise author.

Barry's emotional range inspired playwrights, most notably Thomas Otway. Her first noted tragic performance was in the role of Monimia in Otway's *Orphan* in 1680, followed in 1682 by her creation of Belvidera, the suffering wife, in Otway's greatest tragedy, *Venice Preserved*. Although Belvidera was not the lead character in the play, her role as a helpless victim caught in the machinations of a deadly political plot was, perhaps, the most pathetic. Critics and biographers have noted how Otway's real-life unrequited love for Barry formed her as his tragic muse[20] (Highfill, Burnim, and Langhans 2:315–16). Howe goes as far as to say that Barry's influence on Otway is what caused the focus of tragedy to shift from the hero to the heroine (113). Inspired by Barry's incredible gift for arousing pathos in the audience, other playwrights began writing plays for her tragic acting skills. Thomas Southerne, for example, designed his most successful tragedy, *The Fatal Marriage* (1694), specifically for the talents of Barry. In his dedication, Southerne writes of Mrs. Barry, "I made the play for her part, and her part has made the Play for me; . . . by her power, and spirit of playing, she has breath'd a soul into it" (Jordan and Love 10–11). High praise from critics and the public further make clear Barry's contribution to the successful initial run of *The Fatal Marriage* and the pathetic appeal of the she-tragedy, a genre that prefigured the rise of the sentimental novel.

SENTIMENTAL HEROINES

Sentimentalism, as a feminized mode and a rhetorical appeal to virtue, garnered increasing cultural and artistic capital during the eighteenth century. Sentimental stage heroines might appear as victims in tragedy, but in comedy they possessed intelligence and wit (similar to the prototype of Gwyn's witty woman but less naughty and more likely to claim the moral high ground). The fashionableness of witty yet pathetic femininity, and his unrequited love for Anne Bracegirdle, led playwright William Congreve to create a new type of sentimental heroine: the witty heiress. As Howe explains, "The irresistible heiress who is pursued by admirers" differs from libertine heroines in that she is most often "passive; her task is to protect her reputation and discern if her lover is worthy of her, not to initiate action" (88). Many of Bracegirdle's most famous roles were written especially for her by Congreve, including Angelica in *Love for Love* (1695), Almeria in *The Mourning Bride* (1697), and Millamant in *Way of the World* (1700). The Bracegirdle heroine had universal sentimental appeal because she was something of a rhetorical compromise. She was acceptable to men, to women, to aristocrats, and to the rising bourgeois public. In Roach's terminology, Ann Bracegirdle had "It." The paradoxical quality of It, as Roach explains, incorporates "the power of effortless embodiment of contradictory qualities simultaneously: strength *and* vulnerability, innocence *and* experience" (8). Citing Diana Solomon's work on the frequency of Bracegirdle's delivery of sexually suggestive prologues, Erin Keating notes that "the tension between Bracegirdle's celebrity virgin persona and her performance of paratexts . . . seemed to offer . . . the paradox between virgin/seductress . . . essential to her own 'it' factor" (53). The development of this ethos of opposing attributes, I would argue, was the work of the double speaker—the writer working with the actress—to purposefully cultivate the interiority effect, simultaneously producing and responding to the accretive influence of audience demand.

The collaboration of Bracegirdle and Congreve is well represented in her most famous role, the coquette Millamant in *Way of the World*. Cibber states of Bracegirdle's portrayal of Millamant that "all the Faults, Follies, and Affectations of that agreeable Tyrant, were venially melted down into so many Charms, and Attractions of conscious Beauty" (102). Millamant's mode is one of constant witty repartee, affectation, and raillery. True to the comedy of manners, Millamant is a highly stylized and exaggerated rather than realistic character, but what makes the role so interesting is its ring of truth in relation to upper-class women of the day. As Pat Gill notes, "Unlike most Restoration heroines, but . . . presumably like most Restoration women, Millamant worries about life after marriage" (167). One of Millamant's chief concerns, illustrated in the famous proviso scene in which she and her lover, Mirabell, set terms for their relationship, is that she is able to maintain some of her own private space as well as her feminine mystique even after marriage. Gill points out that Millamant's seemingly small worries are legitimate concerns for any woman about to enter marriage (168).[21] In a protofeminist appeal to women in the audience, Millamant, underneath all her exaggerated behavior, uses her intelligence to succeed as a heroine who gets what she wants in the end.

ENSEMBLES OF WOMEN

Restoration playwrights took advantage of the pool of talented star actresses to write dramas sharply contrasting the story lines of multiple women. For example, Barry and Bracegirdle often teamed up onstage, acting together in fifty-six plays over two decades (Howe 190–91). Barry parlayed the image of strength against adversity, while Bracegirdle signified genteel refinement. In Mary Pix's *Beau Defeated* (1700), the Barry/Bracegirdle pairing provides something of a protofeminist tour de force in which an early eighteenth-century woman playwright collaborated with the two top actresses at the time to form a triple female speaker. Pix's work is markedly woman-focused and protofeminist in its ensemble depiction of women of a variety of ages, classes, and social standing as individuals with unique goals and aspirations. Through the serious plot of the intelligent widow, Lady Landsworth (played by Bracegirdle), and the comic plot of the pretentious widow, Mrs. Rich (played by Barry), Pix explores the psychology of feminine desire as a simultaneous yearning for power, independence, and the ideal man. In this quest, Pix imbues her women characters with Whiggish values of mercantile consumerism, symbolizing the rejection of status quo Tory patriarchy, from a uniquely feminist perspective.

Structurally, the play contrasts the action surrounding the widow Rich with those surrounding Lady Landsworth. Mrs. Rich is a ridiculous comic character who aims to ignore the sensible advice of her relatives and enjoy the freedoms of widowhood, but who is foiled by her own foolishness, while Lady Landsworth is an attractive widow empowered by intelligence and the desire to choose her own man and pursue him. As London's virtuous sweetheart, Bracegirdle in the role of the assertive Lady Landsworth was cast somewhat against her type. But Bracegirdle's refinement was key to her delivery of the role. Lady Landsworth says of her design to obtain a man, she will "invert the order of nature and pursue, though he flies" (Pix 815). She outlines the ideal man as "genteel, yet not a beau; witty, yet no debauchee; susceptible of love, yet abhorring lewd women; learned, poetical, musical . . . modest, generous . . . and . . . mightily in love with me" (Pix 815). This line is a prime example of the double female speaker. Pix, as a woman writer, clearly had a strong image of what many women wanted, and Bracegirdle possessed the ethos to credibly deliver this request to theater audiences. Furthermore, in her position as a widow, the character of Lady Landsworth is able to turn the patriarchal table and make a commodity of men. She uses the language of mercantilism to go shopping for a man when she states, "Being once condemned to matrimony without ever asking my consent, I now have the freedom to make my own choice and the whole world the mart" (Pix 815). With Pix's reversal of the commodity metaphor, Lady Landsworth becomes a symbol of the feminine property owner who can partake directly in the masculine marketplace of products and profits. And partake she does.

By contrast to Lady Landsworth's conquest, the second widow of the story, the foolish Mrs. Rich, is duped into a disadvantageous second marriage. Played against type by the powerful and emotive Elizabeth Barry, the character of Mrs. Rich is a silly and obtuse woman. She is, however, a very comical character, and Barry would have had the skill to portray her as simultaneously ridiculous and sympathetic. An example of Mrs. Rich's comic arrogance can be seen when her brother-in-law tries to give her advice, and she states:

> I pretend to live as I please and will have none of your counsel. I laugh at you and all your reproofs. I am a widow and depend on nobody but myself. You come here and control me, as if you had an absolute authority over me. Oh my stars! What rudeness are you guilty of? (Pix 824)

The Widow Rich may not use her freedom wisely, but one can imagine that Elizabeth Barry had the presence to deliver this speech in such a way that its meaning transcended the superficiality of the character and touched the hearts of women in the audience.

Conclusion

The first generation of English actresses, those of the Restoration era, have been grossly underestimated in their contributions to the history of women's rhetoric. Restoration actresses embodied and exemplified British women's earliest public appropriation of neoclassical delivery methods, which they parlayed into their own versions of late seventeenth-century masculine wit, libertinism, and the increasing emphasis on feminine virtue that would continue into the eighteenth century. The public debut of the actress initiated a new phase of performative gendering in London's public theaters in which middle-class women entered the rhetorical ecology as public figures, artists, and vocal members of society. As soon as actresses began appearing on the public stage in England, their influence on audiences, plays, and British culture in general was immediate and profound. In their performances, actresses embodied the complexity of women's issues, especially their subservient and dependent status in patriarchal society, and ironically this captivated audiences. The British Restoration stage presents a feminist kairos for rereading and re-visioning the first English actresses as practitioners of rhetoric. The popularity of the actresses, as well as disillusionment with the male-dominated government and system of patriarchy, contributed to a woman-focused theater.

Recognized in cultural studies as "It" by Joseph Roach and "interiority effect" by Felicity Nussbaum, the phenomenon of Restoration actresses' performative rhetoric and their reception by audiences reflects the charisma and elocutionary skill of the best actresses of the period, including Nell Gwyn, Mary Saunderson Betterton, Elizabeth Barry, Anne Bracegirdle, and Susannah Mountfort Verbruggen. As a professional group of public speakers, these women inadvertently revolutionized feminine gender identities and kick-started protofeminist public discourse in England. The talents of women players (those named in this chapter and dozens more) inspired and created provocative and memorable women characters whose existence challenged simplistic feminine stereotypes by arousing public interest in what a woman could actually do or how she might truly feel. Their enthusiastic reception by mixed-gender audiences, as well as the development and performance of new feminized dramatic genres, validated their cultural capital and ultimately stamped their impression on the imagination of the modern public. Life as a Restoration actress was neither cushy nor socially respectable, but it offered women a rare professional opportunity, a public identity, and a community of artistic peers.

Professional actresses continued to flourish on the British stage throughout the eighteenth century and have since remained a vital component of contemporary British theater. Many new actresses with a variety of personas took the stage in the eighteenth century, with some achieving celebrity and star status—as Nussbaum details in *Rival Queens*.[22] The great mid-eighteenth-century actor David Garrick became the textbook example of the "naturalized" style of elocution, and his legacy influenced acting theory all the way to the twentieth century.[23] But the popularity of actresses remained high; Sarah Siddons replaced Elizabeth Barry as the greatest actress who ever lived, inspiring a "cult-like following" and "a mania" for her representations in paintings, drawings, engravings, statues, and porcelains (Buchanan "Sarah Siddons" 418). Siddons also appeared as an exemplar of delivery in important nineteenth-century elocution texts, such as Gilbert Austin's *Chironomia or, a Treatise on Rhetorical Delivery* (1806) and Henry Siddons's *Practical Illustrations of Rhetorical Gesture and Action* (1807); however, with the decline in popularity of elocution, Siddons's rhetorical legacy was also buried.

By the close of the Restoration era at the turn of the eighteenth century, conservative religious groups in British society voiced concerns about indecency on the stage affecting the public, particularly women audience members. In *A Short View of the Immorality, and Profaneness of the English Stage* (1698), Jeremy Collier argues that the Restoration stage was enacting lewd conversations and behaviors, which insulted feminine virtue and corrupted the young by encouraging their passions and discouraging their natural modesty. Marsden describes the paranoia of ecclesiastics in early eighteenth-century British society who saw a slippery slope in which "uncontrolled female [sexual] appetites could result in the downfall of the emerging British Empire. Dramatic representation of transgressive sexual behavior could, it was feared, set a bad example and influence otherwise virtuous women in the theater audience, in effect shattering national security" (5). In the political context of 1715 to 1737, as tensions between Whigs and Tories increased, pressures on the theater from the Whig-dominated Parliament resulted in a vicious circle of theatrical satires and censorship.

The situation culminated in the Licensing Act of 1737, which, as Canfield notes, "enforced zero tolerance for criticism of the ministry and effectively disciplined playwrights into conformity" (xvii). At issue was the right of free speech, political critique, and artistic expression versus suppression of antigovernment propaganda and the public's desire for propriety and decorum. Protestant critics continued to reject plays that flaunted vocal, tricky, and especially libertine women, and Parliament increasingly disapproved of plays that satirized the government. Nussbaum speculates that the Licensing Act, which restricted actors to perform only at two London patent theaters (Drury Lane and Covent Garden), resulted in a decrease in demand for actresses "of ordinary talent who were relegated to provincial theater or traveling companies, while star actresses in the patent theaters benefitted from less competition . . . thus foregrounding the talents of the fortunate few" (12).

While censorship tightened the reins on theatrical performance, interest in the practices of oratory increased along with a growing obsession with decorum and politeness. Answering charges that the theater incited immorality, theater owners and companies could make the counterargument that the stage could serve as a vehicle for communicating correct moral conduct. Goring contends that "the bodies of orators and actors were important to the growth of politeness because they occupied supremely public positions in eighteenth-century life, and thus were ripe for dispersing this quality through a broader public" (25). The debut of the actress helped move British oratory toward politeness, a mode that dominated Enlightenment rhetorical practices, both spoken and written. However, the rigid gender divide inherent in the patriarchal society that persisted in eighteenth-century culture remained evident in the sharp division between oratory and drama.

Because of these gendered and disciplinary divisions, Restoration and eighteenth-century actresses have received scant attention as rhetoricians. What makes this dismissal seem unjust is that elocutionists such as Thomas Sheridan, the prominent elocutionary theorist of the period, frequently drew from practices of dramatic acting as models and examples for effective oratory. The elocutionary movement's reaffirmation of public speaking as a male-only practice was one way that the newly minted actress, although she maintained her professional niche, lost some prominence of voice. During the height of the eighteenth-century elocutionary movement of rhetoric, former actor Sheridan published his lectures, and male stars such as David Garrick were lauded as models of elocutionary skill in textbooks on acting, rhetoric, and declamation. As Buchanan notes, the pathetic delivery style of Sarah Siddons found its way into elocutionary textbooks of the later eighteenth century, suggesting that feminine-style elocution persisted. But the conflation of acting and oratory lost credibility as a vehicle for rhetorical training. As Catherine Macaulay states of elocution in her 1790 treatise *Letters on Education*, "Such exercises induce a swelling bombast style of speaking, with an unnatural gesture and action. The stage actors are of all persons the worst models for oratory" (132). By the early nineteenth century, critics pronounced elocutionary rhetoric's classifications of speech and gesture artificial, impractical, and unusable, thereby contributing to the excising of actresses from the history of rhetoric. Nevertheless, in the latter part of the eighteenth century, elocution became a popular subject, and some actresses made use of their oratorical skills outside the theater in a new venue: debating clubs.

CHAPTER 3

In Sociable Venues: Clubs, Salons, and Debating Societies

A female senate now with pleasure see
Flowing alike with eloquence and tea:
The hammer now yon President shall hold,
By whom the ardent orators are told
How far, with reason, and with wit, the theme
Runs glibly o'er the tongue; and when they dream—
Hard task indeed! restraining female wit.
—from "La Belle Assemblée," *The
London Courant*, March 24, 1781

ESTRAINING FEMALE WIT was, indeed, a difficult task in the sociable and increasingly literate society of eighteenth-century Britain. By the early eighteenth century, actresses playing women's parts in public theatrical performances had become the norm, and throughout the century women participated in many public sites of mixed-gender sociability, yet public displays of eloquent female speech defied the deep rhetoric of the patriarchal social order. The idea of a female orator engaged in public speech outside of the theater struck many eighteenth-century people as obnoxious, low, and decidedly unfeminine. The prevailing attitude held that female speakers were no more than chattering viragos stepping out of their domestic place to usurp masculine authority. Investigating this prejudice, Betty Rizzo explains, "While male rhetoric was almost universally, perhaps unprecedentedly, valued and studied" in eighteenth-century England, "women made many particular efforts to be heard . . . in a struggle against the male view that women's speech was insurrectional, irrational, either prate or termagancy" (23). Despite these ingrained prejudices, as literacy and education increased across the social spectrum, women naturally sought opportunities for intellectual exchange.

Polite forms of sociability became an important feature in eighteenth-century Britain's rhetorical ecology, and women socialized in a variety of settings. Those of the middling classes developed rituals of tea table conversation in the privacy of their own homes. For women in the upper echelons of British society, intellectual sociability could be found in elite salons, such as those formed by the Bluestocking women of London. As exclusive private spaces situated in the opulent homes of wealthy hostesses, Bluestocking salons admitted only select groups of learned ladies, prominent men, and up-and-coming literati. The demand for venues catering to feminine topics and tastes had also begun to infiltrate London debating societies, which were a type of public club designed for the practice of oratory and elocution. Traditionally a form of entertainment targeted at middle-class men, debating societies gradually became feminized over the latter half of the eighteenth century until, by the century's end, women speakers performed regularly in mixed-gender debating venues, as well as in predominantly female debating societies, such as La Belle Assemblée.

In this chapter, I compare several types of formal sites in which middle- and upper-class women practiced spoken rhetoric, and I argue that London debating societies developed as unique hybridized sites of rhetoric influenced by both classical rhetorical practices and contemporary trends in sociability. The challenge in making this argument is that eighteenth-century debating societies kept no reports of their events. Unlike the salons, preserved in the voluminous writings of Bluestockings who published in a variety of genres and left behind a large corpus of letters, or even the theater with its rich trove of critical reviews, dedications, scripts and promptbooks, prologues, epilogues, and play bills, debating societies left scanty material, consisting chiefly of newspaper announcements of dates, venues, and topics, as well as the occasional mention of public debates in a poem, letter, or essay. The piecemeal evidence on debating societies and the venues where they met provides only minimal descriptions and, unfortunately, does not include much information about the identities of debate speakers, male or female. To reconstruct debating societies as increasingly feminized sites of Enlightenment rhetoric, I rely on the feminist rhetorical method of critical imagination to examine available data and then hypothesize about the "contexts, conditions, lives, and practices" of women at these sites (Royster and Kirsch 71). Drawing from historical records in newspaper announcements, descriptions of popular speaking practices from elocutionary handbooks, and recent analyses of debating societies from scholars of literary and cultural history, I situate the feminization of debating societies within the rhetorical ecology of late eighteenth-century England. To provide context, this chapter begins with identifying cultural influences that impacted debating society origins and development, including the rise of British club culture, the marketing of elocution as a commercial entertainment product, and the widespread influence of salon rhetoric as a code of conduct for women aspiring to climb the social ladder. I then compare the waves of popularity of debating societies to the parallel rise of Bluestocking salons by analyzing both spaces as rhetorical venues and examining the practices of women as speakers in each. Finally, I analyze topic announcements and reports on debate attendance and response during three distinct periods: the first attempts of the 1750s; the heydays of the early 1780s; and the progressive climax of the 1790s. Throughout the chapter, I compare the rhetorical models and practices of the debating societies with those of the Bluestocking salons, and I invoke critical imagination to reconceptualize women's participation in these club-like contexts.

Sociable Contexts and Influences

The eighteenth century ushered in a new era of commercial sociability and entertainment in Britain catering to everyone who was middle class or above—that is, everyone who could pay for it. Three innovations of eighteenth-century British sociability that served to increase the middle-class woman's participation in rhetorical practice included: the rise of club culture, the fad for popular elocutionary performance, and the publicized ethos of salon rhetoric. The venues that hosted these new customs enabled women across the class structure to practice the new bourgeois value of politeness, a posture reflecting virtue and educated taste, which superseded the (often vulgar and libertine) wit that had defined the ethos of Restoration sociability.

CLUB CULTURE

Throughout the eighteenth century, clubs sprang up as sites of sociability for all types of interests. As Peter Clark notes, clubs "became one of the more distinctive social and cultural institutions of Georgian Britain" (2). A multigendered phenomenon not only of the upper class but also the rising middle class, the popularity of club culture in eighteenth-century Britain contributed strongly to structured practices of feminine sociability. For women, club culture offered an entrée into semipublic, professional, and intellectual activities. A mid-century pamphlet, *The New Art and Mysteries of Gossiping, Being an Account of all the Women's Clubs in and about the City and Suburbs of London* (1756), provides a list of occupationally oriented women's clubs, such as the Weaver's Wives Club, the Milliners Club, the Quilters Club, the Basket Women's club, the Mantua Makers Club, the Shoemakers Wives Club, the Penny Barbers Wives Club, and the Whores and Bawds Club, which sprang up to support professional networks of working women or those who assisted their spouses (Tarbuck 378). While these clubs focused on women's roles in the trades, a parallel trend for women's intellectual clubs also began.

The earliest known women's club in Britain, the Fair Intellectual Club, which began meeting in Edinburgh in 1717, provides evidence of how educated young ladies adapted club culture to a feminine rhetoric of virtue. As Tarbuck notes, this all-female group developed a formal structure for their "secret" literary club, which included limiting their membership to no more than nine members, designating a lead speaker and secretary, meeting for weekly discussions of preselected texts, and keeping minutes of their meetings (376–77). The main purpose of the club was to provide a forum and a society for female intellectual improvement. Admittance to the club required prospective members to demonstrate effective written composition and speaking skills. Their procedures and practices demonstrate that the Fair Intellectual Club prefigured the British elocution and salon conversation movements.

Published a few years after the club's formation, *An Account of the Fair Intellectual Club* (1719) outlines its mission and belief in female civic virtue and intellectual development. The document consists of two parts: a short letter of introduction followed by a lengthy pamphlet enumerating the club constitution and by-laws. The letter contains a brief statement from two of the club members justifying their aims as intellectual, peaceful, and virtuous (M.C. 42). The pamphlet that follows details their mission, activities, and procedures. Foremost the pamphlet stresses that members maintain "sincere and constant mutual friendship," as well as implicitly-shared Protestant values, explicit nonjudgment of each other's personal political opinions, and the assurance of freedom from ridicule or censure; admittance requirements state that applicants must be female and between fifteen and twenty years of age, have the recommendation of a current member, perform "a written harangue," and pay ten shillings (M.C. 7–8). The required performance of a "harangue," which in this context means a speech addressed to an assembly, emulates Scottish parliamentary proceedings, and thus provides evidence that this group of teenage women were performing formal oratory in a club setting.

The young women of the Fair Intellectual Club purposely designed their own rhetorical space to emulate and further the ideals of education that they had acquired in their early schooling. After learning to read, write, and study, these women were not content to limit these skills to domestic usage. They were not agitating for radical protofeminist reform; they simply wanted to continue with a life of the mind. As Tarbuck points out, the Fair Intellectual Club integrated "religious sentiments and Enlightenment ideas" into the fabric of their organization as two essential threads, and she notes that this perspective was a common combination in many polite circles of sociability (381). Furthermore, this club of young, unmarried Scottish women reflects growing awareness of the applicability of the Lockean social contract to feminized spaces of sociability where women could collaborate on shared projects of intellectual significance.

A few decades later, during the 1740s, London debating societies, or spouting clubs, arose as a nonprofit form of masculine entertainment in alehouses. These societies targeted a male-only artisan crowd, as Mary Thale explains, in an effort to provide men of the middling station an intellectual entertainment forum "to debate questions on religion, politics, commerce, etc" (31). The earliest London debating societies did not admit women even as audience members. Before the 1750s, attendance at London's public debating societies consisted chiefly of middle-class tradesmen who came to discourse on their rights and civil liberties in lively, and at times rowdy, debate forums. As debate venues became very popular, the owners and managers of these London clubs sought to commercialize them to maximize profits. The financial success of clubs such as the Robin Hood Society, which continued to donate its proceeds to charities, caused entertainment entrepreneurs to envision the commercial potential of attracting larger, more affluent, mixed-gender audiences.

By the 1750s, both salons and debating societies were thriving as sites of mixed-gender sociability, surging in popularity in the same decades but addressing different levels of social class. While the practice of public oratory for women clearly transgressed prescribed gender norms, salon sociability seemed to fall within the guidelines of social decorum. Gentility, education, and wealth protected salon attendees from public censure for the most part but not entirely. Although the high-brow Bluestockings saw themselves as leading a virtuous life of the mind worlds apart from the middle-class venues of debating societies, like the female orators, they were targets of ridicule in satires, lampoons, and satiric cartoons, such as in figure 3.1. Depicting a group of well-dressed women engaged in a rowdy squabble around a tea table, Rowlandson's satiric print taps into the belief that allowing women to gather socially would produce unruly and malicious behavior. Despite unflattering critiques and caricatures, salon culture became an important model for British women's sociability. By the 1770s, the terms *bluestocking* and *learned lady* had become sobriquets for an intellectual or well-read woman, yet these terms often carried a negative undertone.

From the 1770s to the 1790s, both salons and debating societies reached their zenith as mixed-gender rhetorical sites. Their coinciding timelines show that the growth of sociability among the middle and upper classes during this era produced conditions favorable to women's rhetorics. In efforts to expand their clientele, debating club managers commenced the feminized commercialization of debating societies as a purposeful move, beginning with the infusion of

FIGURE 3.1. *Breaking Up of the Blue Stocking Club*, Thomas Rowlandson (1815). The Met150, https://www.metmuseum.org/art/collection/search/811678, public domain. The Elisha Whittelsey Collection, the Elisha Whittelsey Fund, 1959. Accession no. 59.533.1591. Wikimedia Commons.

salon ambience and décor, adding debate topics designed to appeal to female audiences, and eventually announcing the addition of female speakers.

THE COMMERCIALIZATION OF ELOCUTION

The commercialization of debating societies indicates that the skills of acting and oratory became increasingly marketable commodities in eighteenth-century society. As Paul Goring notes, over a half-dozen short publications on elocution published from the early to mid-eighteenth century provide further evidence of general interest in public speaking (10–11). The phenomenon of speechmaking as entertainment served as an economic driver in women's Enlightenment rhetoric. Entertainment entrepreneurs and publishers realized that women with their pin money represented a sizable consumer demographic that was interested in works such as John Hill's *Actor: A Treatise on the Art of Playing* (1750) and Aaron Hill's *Art of Acting* (1753), which provided packaged theatrical performance and delivery theory. Although these popular books focused much more on male actors than on female actresses, they presented the techniques of acting and dramatic delivery as proper models for public speakers and spurred interest in elocution and declamation. Betty Rizzo lists eighteen treatises on elocution published from the 1750s to the 1780s, with fourteen of those appearing between 1770 and 1780. With the popularity of instructional texts on elocution, the idea that anyone could learn the art of public speaking was gaining ground.

Scholars agree that London debating societies, the main public sites for the practice of amateur elocution, increasingly welcomed the participation of women over the latter half of the eighteenth century, but this development was not without its challenges. As Thale notes, entrepreneurs in the 1750s succeeded in the "feminizing of masculine entertainments for commercial ends" by attracting female audiences and catering to feminine tastes in décor, but they failed to obtain public acceptance of female speakers, an extreme change that did not succeed with audiences until the 1780s (31). Betty Rizzo concurs, stating that, in the 1750s, "women appeared regularly if infrequently as public orators," but by 1779, evidence shows their "more active participation" as speakers (28, 36). In superbly contextualized discussions, Thale and Rizzo offer venue-based historiographic analyses of women's entrée into debating clubs from the 1750s to the 1790s. In addition, Donna Andrews's informative compilation, *London Debating Societies, 1776–1799*, aggregates and editorializes postings from London newspapers for the different debating clubs and events during their highest period of popularity. These scholars show that the feminization of London debating societies occurred in several concentrated peak seasons over this extended time span and that the infiltration of women—first as audience members and as a topic of discussion, then as speakers—was a driving factor in the success of these venues despite ongoing strictures against public female speech.

Notwithstanding British women's inroads into public speaking, throughout the eighteenth century, the deep rhetoric of patriarchy prescribed the civic practice of public oratory as a masculine activity—with women allotted only a passive role as spectators (Goring 10). The gender bias is clear in pamphlets, manuals, and lectures on oratory and elocution, which ostensibly address male readers. Leading publications on elocution, such as Thomas Sheridan's *Course of Lectures on Elocution* (1763) and Gilbert Austin's *Chironomia* (1806) primarily use examples of famous actors to describe effective delivery styles for the podium and pulpit. However, these texts were read by men and women, and examples describing actresses were not entirely absent from them. Furthermore, some handbooks, such as *The New Art of Speaking, or, A Complete Modern System of Rhetoric, Elocution, and Oratory* (1785), specifically announced that women were part of their target audience. This neoclassical compendium defines rhetoric as "the theoretical part of Elocution" and provides a synthesized handbook of classical tropes, figures, and styles; a detailed breakdown of passions and manners similar to those in book 2 of Aristotle's *Rhetoric;* a collection of sample letters and orations, including one woman's speech from the *Aeneid,* that of Andromache to her husband Hector; and even instructions on making cards for a game that improves conversation (13, 90, 142–46). While the handbook exhibits the canons and elements of the masculine rhetorical tradition, its emphasis on passionate and mannered delivery also shows the influence of feminized Asiatic dramatic elocution.

The connection of elocution with drama carved a space for feminine rhetorical delivery and exemplary women speakers. Just as premier Restoration actress Elizabeth Barry figures prominently in Charles Gildon's *Life of Mr. Thomas Betterton* (1710), Gilbert Austin's *Chironomia* features illustrations of Sarah Siddons, the most renowned British actress of the late eighteenth century, as a model for proper elocutionary gestures and delivery. Lindal Buchanan argues that Sarah Siddons's appearance in *Chironomia,* and her focus as the main feature in Henry Siddons's *Practical Illustrations of Rhetorical Gesture and Action* (1807), "signifies a growing acceptance of women on public platforms" in the later eighteenth century (415). I would add as a caveat to Buchanan's remark that—while these publications widely marketed the skills of delivery and elocution to women readers—in reality, it was only a small percentage of mostly middle-class women who appeared as public speakers in theaters and debating clubs. Uneducated women of the lower classes were not likely to have the opportunity to attain elocutionary skills, and public performance of any kind remained taboo for upper-class women who almost invariably aspired to the status of a proper lady in polite society.

SALON ETIQUETTE

While debating clubs and elocutionary entertainments attracted middle-class men and women (and also men of higher social ranks), the London Bluestockings built a more elite and genteel model for upper-class, female-led intellectual sociability, following in the seventeenth-century European salon tradition. As Elizabeth Eger describes, the Bluestocking salons developed as a "culture of opulent yet regulated assemblies . . . indebted to their French predecessors and contemporaries," but the Bluestockings saw themselves as "pursuing a more rigorously virtuous and apolitical identity than their French sisters" (60). Nevertheless, the bluestocking model of sociability and conversational rhetoric had its precedent in serious women-led and mixed gender intellectual traditions, particularly in the tradition of the French salonnières. Bluestocking culture also took inspiration from earlier eighteenth-century British intellectuals, including John Locke, Anthony Ashley Cooper, Mary Astell, Catherine Trotter

Cockburn, Samuel Clarke, Joseph Butler, and Alexander Pope (particularly his *Essay on Man*) (O'Brien 49–56). Even before the bluestocking name caught on, mixed-gender intellectual gatherings of the Neoplatonists (including Astell) and the Lockean empiricists (including Cockburn and Masham) and women's literary and religious groups, such as the Fair Intellectual Club in Edinburgh, were happening in London and throughout Britain. In the 1740s, for example, Sarah Kirkham Chapone and Mary Granville Pendarves were active in discussions with John Wesley, founder of Methodism; Chapone was also an admirer of Mary Astell's work, a close friend of grammarian Elizabeth Elstob, and would later become mother-in-law of Hester Chapone, author and member of the next generation of bluestockings (Orr "Sappho of Gloucestershire" 92, 96–97). Thus, the early British bluestockings derived the rhetorical practices of social networking from a long tradition of women's involvement in the leading intellectual circles across England and Europe.

Continuing the tradition of intellectualism, and adding their own philosophical rhetoric of virtue, women of the later famous circles of Bluestocking intellectuals, such as Catherine Talbot, Elizabeth Carter, and Elizabeth Montagu, weighed in on the ideas of Scottish Enlightenment theorists, such as Samuel Butler on Christianity, and James Beattie and Lord Kames on common sense and moral philosophy. As Karen O'Brien details in *Women and Enlightenment in Eighteenth-Century Britain,* the Bluestockings' participation in the debates of the Scottish Enlightenment resulted in women's emergence as "a distinct discursive category" without which the later emergence of nineteenth-century feminism "would not have been possible" (2).[1] Yet O'Brien also notes that neoclassical influences in eighteenth-century society reaffirmed the public realm as a place for men to speak while women were to remain sequestered and silent in private domestic spaces. The pervasiveness of this deep patriarchal rhetoric helps account for the double standard of the Bluestocking circle, who promoted a ladies' rhetoric modeled on and confined to private conversation, while many of their members actually engaged in literary publication and other forms of public and semi-public intellectual performance.

The Bluestockings were major proponents of polite conversation, but they were also active in literary criticism, letter writing, and the study of belles lettres, and they contributed significantly to important critical conversations of the Johnsonian literary circle and the Scottish Enlightenment philosophers. Bluestockings of the late 1750s began meeting in the homes of Elizabeth Montagu, Elizabeth Vesey, and Frances Boscawen where they solidified their practice of female intellectual networking and developed their skills as scholars, critics, and arbiters of national literary taste. In particular, Montagu, who was known as Queen of the Blues, played a "central role in fostering the female 'life of the mind' during the eighteenth century" and developing the Bluestocking philosophy, which Eger describes as "the social expression of an Enlightenment belief in freedom of enquiry" (Eger 11). Montagu corresponded with leading men of Enlightenment belletristic theory and also contributed her own volume of Shakespearean criticism. Others, such as Hester Thrale, Catherine Macaulay, Maria Edgeworth, and Hannah More published their own pedagogical plans for girls' and women's education. Catherine Talbot's *Reflections on the Seven Days of the Week* (1770) and *Essays on Various Subjects* (1772) were published in numerous editions and, as O'Brien notes, advocated a "moral philosophy of active, amiable sociability balanced by intellectual cultivation and reasonable self-love" (65). In their intellectual and professional pursuits, the Bluestockings embodied the lifestyle of a good woman speaking well.

The Bluestockings' salon model of rhetoric consisted of informal mixed-gender conversation focused on intellectual topics and dominated by the female point of view. In contrast to elocutionary venues in which solo speakers delivered traditional orations to an audience of spectators, the salon model centered on collaborative communication, and women assumed positions of leadership. The female host, or salonnière, designed the guest list, informal codes of conduct, and rules for conversation, and she often directed the form and content of the interactions, but the main mode of the rhetoric was dialogic and conversational. The salon model offered eighteenth-century British culture an alternative feminine model of social interaction, which proliferated across tea tables and other polite spaces nationwide, helping to steer norms of manners and taste.

Polite salon etiquette suggested a model or path for upward mobility, a way for middle-class individuals to attain a more genteel identity. As noted by Hannah More, Bluestocking ideology was focused on the educated elite and "the principles and conduct prevalent among women of rank and fortune" (title page). Class consciousness pervaded all levels of eighteenth-century society, and British women of all social ranks knew that polite behavior was a requirement for respectability. Hannah More, for example, lists the following behavior for ladies in her *Strictures on the Modern System of Female Education* (1799):

1. Study to promote both intellectual and moral improvement in conversation.
2. Labour to bring into it a disposition to bear with others, and to be watchful over yourself.
3. Keep out of sight any prominent talent of your own, which, if indulged, might discourage or oppress the feeble-minded.

4. If you know any one present to possess any particular weakness or infirmity, never exercise your wit by maliciously inventing occasions which may lead her to expose or betray it.

5. Give as favourable a turn as you can to the follies which appear, and kindly help [others] to keep the rest out of sight.

6. Never gratify your own humour, by hazarding what you suspect may wound any one present in their persons, connexions, professions, or religious opinions.

7. Give credit to those who without your kindness will get none.

8. Do not talk at any one whom you dare not talk to, unless from motives in which the golden rule will bear you out.

9. Seek neither to shine nor to triumph, and if you seek to please, take care that it be in order to convert the influence you may gain by pleasing to the good of others.

10. Cultivate true politeness, for it grows out of true principle, and is consistent with the Gospel of Christ.

11. Avoid those feigned attentions which are not stimulated by good will, and those stated professions of fondness which are not dictated by esteem.

12. Remember that the praise of being thought amiable by strangers, may be bought too dear, if it be bought at the expence of truth and simplicity.

13. Remember that Simplicity is the first charm in manner, as Truth is in mind; and could Truth make herself visible, she would appear invested in Simplicity.

14. Remember also, that true good nature is the soul, of which politeness is only the garb. (More 88–90, numbering is mine)

The list above notably conforms to the traditional patriarchal view that female behavior should be restrained and self-effacing. Ladies should keep their communications simple and not venture to express their opinions except in the direct service of helping others. The difficulty with taking More's strictures at face value is that Bluestockings not only published their written work; some engaged in business and nonprofit ventures. For example, as heiress of a successful coal-mining manufactory, Montagu oversaw the business and related community philanthropy projects, and Hannah More led a movement to establish Sunday schools across England. While Montagu and More could justify their leadership as service to others, they clearly took charge of organizations involving many people.

The Bluestocking elite knew that their practices challenged the image of the domestic woman within the deep rhetoric of the patriarchal tradition, but they justified their intellectual activities through their privileged rank, virtuous activities, and decorous private settings. They saw the emergence of middle-class women taking to the stage in public debates as very different from their salon model and as doubly violating the social order—in terms of gender and social standing. Written evidence shows that Bluestockings, such as Frances Burney and Hannah More, frowned upon debating societies as improper plebeian entertainment not appropriate for ladies of quality (Rizzo 40). In her *Strictures on the Modern System of Female Education,* More explicitly states that "a lady studies, not that she may qualify herself to become an orator or a pleader; not that she may learn to debate" (1–2). More's comment is typical of the Bluestockings, who upheld the taboo against ladies appearing, much less speaking, in general public assemblies. As part of their rhetorical model, educated ladies had great concerns for where they should not be seen. Ironically, in order to create an atmosphere to attract upper-class ladies as customers, London debating societies, as we shall see, attempted to emulate the salon model; however, debate attendees more likely reflected Mary Wollstonecraft's stated target audience of "the middle class" whom she describes in her *Vindication of the Rights of Women* (111).

Venue Accessibility and Ambience

Constraints both of social class and gender dictated access to eighteenth-century British salons and debating societies. Bluestocking salons were situated in exclusive private homes whereas debating societies met in public assembly halls, or clubs. While the doors of debating societies were open only to men before the 1750s, by the latter half of the eighteenth century they admitted any male or female who could pay the price of admission. Salons, on the other hand, always encouraged mixed-gender participation, but admittance was by invitation only and was restricted to select circles of the rich, refined, and highly literate types of people. London debating societies attracted large middle-class audiences who came to listen to speakers declaim on preplanned topics of social and political interest, which were advertised in the newspapers several days in advance. In contrast, the interactive ambience of the Bluestocking salons centered on spontaneous conversation among mixed-gender groups; the interaction was facilitated and groups arranged by the hostess or salonnière.

The three most celebrated London salons were in the homes of Elizabeth Montagu, Elizabeth Vesey, and Frances Boscawen. Montagu was undisputedly the most famous of the Bluestocking hostesses. She cultivated her two homes—

the first on Hill Street from 1744 to 1780 and, starting in 1781, a much larger mansion on Portman Square—into cultural centers renowned for elite intellectual gatherings. Montagu's friend, Elizabeth Vesey, known as "the Sylph," also hosted very successful salon assemblies in her wealthy home. The social interactions within Bluestocking salons followed the protocol of the hostess; the arrangement of chairs, in circles at Montagu's salon and in random groupings and zig-zags at Vesey's salon, was calculated to maximize the potential for conversation and sociability (Eger 109–110). The arrangement also included the strategic placement of books and art as devices of conversational invention for attendees to examine. Bluestocking conversation gravitated toward matters of the belles lettres tradition: literature, art, and architecture. The physical design and ambience of salon space was a critical component of the Bluestocking rhetorical model. Attention to "visual ornament," including furniture, paintings, sculptures, and even the clothing worn by attendees, as Eger explains, "was an almost overpowering aspect of bluestocking assemblies" (110).

Montagu's salons were unparalleled in their rich, historical, and multicultural designs, which included the "juxtaposition of classical and Chinese" motifs, which were intended perhaps to emulate the "gendered characteristics of contemporary aesthetics" in which the femininized "chinoiserie could be seen as a form of resistance to the predominantly masculine sociability associated with classical taste" (Eger 69). The visual rhetoric of Montagu's interior decorations enacted a deliberate invention strategy for promoting diverse, multicultural conversation. The contrasting styles of the different rooms in the Bluestocking salons also served as embodiments of gender fluidity; from the trusted and masculine Attic style of the Grecian rooms to the mysterious and feminine Asiatic style of the Oriental rooms, Montagu provided her guests choices in gendered visual stimulation and cultural styles.

By the 1750s, debating societies were attempting to copy this atmosphere of genteel gendered decorum. The imaginative, diverse, and opulent decor of Bluestocking salons, legendary in their own time, inspired owners and managers of the debate clubs to gentrify their spaces in an effort to attract affluent women into the audiences. Debating societies began running announcements of venues renovated to recreate salon ambience. In the 1750s, entrepreneurs updated the décor of debating clubs to put their establishments on par with other mixed-gender entertainments considered suitable for ladies, such as the theater and the opera. In making these upgrades, club managers sought to attract the upper classes and extend female participation to ladies of quality. Newspaper advertisements inviting ladies to debating societies attempted to dispel ongoing public concerns that the ambience and activities of the venues would insult female decorum or possibly even corrupt women's minds. Promoters further transformed the venues by expanding the programs to include discussion of feminine topics, some of which were light and frivolous, but women's serious issues increasingly came into focus in the 1780s and 1790s. As commercialized profit-seeking venues, debating societies continually adapted visual and thematic elements of the feminized salon sites in order to expand their customer base; however, most upper-class women were too chary of their reputations to attend.

By the 1780s, debating society venues regularly advertised their feminized décor and ambience, emphasizing elegance, propriety, and modesty. For example, an announcement in the February 2, 1780, edition of the *London Courant* on the opening of the Carlisle House describes "a large and elegant room . . . for the purpose of Debate and Public Speaking; where gentlemen and ladies will not be separated" (Andrews *London Debating Societies* 66). The paper also reports plans for an Academy of Sciences and Belles Lettres and School for Eloquence targeted for the oratorical training of gentlemen in preparation for public life. Women did attend the School for Eloquence, which took place at the Carlisle House, which was an event venue, not an actual school. An illustration of the School for Eloquence appears as the frontispiece in *The New Art of Speaking* (1785); the handbook's title page addresses members of Parliament, the clergy, law students, academic lecturers, and "all such of both Sexes as attend public Disputations at: The School for Eloquence; The Palladium, or Liberal Academy of Eloquence; The Cassino, or Female Parliament; The Forum; The Oratorical Society; La Belle Assemblée; and the Apollo Society." This address openly encourages women to learn about elocution and to attend debates at multiple venues.

The feminine focus that the managers integrated into debating societies— although initially superficial and even farcical—involved a strategic emulation of bluestocking salon ambience and polite manners. The dynamics of delivery was one of the biggest differences between the two sites. In salons, the atmosphere was hyperpolite yet also interactive and collaborative. Salon conversations aspired to the intellectual depth of Platonic dialogues, a long-standing tradition in genteel educated circles. Salonnières and salonistes (those who hosted and those who attended salons) took turns speaking, engaging in free exchanges of intellectual conversation. Each salon had a single salonnière, but even for one with a commanding personality such as Elizabeth Montagu, the goal was to facilitate the speech of others much more than to dominate the conversation floor oneself. In theory, to attend the salon was to participate both as a speaker and a listener. The model was that of the classical dialogue.

In contrast to salon rhetorical practice, debating societies maintained their core model of public declamation based on the principles of classical argumentation. Some speakers were amateur orators, some were actors, some were practicing politicians, and some were volunteers from the general public. Speakers in debate clubs knew the debate questions in advance, but the speakers' identities were usually not announced before the event. Some of their speeches were prerehearsed while others were delivered extemporaneously. Each event followed the formula of the two-hour evening debate at the conclusion of which the audience voted to determine the winning side (Thale "Women in London Debating Societies in 1780" 5–6; Andrews "Popular Culture and Public Debate" 409). Gender norms loosened up a bit over the time of the eighteenth-century debate craze; at the outset, the norm for speakers was decidedly male; however, as the century progressed, the debate stage became a mixed-gender space.

Women Speakers in Debating Societies

The most striking evidence of feminization in debating clubs was the shocking appearance of female speakers on the stage. The introduction of women as speakers began in the 1750s with their performances of mock orations on mundane and seemingly insignificant feminine topics. Women who spoke in public debating venues conformed to the masculine tradition of oratory in which individuals delivered speaking performances to large audiences on topics of public interest. The rhetorical model of these interactions involved the direct appeals and declamations of featured speakers to large groups of paying auditors who could then engage with the speakers after their orations during a question and answer period allowed for response.

Evidence suggests that the earliest performances of female orators were dramatized and scripted, like those of actresses in theaters, and this practice likely continued throughout the century. During their first decade on the debate stage, female orators were seen by many as nothing more than a bad joke. Rizzo claims that in the mid-eighteenth century, female orators "appeared regularly if infrequently . . . but usually in the spirit of a freak show" (28). However, Thale argues for the occurrence in the 1780s of extemporaneous debating performances in which "women speakers were . . . determining for themselves what they would say, and competing with men," and—unlike the conversational model of salons where it would be impolite for attendees to directly contradict each other—"men and women could address each other forthrightly" ("Women in London Debating Societies in 1780" 13). The impromptu appearances of random women volunteering to deliver extemporaneous speeches could also have been staged entertainments, planned and rehearsed (not unlike the model of some of today's reality television shows). Occasionally, newspapers announced female speakers in advance. For example, the *Daily Advertiser* reports that Miss Charlotte Elizabeth Meanwell led the "Young Lady's Oratory" at the Robin Hood Club on June 16, 1758. This young woman clearly was using a fictitious stage name. Details of her performance do not exist, so we do not know if she portrayed a comical or a serious persona, but it is likely that she advocated for chaste and polite feminine behaviors, perhaps by satirizing impolite behavior.

Actresses had shown that women were capable performers that enriched the theater by introducing more realistic portrayals of female roles to the stage. Like theatrical actresses, the ethos of female orators derived largely from their authenticity as women; however, their knowledgeability was suspect. Female orators became a provocative novelty, a comical and oxymoronic performative device that entrepreneurs hoped would draw larger audiences of women and men, just as actresses in the theater had done. Based on the factual details of British club culture and the theater, we can speculate that the female speakers who appeared in eighteenth-century debating societies were likely in their late teens or twenties, maybe even their thirties. Regardless of the personas they presented, we can also safely assume that most were trained in elocution and confident in their delivery.

When female orators appeared, the attraction for women spectators included the representation of their own sex in the subject matter and concerns of public discourse. The appeal to men was likely the public female bodily display, which held sexual connotations. Although critics might view women performers as indecent and promiscuous, the advent of female speakers on the debate stage also conformed to Enlightenment ideals of equality in cognitive ability. As Thale contends, "The exclusion of women from this 'rational entertainment' [of public oratory] was at odds with the development of English culture" in the mid-eighteenth century ("Case of the British Inquisition" 32). As is so often the case with cultural change, the regendering of the debate stage occurred sporadically. The few brave women orators of the 1750s blazed the trail, but female speakers did not feature regularly in debating societies until the 1780s.

A Public Stage for Moral Values

The rise in popularity of women orators also had the effect of influencing debate content. Compared to bluestockings, who autonomously cultivated their own learning by choosing for themselves the subject matter they wished to study, female debaters presented topics chosen by the debate club owners and managers who made their selections based on general public interest and potential for profits. Although women in debating societies did not often select the subjects of their speeches, they nevertheless could interject their own tastes and improvisations into their performances. They could publicly embody and model middle-class femininity as a politically significant commodity, and this fact indirectly benefited the average woman in eighteenth-century England. As the following subsections show, the progress of London debating society topics reveals a growing public interest in women's issues as a thematic undercurrent from the 1750s to the 1790s.

FIRST ATTEMPTS: THE 1750S

By the 1750s, debating society managers were attempting to attract a large target market of women into their audiences. Citing primary reports of female speakers in the late 1750s at the Robin Hood and the King's Arms societies, Rizzo explains that these "venturesome young ladies" were likely actresses whom the audiences expected "could declaim with unparalleled skill" (28). The timing of the first female debaters in the 1750s follows roughly a decade after the 1737 Licensing Act, which limited theatrical performances to two patented theaters. Debating clubs offered actresses another venue in which to use their professional skills in an era when theatrical opportunities had become scarcer. These circumstances suggest the theatrical stage as the professional origin of the early female orators and the site where most of them likely received their elocutionary training. As for access to debate venues, the price of entry varied for each event and for the different sections within a venue, and seating was sometimes segregated by gender. Thus, while debating societies were technically open to the public, the price for attendance restricted access for the poorer classes. On the upper end of the class spectrum, access also was affected by social decorum, which dictated against the public appearance of upper-class women in such uncouth venues as debating establishments were reputed to be prior to the 1750s. But the gendering of London debating societies took a decidedly feminine turn toward politeness at mid century.

In 1752, the Temple of Taste, was one of the first debating clubs to admit women. According to Thale, the entrepreneurs behind the Temple of Taste implemented strategies "to attract a large mixed-gender audience," including: a "lofty" name that connoted refinement; a daily newspaper advertisement that detailed a program consisting of musical performances interspersed with spoken prologues, epilogues, poetic addresses, and other topics of "rational entertainment"; and a much higher price than other debate events—two shillings and sixpence compared to the mere sixpence charged by the Robin Hood society—to show that the content of the entertainment was of a more genteel quality ("Case of the British Inquisition" 34). By transforming debating-club ventures from no-frills nonprofit institutions to more elaborate commercial enterprises, the owners hoped to extend their appeal to affluent women, which they saw as a highly lucrative demographic. The Temple of Taste advertised debates on marriage customs, the differences of the sexes, and women's suitability "to fill Civil offices" (Thale "Case of the British Inquisition" 35). These topics suggest the potential for groundbreaking discussions on gender in the presence of large public audiences.

The lavish mixed-gender club known as the British Inquisition was another example of debating society expansion catering to the increased access of women. In November of 1754, Charles Macklin, an actor and former Robin Hood member, opened the British Inquisition as part of an entertainment complex that included "a gentlemen's club, and expensive restaurant, a coffee house, and a card club," and he invited women to attend debates as paying audience members (Thale "Case of the British Inquisition" 37). As Thale explains, Charles Macklin's advertisements promised dramatic soliloquies and lectures on questions related to courtship, marriage, and parenting—"personal and domestic matters that were seldom debated in the all-male societies"—as well as questions concerning women's education and their participation in rhetoric and politics, and he also included an invitation for ladies to speak extemporaneously on a predetermined list of questions (Thale "Case of the British Inquisition" 36–40). It is unclear whether Macklin merely planted the invitation as a marketing device, or if women who answered the invitation actually spoke at the British Inquisition. Conceivably, Macklin could have conducted interviews with trained actresses and any literate young women who responded to the ad, perhaps who were financially motivated.

Macklin's goal was not only to broaden the audience by gender but also to attract members of the gentry and the aristocracy. To spur demand, Macklin promoted the British Inquisition with "an alleged news story, actually an advertisement" depicting the opening night as so popular that "758 Gentlemen and Ladies attended" and stating that many more had to be turned away (Thale "Case of the British Inquisition" 38–39). The advertising suggests that a polite, mixed-gender, upper-class public presence had arrived, but this is doubtful. Attempts at commercialization, gentrification, and feminization of London debating clubs in the 1750s met with skepticism and financial challenges. The Temple of Taste only met four times over the course of four weeks before shutting down, while the British Inquisition fared somewhat better, lasting for four months (Thale "Case of the British Inquisition" 35–36, 40–41).

Ultimately, the mixed-gender debating clubs of the 1750s failed. As Thale argues, the public was not ready for the feminization of oratory; in fact, proprietors of debating venues probably did not intend the female orators to be taken seriously, as illustrated by the farcical "spin-offs" of the Female Lyceum and the Female Inquisition in 1755, which portrayed female speakers as "matter for ridicule and exploitation, not admiration and revaluation" (Thale "Case of the British Inquisition" 44). The taboo against women speakers was apparent in advertisements stating they could perform incognito. For example, one ad offers "masques and dominos" for women to wear in order "to accommodate those, who, from diffidence, or any other objection, may be discouraged as public speakers" (Andrews *London Debating Societies* 66). The perceived need for women to wear masks to shield their identities confirms that the long held belief that women's public speech compromised their feminine virtue was still very much alive—even as the general public deemed women's issues worthy topics of debate.

DEBATE SOCIETY HEYDAYS: THE 1770S AND 1780S

As the most ubiquitous type of primary source on London debating societies, newspaper postings give a daily summary advertising happenings at the debate venues throughout the city, including event and topic descriptions; refreshments and decorations designed specifically for the ladies; questions focused on gender traits and roles; the appearance of female debaters; and sometimes a few sentences on debate outcomes. The London Record Society's list of debate topics from the 1770s through the 1790s, compiled from London newspapers for those three decades, shows debates on women's issues as a consistent thread throughout the entirety of the published record and provides an indicator of the top concerns related to women. Traditionally feminine topics such as beauty and fashion, which had been appearing in debate programs since the 1750s, were still prevalent, but scholars also note a sharp upsurge of new feminized topics and more women speakers in the announcements for the 1779–80 debate season. In "Women in London Debating Societies in 1780," Thale attributes the increase in female speakers and the deeper attention to women's issues in debate discussions in this one particular year to the rise of the English national social reform movements, and particularly events of 1779–80 (17).[2] Angela Escott concurs, noting that eighteenth-century debating societies functioned as "barometers of the swings between political freedom and repression" and women flourished within them "when movements in political reform were active" (63). Due to lack of detailed minutes, it is often impossible to discover the particular controversies or how and if a consensus was reached on the topics of discussion. However, reports of rowdy scenes suggest that agitation was happening. For example, one month after its opening, the School for Eloquence received some unflattering reviews, which upheld the concerns that bluestockings had about debating societies. On February 25, the *Morning Chronicle* reports that the School of Eloquence, attended by gentlemen and ladies, became unruly as people were "interrupting the Speakers repeatedly with hisses and coughing" until constables were called to remove some of the attendees (Andrews *London Debating Societies* 73). These reports of unruliness clearly clash with eighteenth-century rules about politeness and decorum and would surely have deterred the attendance of upper-class ladies.

Nevertheless, as reported by newspapers, the debate venues drew crowds of people, and the sound and style of women speakers was gaining admiration. The *Morning Chronicle* reports on a meeting on February 28, 1780, at Mr. Greenwood's Room, with seven hundred in attendance, where "the ladies spoke well," but the newspaper complains of the poor performance of the male moderator who "after quitting his post . . . gave no proof of his being fit to hold it" whereby "a sprightly female seized it, and entertained the audience highly by an excellent recital of a well-known poetical tale" (Andrews *London Debating Societies* 74). The description of general unruliness as a "female" recited a literary work suggests that the audience's acceptance of women's public speaking was limited to comical entertainment—the enthymemic subtext of which was that women's contribution to oratory was in novelty, not substance. However, the society known as La Belle Assemblée actively sought to refine the practice of public debate to make it suitable for women. In the spring of 1780, the newspapers were noting that the meetings of La Belle Assemblée at Mr. Greenwood's room at Haymarket were becoming so popular among "persons of First Distinction" and so crowded that "the street [was] rendered impassible by the great number of coaches of nobility, gentry, &c. who had left their homes to hear the ladies argue" (Andrews *London Debating Societies* 82). This advertisement aimed at the middle and upper social classes, but appeals to gentility were undercut by the stigma of public crowds.

Other newspaper posts from the 1780s note the gendered styles of oratory in a variety of venues. The *Morning Chronicle* states that, at La Belle Assemblée, ladies learn to overcome their shyness while "gentlemen become familiarized to their pleasing stile"; by contrast, ladies who attend Carlisle House can learn the "gentlemen's stile of reasoning"; and both sexes can "display their talents, and give their unrestrained opinions" to the welcoming and respectful mixed-gender audiences at Free-Masons Hall (Andrews *London Debating Societies* 82–83). These reports are encouraging in their suggestion that the presence of female speakers engaged in oratory on the debating stage enriched the elocutionary style of debates.

By the 1780s, female orators were vocalizing women's concerns and issues, publicly voicing feminine opinions on a wide range of matters, including the rights of women in marriage, education, and the professional world. Women on the debate stage had the difficult job of raising sensitive issues publicly while still maintaining feminine modesty in their personas. For example, the *Morning Post* reports that on April 11, 1780, during a debate at the Oratorical Society at the Old Theatre addressing the question: "Have not the Ladies as good a right to a classical education as the men?", the female speaker was so "greatly confused by the repeated testimonies of applause" that the establishment asked attendees to desist until the end of the speech so as not to upset "the natural timidity of those who have but lately assumed their rights and privileges, by bursting those chains, with which through custom and illiberality, they have hitherto been fettered" (Andrews *London Debating Societies* 89). Apparently, the speaker was intimidated by applause because, as a woman, she was not accustomed to public attention. She was not supposed to enjoy or even understand it; however, the news story insinuates that her feminine virtue called her to speak, and the morality of her cause carried her to victory on the debate stage.

Other sources offer less flattering and more satiric portrayals of feisty female speakers. As Angela Escott notes, "This was the age of satire and caricature, and the fashion for oratory and debating were popular targets" (61). Female orators who performed regularly must have enjoyed a shared sense of professionalism and success; however, they would also have been keenly aware of criticism. The final pages of *The New Art of Speaking,* a lengthy handbook on elocution and oratory, end with a sarcastic song specifically addressing ladies who have developed a hobby of public speaking:

Come all ye Female Orators affecting tuneful Glee,
    Now join our motley choral Group, and bear a bob with me.
For a singing we will go, will go, will go,
    And a singing we will go.
Come Ladies all who fondly aim in high Debate to shine,
    Who carry ev'ry Question through with Eloquence divine.
    For debating we will go, &c.
So mended from our Mouths shall flow what Genius can inspire,
    That ev'ry learned Orator our LIP WORK shall admire.
    For a speaking we will go, &c.
The Senate, Pulpit, Bar, and Stage, with City Speakers sleek
    From Women may improve—for why, they taught 'em first to speak &c.
    For a speaking we will go, &c.

On Measures, Ministers, and Men, we'll never cease to prate;
>> We'll tickle 'em with Politics—good Lord! at what a Rate!
>> For a prating we will go, &c.

On Slander, Dress, and private Talk, we have no Time to waste;
>> O no, we'll talk in public, Girls since that is now the taste;
>> For a talking we will go, &c.

Regardless what the Surly say concerning this or that,
>> Their Ears shall find, and soundly too, we'll have our Share of Chat.
>> For a chatting we will go, &c.

Our Tongues as well as theirs are free; then why should we prolong,
>> By tame Submission to suppress the Clacking of the Tongue?
>> For a clacking we will go, &c.

With feeble Wit some Critics dull attack our Heads so high,
>> We'll be reveng'd, and sneer in Turn, or know the Reason why.
>> For a sneering we will go, &c.

All Macaronies, Male Coquets, and Fribbles we will maul;
>> Our Satire keen shall make 'em smart—we'll lash the Cox-combs all.
>> For a lashing we will go, &c.

The Men are welcome to attend our Meetings when we spout;
>> But if unruly—SENATE-LIKE, egad we'll turn 'em out.
>> For a spouting we will go, &c.

Or should the Sex neglect our Haunts, and keep at home unkind,
>> Why then we'll mag Abroad ourselves, and leave the Churls behind.
>> For a magging we will go, &c.

Disguis'd in ev'ry specious Garb, full Half the World parade;
>> Then to conclude, Experience proves—THE WORLD'S A MASQUERADE.
>> And a singing we will go, &c.

The song paints a spirited and apparently derogatory picture of the female orators, equating their eloquence with incessant chatter and gossip, and describing them as prating and clacking. Looking past the misogynistic statements about women's "free" tongues, however, the song makes several strong claims of fact: women have the natural gift of speech; and female debating societies showcase women aspiring to increase their public voices. The song also describes female orators as possessing skills, ambition, and camaraderie, and excelling in many styles and subjects. Capable of delivering keen satires, as the song states, female orators "aim in high Debate to shine . . . with Eloquence divine." Overall, the satiric song provides public acknowledgement, if not clear approval, of this new female performative role.

Throughout the eighteenth century, genteel women worried that openly appearing at public debates was risking their social disgrace and victimization by satirists. Exemplifying this taboo, the *Morning Chronicle* reports that in March of 1780 a pamphlet called the *Picture Gallery* caused great offense and possible moral injury to nearly two hundred of the "most distinguished" women living in England by including their names on a list of people who were planning to attend the "Ladies Assembly," a debate at which the male author of the pamphlet "intends to open the business, disguised in women's cloaths" (Andrews *London Debating Societies* 80). Although the report takes a humorous tone, it points to the circus-like atmosphere associated with debating societies as well as deeper anxieties about performances of gender fluidity. Despite efforts at gentrification, an aura of disorderliness and danger still surrounded these public clubs and venues. Nevertheless, in 1788, La Belle Assemblée was still reaching out to upper-class women. The *Morning Post* reports an invitation to "the Nobility and Gentry" to attend La Belle Assemblée (Andrews *London Debating Societies* 223). While debate societies never transformed into acceptable upper-class venues, efforts toward feminization continued, as is evident from the greater acceptance of women speakers and feminized topics as the century progressed.

Potentially protofeminist debate topics in the lists of the London Record Society can be divided into the categories of courtship and marriage; the appreciation of women's minds and bodies; the value of women's education; safeguards and legislation to protect female workers; and the right of women to engage in public speech and other political processes. Debate questions related to courtship and marriage addressed many practical economic matters that women faced, including discussions of female sovereignty. Even superficial topics, such as ladies' fashion, had the potential to generate heated, substantive, and progressive debate, depending upon the political climate at the time of the event and the composition of the audience. Questions on women's fashion not only touched on matters of artistic taste but also the business of fashion and the professional expertise of middle-class women in the audience who might have worked as milliners, dressmakers, and seamstresses.

The appearance of woman orators opened up public discussions of feminine power and female intelligence. A sampling of London newspaper announcements from the year 1777, for example, includes questions focused on women's capacity for reasoning, their physical appearance, and attitudes about marriage. The February 5 issue of the *Gazetteer* advertises for the Debating Society at the Queen's-Arms, Newgate Street the following debate question: "Which tends more to establish female power, wit or beauty?"; while the October 13 *Morning*

Chronicle reports that the Robin Hood Society will debate: "Whether the female part of a theatrical audience should be allowed to wear hats during the performance?" (Andrews *London Debating Societies* 16, 24). The first question prompts a potentially productive discussion of female capability and influence. The second question seems silly, but it draws attention to women's participation in public life.

Debates on topics pertaining to marital status and morality put a spotlight on women's roles. The Robin Hood Society entertained the following two questions: "Whether maids or widows have the greatest propensity to matrimony? And, which situation is more favourable to female chastity, a nun or a maid of honour?" Andrews reports a later announcement of the debate results: "On the first question, it was decided that 'widows have the greatest propensity.' The second question was dropped" (*London Debating Societies* 27). Together these questions consider the traditionally acceptable adult female roles—wife, widow, maid, and nun—and their implications for moral female sexual activities, which were restricted to the wife's compulsory performance of sexual duties with her husband in marriage and sexual abstinence for women outside of matrimony. The debate result, the conclusion that widows were more likely to marry than maids, alludes to the widow's greater likelihood of possessing sexual experience. Perhaps the second question, on female chastity, was dropped due to time limitations, or it may have been too risqué to those in attendance. While these questions about sexuality might seem less than enlightened by today's standards, they signal that public venues for discussing women's issues were opening up in British society.

Debating societies also entertained topics related to women's education, from questions about appropriate sites and content to the value of learning for girls and women. In March of 1780, the Coachmakers Hall Society debated the effect that boarding schools had on the corruption or reform of manners in the "rising generation" of young ladies; the topic for April, "What is the most Amiable accomplishment in Woman, Fine Natural Sense or Extensive Learning?," reflects concern about the purpose of education for girls (Andrews *London Debating Societies* 79, 95). In 1788, the *Morning Post* announced that the Westminster Forum had debated the question: "Is the virtue of the female sex most in danger from their own natural frailty, parental restraint, or the defects of modern education?" (Andrews *London Debating Societies* 216). These questions reflect the state of flux in education during the eighteenth century. Education theory and practices were also a main focus of Bluestocking authors, including Hester Chapone, Catherine Macaulay, and Hannah Moore, which I shall discuss in the next chapter.

Published debate questions also reveal concerns about women in relation to professions, economics, and business-related topics. A large percentage of middle-class women worked for pay in eighteenth-century Britain (Hunt 169). And so, it is not surprising to see the debate question: "Are not Male Encroachments on Female Occupations, an hardship on the Sex, which ought to be remedied by a restrictive Law?" (Andrews *London Debating Societies* 95). This question refers to protections for common women's occupations, such as dressmakers, seamstresses, milliners, and perhaps midwives. Furthering the discussion of gendered professions, La Belle Assemblée held multiple debates on the national budget in which attendees particularly discussed taxing those whose occupations crossed standard gender designations, such as male milliners, mantua makers, and marriage brokers as well as female fox hunters, playwrights, and military workers (Andrews 133). This line of debate shows that women sought to gain a public voice on economic matters.

By the early 1780s, questions increasingly extended to progressive discussions of women's rights, including the right to public speech. Thale notes that 32 percent of the 279 documented debates in London in 1780 focused on gender relations, identities, and roles or specifically on "women's matters, both trivial and serious," and the following year nineteen debates focused on "women in non-domestic roles" ("Women in London Debating Societies in 1780" 18). Advertisements openly invited ladies to participate in debates about the fittingness of women to practice oratory. For example, on February 26, 1780, the *London Courant* announced that the female society of La Belle Assemblée would address the topic: "Whether Oratory is, or should be, confined to any sex?" (Andrews *London Debating Societies* 73). A debate at the Liberal Academy of Eloquence at Free Mason Hall, announced the topic: "What reason can be assigned for precluding the Fair from the privilege of Civil Society, or from a liberal participation in their discussions?" (Andrews *London Debating Societies* 81). However, as Andrews reports, one debate on the topic of public speaking by ladies concluded "almost unanimously against" the propriety of this activity for women in general; but in the same week the *London Courant* published "grateful thanks" to La Belle Assemblée for their donation of Twenty Pounds to the victims of a fire on Princes-street, Cavendish Square (*London Debating Societies* 87). These announcements suggest that, even though women's public speech was not universally supported, some women had become activist rhetoricians and were using their public platform to advertise their philanthropy.

The newspapers also reveal that female oratory in the London debating societies regularly delved into political topics. For example, on several evenings in March of 1780, women in La Belle Assemblée debated the ethics of the

Salique Law, a European law dating from ancient times, which prohibited any monarchical line of succession based only upon claims of female lineage and contained other provisions to block women's inheritance of property. As reported by the London Courant, the ladies "displayed in the debate such superior accomplishments and refined understandings, as may truly be said to *win the soul*" on both sides of the debate, with some for "abolishing a law so tyrannical to the softer sex" while others supported "declining all female pretension to imperial sway" because women as sovereigns "were too liable to be seduced from their attention to the public weal by the smooth and silken parasites who infest a court" and had not the stomach to pronounce the death penalty on those who warranted it (Andrews *London Debating Societies* 75–76). This commentary shows the public's readiness to debate laws that discriminated based on gender but also that misogynistic stereotypes about female moral weakness persisted in the deep rhetoric of the Enlightenment era and illustrates that anxiety about primogeniture was still strong despite the historical success of women monarchs in England.

Patriarchal anxieties pertained not only to British female royalty but extended to the place and the rights of the average woman as a female subject of Britain. Thale reports that with the decline of reform movements women's participation in debates waned from 1782 until around 1788 when a new version of La Belle Assemblée debuted and London debating stages saw a resurgence of women speakers (Thale "Women in London Debating Societies in 1780" 20). However, the questioning of women's political rights is evident in a 1784 issue of the *Gazetteer* announcing a debate at Coachmaker's Hall on whether it is "consistent with decency for the female sex to interfere in elections" (Andrews *London Debating Societies* 159). Debates questioning British women's roles in the political processes of the 1780s prefigure the later national suffragette movement of the Victorian era. As Anna Clark notes, the debating societies of the 1780s provided a public forum through which middle-class women could "associate and organize" and "occasions on which the germs of feminist ideas— criticisms of women's subordination and advocacy of women's rights—could be discussed" (573–74). While aristocratic and gentry women might enter into political work and advocacy through hosting and fundraising, the debating societies provided an avenue for middle-class women to shape political rhetoric.

By 1788, La Belle Assemblée was hosting discussion of more radical political topics, such as women's right to vote and hold public office. The *Morning Post* reports the following topic at La Belle Assemblée: "Do not the extraordinary abilities of the Ladies in the present age demand Academical honours from the Universities—a right to vote at elections, and to be returned Members of

Parliament?" The newspaper also briefly comments on the discussion itself and the results, noting that "the audience . . . was numerous and polite—the debate a brilliant assemblage of wit, elegance, and pleasantry, the decision terminated in favour of the affirmative of the question" (Andrews *London Debating Societies* 223). Yes, was the published answer; those present at the debate voted in favor of the rights of women to attend university, vote in parliamentary elections, and have their interests represented in Parliament. This record captures an early ground-breaking moment of protofeminism and provides proof that eighteenth-century London debating societies were host to women's Enlightenment rhetoric. Foreshadowing first-wave British feminism, this public assertion came ninety-two years before women would be admitted to universities (in 1880) and 130 years before women gained the right to vote in England (in 1918). Undoubtedly, there were many legal and social barriers to women achieving the equality for which the speakers at this event voiced support. The newspaper announcement later states that women speakers could wear veils while debating if they chose (Andrews *London Debating Societies* 223). Within the same announcement, the juxtaposition of progressive views on women's rights and the regressive suggestion that women who speak publicly may not want to show their faces illustrates the tension between the deep rhetoric of Georgian patriarchy and the simultaneous desire for change.

Protofeminist debate topics continued to appear; however, antifeminist topics continued to be recycled as well. In 1789, a topic that had been circulating for the past twenty years was still being announced at Coachmaker's Hall: "Which is the most attractive in the Female Sex, Wit, Beauty, or Good Nature?" and another debate in the same venue concluded that the "Foppery of the Men and the forward Boldness of the Women . . . is a principal cause of many modest Ladies being obliged to live in a State of Celibacy" (Andrews *London Debating Societies* 258, 256). These lines of discussion imply the reiteration of traditional gender roles emphasizing the necessity of beauty, acquiescence, and silence in women and the need for men to resist the feminine preoccupations of fashion. It is interesting to envision how these conclusions were reached among the speakers and audiences. Some may have viewed the proceedings as a restatement of proper gender order, while others likely viewed the event as humorous entertainment, but some may have felt indignation about the stereotypes put forth.

CLIMAX AND SHUTDOWN: THE 1790S

The ebbs and flows of debate content continued. By the 1790s, more progressive debates about gender were regularly on the programs. Debating venues entertained serious discussions of radical protofeminist arguments, specifically those raised by Mary Wollstonecraft's *Vindication of the Rights of Women,* along with other politically charged topics of social reform. Arguments for women's rights evinced close connections to the radical Jacobin line of thinking espoused by Wollstonecraft and other progressives. Public display of support for progressive causes suggest middle-class sympathy, or at least concern, for the French Revolution. Due to continual inclusion of politically subversive subject matter, clubs where debate societies met experienced continual harassment by the British government, which was cracking down on public gatherings in London and elsewhere in reaction to the French Revolution (Thale "London Debating Societies in the 1790s" 58). Despite continual harassment, and the introduction of a series of Seditious Meeting Bills, debating societies continued to host discussions of Wollstonecraft's ideas.

In 1797, several debates took place regarding Wollstonecraft's treatise. The *Morning Chronicle* announced that on April 10 a debate titled "What is woman?" would take place at the London Forum with the chief topic "Which is more Repugnant to Truth and Experience, the Doctrine of Mahomet, that Women have no Souls, or the Opinion of Mrs. Wollstonecraft, that they possess Mental Endowments equal, if not superior to Men?" (Andrews *London Debating Societies* 358). Beyond the fact that the question inaccurately states Islamic doctrine, the tone of the advertisement implies a satiric bent in pitting Islam against Wollstonecraft's feminism. Upon close inspection, however, the debate questions really suggest, not two, but three options: women are inferior to men; women are equal to men; or women are superior to men. While the Enlightenment philosophy of equality should have led attendees to a discussion of gender and human rights, as Thale notes, the derogatory tone of the debate at the London Forum was meant to discredit women. The wording of a similar debate topic at Westminster Forum was friendlier to Wollstonecraft's protofeminist ideas, but records show only mixed audience support (Thale "London Debating Societies in the 1790s" 83–84). Nevertheless, the theme of women's equality was carried on throughout April 1797 with at least three other debates addressing the topic that month.

The trick for debating society owners and managers was to advertise topics that would attract interest for customers, many of whom were sympathetic to progressive reform, but to avoid the scrutiny and censure of the government. In April 1798, a year after Wollstonecraft's death, we find public support of her *Vindication of the Rights of Women* in a post in the *Morning Herald,* which reports it as "the leading Proposition of a Work every day rising in Public Estimation" and as the major topic of an upcoming debate at the London Forum (Andrews *London Debating Societies* 377). However, this positive opinion of Wollstonecraft's *Vindication* was not universal. Bluestocking conservatives eschewed the Wollstonecraftian subversion of social classes. Hannah More, as Miriam Brody notes, found the title of Wollstonecraft's treatise "so patently ridiculous" that she "would certainly not read it" (108). Meanwhile, Wollstonecraft's posthumous influence persisted in the debating societies until they were shut down by the government in 1799.

Conclusion

Throughout their evolution in the eighteenth century, debating societies produced several distinct innovations in the history of women's rhetoric: the admittance of women audiences to public sites of open declamation and political debate; the public exhibition of female elocution outside of theatrical performance; and the gradual emergence of progressive, and even radical, protofeminist performances by middle-class women speakers. Although the venues of the Bluestocking salon and the London debating societies were dissimilarly class inflected, progressive gendering within Enlightenment culture precipitated the development of both the salons and the debating societies as feminized institutions. The deep rhetoric of propriety and social class distinctions ruled elite Bluestocking salons, the more politically conservative of the two venues. In contrast, Enlightenment developments in bourgeois capitalism propelled the success of public debating societies and enabled new lines of protofeminist rhetoric performed by middle-class women speakers.

London debating societies rose from plebeian origins to achieve prominence among the middle class by the close of the eighteenth century. Although the managers of debate society venues failed in attempts to attract women of the gentry, the content of debating society rhetoric ultimately transcended salon rhetoric by supporting open discussion of socially progressive topics and their impact on the populace as a whole. Although women in debating societies violated the model of private sociability for women, which was endorsed (but not always followed) by the Bluestocking leaders, ironically, the popular demand for mixed-gender and feminine public debate was largely inspired by salon culture, which had become famous through word-of-mouth descriptions, correspondence, and the publications of learned ladies.

In terms of subject matter, while the social status of their members differed, both salons and debating societies exemplified women's Enlightenment rhetoric in their speakers' reliance on the combined appeal of wit, virtue, and taste. For both groups, appeals to wit were conveyed through reason and logic, as well as the artful arrangement and clear presentation of arguments and examples. While virtue for bluestockings was connoted by polite and dignified interactivity, in debating societies, appeals to virtue increasingly included discussions of equality, women's rights, and an honest day's work. Arguably, interactive discussions in Bluestocking salons focused more on intellectual, philosophical, and literary topics and artistic taste and aesthetics—the subjects of belletristic rhetoric. In contrast, debating societies followed the neoclassical elocutionary model of delivery, and women orators performed a middle-class female aesthetic, reflecting their audiences' professional knowledge in trades related to fashion, theater, pedagogy, and other areas of women's work experiences and sites of sociability. A strong line of argument pursued by women speakers in debate venues had to do with methods of achieving upward mobility and economic prosperity. In many cases, the owners and managers of debate societies designed, and probably even scripted, the performances of women speakers to help ensure that their oratory conveyed some semblance of bluestocking style.

Within both debating clubs and salons, women speakers raised many questions about unequal gender roles, the unjust patriarchal subordination of women, and the need for education for girls and women. Both groups were also victims of patriarchal prejudices and strictures limiting female speech. They also shared in the performance of feminine intellectual exchange, which some people considered transgressive in a society where traditional women's roles exemplified subdued politeness—if not complete silence—and passive moral virtue. The omission of female orators, as well as bluestockings, from the twentieth-century construction of rhetorical history is symptomatic of the cognitive blind spots that naturally occur within deep rhetoric, in this case resulting from the persistence of patriarchal prejudices even during the progressive political climate and so-called egalitarianism of the Enlightenment. The next chapter analyzes how bluestocking women appropriated written forms of rhetoric and rhetorical theory to advocate for women's intellectual development and optimal education models for girls and women.

CHAPTER 4

On the Page: Written Rhetoric and Arguments about Education

I have not yet read Mrs. Wollstonecraft's *Rights of Women*, but I am promised them by a friend, and I will afterwards give you my opinion, if you think it worth your attention.
　　—Clara Reeve, in a 1792 letter to the *Monthly Magazine*

ℛISING LITERACY AND the explosion of publishing in eighteenth-century England produced a booming literary marketplace in which a new professional class of woman writers churned out a proliferation of titles across a wide range of literary genres answering the reading public's demand for popular and polite publications. As historian Margaret Hunt reports, "Women's literacy rose from about ten per cent in 1600 to fifty per cent in 1840" (262). More women were reading, and reading aloud was a popular pastime. Not only stand-alone books, but also the new media form of the periodical passed into consumers' hands through booksellers, circulating libraries, and other commercial venues. While the deep rhetoric of patriarchal ideology continued to cast women into domestic roles in the private realm of the home, the publishing industry was capitalizing on women as a massive subaltern group rapidly transforming into a self-aware counterpublic.

Within this new literary public realm, the genre of the novel appealed to the imaginations of women readers through stories that played with and challenged gender norms. The treatment of women became a popular common theme of eighteenth-century British fiction, and prominent authors wrote bestselling sentimental and Gothic works targeting women readers. Bodice-rippers such as Eliza Haywood's *Love in Excess* (1719–20) were popular early in the eighteenth century, but by mid-century, sentimental novels celebrated feminine virtue. In *Pamela* (1740), the most popular novel of the mid-eighteenth century, Samuel Richardson engrossed English readers with the suffering and purity of his sentimental heroine. *Pamela* was enthusiastically read aloud in many middle-class homes across the nation, captivating readers and intimate circles of auditors, both male and female. The literary theme of the suffering woman continued its ascendancy with spine-tingling gothic novels, such as Ann Radcliffe's *Mysteries of Udolpho* (1794), which offered romance and excitement, and also pointed out the malevolent side of patriarchy. Even into the early nineteenth century sentimentalism extended to the plight of the black heroine in *Woman of Colour: A Tale* (1808), an anonymously written novel published in the era immediately preceding abolition in England. Beyond their main purpose of entertainment, novels about women often carried cautionary messages and performed subtle didactic functions.

Countering what many people viewed as the harmful and potentially incendiary effects of novel-reading, conduct literature attempted to directly inculcate proper behavior in women readers. Works such as *Ladies Library* (1714), John Gregory's *Father's Legacy to his Daughters* (1761), James Fordyce's *Sermons to Young Women* (1766), and Thomas Gisborne's *Inquiry into the Duties of the Female Sex* (1797) prescribed a virtuous course of feminine studies and practices, including reading and writing, and warned women away from frivolous and dangerous novels.[1] Ironically, while their purposes and styles differed—novels and conduct literature both offered intimate and descriptive conversational prose, prescribed real-world gendered behaviors, and issued warnings for not following them, and both genres delivered social critiques that attempted to play on the emotions of eighteenth-century women readers.

Seeing the market potential for works that instructed and appealed to women readers, publishers sought additional genres to commercialize. Traditionally private genres of women's rhetoric, such as the conversation and the letter, were commodified into nonfiction publications that explored women's rhetorical practices and learning. Publishers "transformed" women's genres and writing practices into "print forms that could be sold," Hunt argues, but they were not "dragging women or their words from the private sphere out into the public (though sometimes that was the rhetoric)"; rather, they were textualizing, typesetting, printing, and selling existing "persuasive practices [already at work] in . . . kinship networks, literary coteries, religious movements, and politics" (265). The publication of a diversity of feminized print genres enabled women of many backgrounds, talents, and viewpoints to become professional writers, marketing their work to an exponentially larger group of women readers. Furthermore, within the rhetorical landscape of Britain's eighteenth-century literary marketplace, professional women authors found support and patronage from learned ladies (Gallagher 227–31). In effect, the literary market fostered networks of literate women that included authors, readers, patrons, and mentors.

This chapter contextualizes the British Enlightenment as an era of kairos for women writers and protofeminist written rhetoric. I begin by analyzing the conditions that encouraged women writers to engage in and write about rhetoric. I then examine several important treatises dedicated to the subject of British women's rhetoric in their offering of practical and helpful advice on how to write for different purposes, and how to reason effectively in writing and speech. These treatises discuss women's appropriation of the finer points of persuasion, including purpose, tone, and style. To see how eighteenth-century women writers put rhetorical theory into practice, the final section of this chapter offers a comparative case study of the rhetorical strategies eighteenth-century British women writers used in their arguments about education, which I group into three categories: arguments of gentility; arguments for domestic education; and progressive plans for institutional education.

Women Writers Writing Rhetoric

Women writers were not isolated savants, working alone, but rather educated members of familial writing groups and local literary circles. Like many eighteenth-century writers, women who published treatises and other works of nonfiction were highly knowledgeable about the principles of classical rhetoric and argumentation. Many were from studious middle- and upper-class families and had received rigorous domestic educations at the hands of a parent, relative, tutor, or governess. Most upper-class and some middle-class girls grew up with access to libraries containing classic and contemporary works of literature, history, philosophy, and religious writings. While girls' education did not typically include classical languages, quite a few women writers were well read in English and French translations of Greek and Roman literature and selections of classical rhetoric, especially Plato, Aristotle, and Cicero. An educated woman's knowledge about philosophy and rhetoric would have included the work of Descartes, the French Belletrists, John Locke, and, in the latter part of the century, David Hume, Adam Smith, and Hugh Blair, among others. Daughters in literary and politically progressive families also might have had exposure to mixed-gender intellectual circles and encouragement to engage in protofeminist literary activities.

The growing contingency of serious amateur and professional women writers developed rhetorical strategies to refute criticisms of their profession. As Hunt explains, British women writers argued that pursuit of virtue and moral obligations "outweighed their 'natural' feminine aversion to publicity," especially as they saw authorship as a viable means to gain "a considerably larger sphere of influence" and an independent source of income (265). Thus, the long eighteenth century witnessed a proliferation of arguments written by women in defense of women. Women who wrote and published works of persuasive nonfiction—including polemical essays, tracts, and treatises—skillfully employed classical appeals and masculine strategies of argumentation in their writing. They also drew on commonalities of female experience and contemporary Enlightenment philosophies regarding gendered social constructs. As Apetri notes, at the turn of the century, the woman question reached an unprecedented "intensity" with publications such as "The Woman's Right: Or Her Power in a Greater Equality to Her Husband" (1680) by London portrait painter Mary More, Judith Drake's *Essay in Defence of the Female Sex* (1696), and Mary Astell's *Serious Proposal, Part I* and *Part II*, and *Reflections upon Marriage*, as well as devotional writing by women such as Damaris Masham, Alicia D'Anvers, Elizabeth Singer Rowe, and Susanna Hopton (6–9). Appropriating humanist genres, such as the dialogue and the defense, women writers composed and published detailed enactments and analyses of controversial topics relating to the feminine gender, such as arguments for women's roles and rights in British society, as well as their cognitive capabilities, educational needs, and rhetorical theories and practices.

In terms of style, eighteenth-century British women writers, following the composition prescriptions of their times, excelled in extremely intricate description, clever reasoning and sentimental appeals. Wit, a main feature of Enlightenment rhetoric, is apparent in their strategic arrangement of evidence as well as their various tones (lofty, plain, or humorous). Additionally, women writers developed ethos based on constructing authorial identities imbued with virtue and sensibility—a stance involving both emotion and taste. In their creation of feminine styles and genres, as JoEllen DeLucia argues, women writers helped situate "emotion's place in discussions of social and commercial progress in Enlightenment Britain" (4). As a sign of virtue in Enlightenment rhetoric, emotion (or affect) represents a feminine form of ethos, as well as an appeal of pathos.

While uniquely feminine appeals to pathos distinguish eighteenth-century women writers, women also gained credibility through effective use of traditional authorial practices and logical structures. They often directly announced their targeted readers in the title or preface of their work. They created rational arguments and artfully employed numerous rhetorical devices and layers of direct and indirect rhetorical appeals. In conformance with their era's penchant for satire, women writers often developed purposeful irony as a dual appeal to wit and emotion—by which they aimed to arouse sympathy for issues women faced. Feminine humor and the woman's point of view functioned as popular persuasive devices (which male writers often imitated in drag authorial performance). Gender was certainly a topic that authors played with in their usage of terms and meanings that could be doubled. For example, the term a "man of parts" describes an educated and knowledgeable man of wealth and means; however, depending on the context, it also could signify a pretentious fool. Likewise, the term "learned lady" could refer to an educated woman, but it also could be used sarcastically to characterize women intellectuals as silly and pretentious. Women writers found myriad ways to adopt wit, humor, irony and other neoclassical devices, and there were at least several works that provided style guidelines for women's rhetorics.

Protofeminist Persuasive Genres and Rhetorical Theory

Discussions of women's practices of persuasive writing appear in a variety of nonfiction genres, and many frequently employ dialogue as a presentation format and a rhetorical technique. In neoclassical dialogues and defenses, women writers participated in the debate of the *querelle des femmes,* which had been waging since medieval times. The dialogue tradition, as Ekaterina Haskins explains, dramatized arguments as conversations "between the author and his or her opponent or a sympathetic listener" (289). Alternatively, the genre of the treatise presented arguments more directly, undramatized—although treatises did sometimes contain embedded dialog. Protofeminist treatises, dialogues, and defenses engaged in progressive conjecture about rhetorical theory and could feature high, plain, or humorous style. These highbrow academic genres, as practiced by British women writers of the era, display both rationalist and empirical philosophies and advocate polite conversation and writing as the primary modes of persuasion.

Several nonfiction works stand out as specifically focused on women's rhetoric during the long eighteenth century. Mary Astell's *Serious Proposal to the Ladies, Part I and Part II,* (1694, 1697) remains one of the most important early works of women's Enlightenment rhetoric. As its title implies, Astell's treatise presents a scholarly exhortation written in a "serious" intellectual voice. In *Serious Proposal, Part I,* Astell enumerates the many reasons that women have faulty educations. Astell expresses her belief that women were enslaved not only by the laws of their patriarchal society but also by their own lack of effort to employ logical reasoning—a skill she thought could and should be learned by all human beings. Astell's major claim in *Part I* lies in her model for a secluded and communal female academy for learning. In *Serious Proposal, Part II,* Astell focuses more specifically on the curriculum for optimal feminine education, including rhetorical theory and the need for girls and women to develop the skills of written composition. In both *Part I* and *Part II,* Astell uses logical persuasive argument, appeals to Christian values, Enlightenment philosophy, and common sense to put forth her vision.

Besides Astell's *Serious Proposal, Part II,* two other notable neoclassical texts theorizing women's use of rhetoric emerged at the turn of the eighteenth century: Judith Drake's *Essay in Defence of the Female Sex* (1696) and an anonymously authored handbook, *The Lady's Rhetorick: Containing Rules for Speaking and Writing Elegantly* (1707). When compared, these three very distinct texts offer a panoramic snapshot of women's early Enlightenment rhetorical theory. In terms of subject matter, Drake's defense makes similar points to Astell's, drawing mainly from Cartesian rationalism and (to a lesser extent) Lockean empiricism, to argue in favor of women's rhetorical capabilities. Drake uses humanist dialogic dramatizations and a light satirical style as compared to Astell's philosophical logic and direct, plain style. These differences might be better understood by a reading of the third text, *The Lady's Rhetorick,* which, of the three, looks and sounds the most like a handbook or style guide. From the explanations about writing provided in *The Lady's Rhetorick,* readers can deduce that the light humorous tone found in Drake's essay is an example of the jesting style. Striking a middle ground of polite-yet-light conversational style, in its focus on the usefulness of rhetorical theory for women, *The Lady's Rhetorick* makes explicit connections between French and English belletristic and conversational rhetoric, as does Astell's *Serious Proposal, Part II.* While differing in style, all three of these early treatises demonstrate the importance of belletristic rhetoric to the literate British female population and connect English rhetorical practice both to French and classical sources.

The most scholarly and philosophical of the three works, Astell's *Serious Proposal, Part II* embeds rhetorical theory in a larger argument about the need for women to subdue their own vices and passions and tap into their capacity for learning. Astell was a strong proponent of Cartesian epistemology, which relied on "natural logic" and "recognized that extensive professional education was not necessary in order to engage in the life of the mind"; like Descartes, Astell believed pursuing excellence in the vernacular of one's own culture was more important than studying classical languages (Sutherland 125–26; 56–57). Throughout her proposal, Astell connects Cartesian philosophy and seventeenth-century French rhetorical theory with the emerging philosophical developments of the British Enlightenment. In *The Eloquence of Mary Astell,* Christine Mason Sutherland notes that Astell's "primary audience was women," but that in *Serious Proposal, Part II,* Astell was also addressing men, specifically "those contemporary philosophers and theologians" with whom she disagreed (125). Astell was writing herself into the Western philosophical tradition, and the rhetorical theory that Astell describes often tends to follow earlier humanist, rather than Enlightenment, principles of rhetoric. Foremost,

Astell aligns invention with logic, not rhetoric, as in the French tradition of Descartes; the Port Royalists, Antoine Arnauld and Pierre Nicole; Blaise Pascal; and Peter Ramus (Sutherland 125–36; Bizzell and Herzberg 845). From the Port Royalists, Astell finds a connection between logical reasoning and Christian theology, that is, an ethical connection between reason and faith wherein human error results from a lack of faith (Sutherland 132–133). In her mistrust of strictly empirical reasoning, we can see Astell's differences from Locke.

Furthermore, Astell's six rules of invention mirror the four rules that Descartes includes in his *Discourse on Method,* as Sutherland points out (127–28). In terms of rhetorical theory, Astell's Cartesian-inspired rules cover not only classical *inventio* (thinking) but some aspects of *dispositio* (organization) as well (Sutherland 130). Concisely paraphrased below, Astell's rules lay out the process by which a rhetor or writer should approach discourse on a topic:

1. have a "distinct notion of [the] subject" and precise terms to describe it;
2. cut out extraneous or irrelevant material;
3. order one's thoughts from the simple to the complex;
4. treat a subject thoroughly and divide it into as many parts as needed to make it comprehensible;
5. keep the subject in close focus; and
6. "judge no further than we perceive, and not take anything for Truth, which we do not evidently Know to be so." (Astell 128)

Even though Astell categorizes the above rules within the province of logic, and not rhetoric, we can read them as rhetorical theory in that their purpose is to help inform women writers how to build and articulate verbal analyses and argumentation.

For Astell, however, the proper focus of rhetoric and rhetorical theory mapped to the classical canon of *elocutio* (or style). Chapter 3, section 5 of *Serious Proposal, Part II,* is where Astell most directly theorizes rhetoric as she sees it pertaining to women—in their style of speech and, even more so, in their style and practice of written composition. Astell saw the purpose of rhetoric—meaning elocutio or style—not as the winning of arguments but rather to "remove those Prejudices that lie in the way of Truth . . . and excite our Hearers to a due consideration of it" (190). The difference between victory over an opponent versus the removal of falsehood may be subtle, but in this statement, Astell truly shows herself as a Platonist and an absolutist, therefore, not so much an empiricist. She does, however, concede to the practical wisdom in Locke's theories of language and learning. For example, in *Serious Proposal, Part II,* as Ruth Perry points out, Astell identifies one impediment to women's abilities in logical reasoning as their inability to properly use "particles—what we call conjunctions" and prescribes that they read the section about particles in book 3 of Locke's *Essay Concerning Human Understanding* (362). Moving from the finer points of style to the canon of delivery, which she terms "pronunciation," Astell asserts that women have an advantage because they possess more naturally pleasing voices than men (Bizzell and Herzberg 845).

In terms of her own written composition style, Astell's *Serious Proposal, Part I* and *Part II,* provides an expertly crafted example of protofeminist Enlightenment rhetoric. Both parts of Astell's treatise innovate in their direct address to women readers and in masterfully layering persuasive devices. Sutherland explains the appeal of *Serious Proposal* in several ways: "It was the brilliance of Astell's rhetoric that made her proposal so arresting. . . . She prepares the ground very carefully before setting forth her proposal, making full use of suspense, luring her audience to read out of sheer curiosity," and she "adopts the commonsense stance of the mentor, even the mother, not aspiring to the dignity of authority" (60–61; 134). While Astell appeals through brilliant organization and personalized tone, it is perhaps the latter quality, her personal tone of mentoring, that resonated most with women. Her model for a female learning community in *Part I*, which I describe later in this chapter, was influential among her contemporaries and with the next generation of British women intellectuals. Furthermore, in combining attention to the needs of a specific audience with attention to belletristic principles, Astell's approach to rhetoric was ahead of her time, prefiguring George Campbell's *Philosophy of Rhetoric* (1776) and Hugh Blair's *Lectures on Belles Lettres* (1783) by many decades.

Just as Astell drew from past and contemporary sources in the development of her theories about moral philosophy and rhetoric, Judith Drake also combines points from rationalism and empiricism together with traditional humanist devices to argue in favor of women's rhetorical capabilities. As her lengthy title foretells, in *An Essay in Defence of the Female Sex in Which Are Inserted the Characters of a Pedant, a Squire, a Beau, a Virtuoso, a Poetaster, a City-Critick, &c. in a Letter to a Lady* (1696), Drake employs wit and hyperbole to enter the Enlightenment debate on gender and human character. Striking a unique note with her duel appeal to empirical and rationalist humor, Drake denies the "existence of innate ideas and the distinction of sexes in souls" and argues that, if merely biological differences be considered, the physically weaker female sex is better designed for intellectual pursuits (2).[2] In her satiric essay, Drake encourages all women to read romances, novels, plays, and poems to help their "wit, humanity, manners, and conversational skills" (Todd and Dow). After an effusive dedication to Princess Anne of Denmark,

Drake—herself an upper middle-class, educated, married woman—presents her defense of the female sex in an informal epistolary address from one unnamed woman to another. The unnamed narrator states her purpose as "The defence of our Sex against so many and so great Wits as have so strongly attacked it," and continues sardonically, "Not that I can, or ought to yield, that we are by Nature less enabled for such an Enterprize as Men are" (Drake 26). The tone and voice of the text makes it readily apparent that the narrator's plan is to deflate male egos and to show that women are, in fact, equal to the task of their own defense.

The defense begins by disabusing women of their reputation for shrewishness and showing that rude and aggressive communication styles are applicable to males as well as females. She then defends women's speech, education, and learning based on the ideas that all humans have minds for the purpose of making sense of the world—here showing with light humor her knowledge of Descartes and Locke. Like Astell, Drake states that the skill of logical reasoning does not require knowledge of the classical languages. She later argues that the study of classical languages in eighteenth-century British male education is not only irrelevant and impractical, it takes so much energy that it stunts boys in their emotional development and causes them to lack the maturity of girls at the same age (Drake 49, 61–64). While her tone is playfully pedantic, the detail with which Drake renders this argument makes it seem simultaneously serious and ridiculous. As Ektarina Haskins concludes, Drake's finely crafted text melds Platonic dialogue and allegorical (Theophrastean) male character portraits, both devices of the traditional querelle des femmes genre, with the "egalitarian philosophies of Descartes and Locke" to reiterate age-old arguments well known to late seventeenth-century readers using more contemporary and humorous examples (298). More plainly, Drake successfully uses humor to dismantle misogynistic stereotypes of gendered learning.

Another witty, pseudoserious, and largely overlooked, treatise, the anonymously authored *The Lady's Rhetorick,* explicitly delineates feminine strategies for persuasion based on the classical canon of Greek and Roman rhetoric and on the belletristic theory and salon rhetorics of seventeenth-century France. The title page of *The Lady's Rhetorick* announces its content and its form as "Rules for Speaking and Writing Elegantly in a Familiar Discourse Directed to an Honourable and Learned Lady . . . Enriched with Many Delightful Remarks, Witty Repartees, and Pleasant Stories, Both Antient and Modern . . . Done from the French with Some Improvements." In providing extensive rhetoric and composition guidelines for women—as Tania Smith describes, *The Lady's Rhetorick* evinces "the tip of an iceberg . . . of women's informal rhetorical practice and education" (Smith "Lady's Rhetorick" 349). Written in the style of a framed Platonic dialogue, *The Lady's Rhetorick* employs a conversational tone but presents only one side of a conversation, an address from an unnamed gentleman to a fictitious feminine auditor, Lady Sophia. This one-sided conversation presents a model of male authority and suggests dominance over the female; however, the instructive subject matter encourages and supports women's education in the methods and feminine uses of rhetoric. While the speaker's language flows informally, as a conversation would, the discussion is comprehensively organized into a structured handbook.

Although scholars of rhetoric in that time period and today would likely view *The Lady's Rhetorick* as a watered-down version of classical theory, its examples are instructive and broad-based, including references to Queen Anne and other contemporary English figures as well as French authors, such as Bernard Lamy and Balzac, and ancient orators, most prominently Cicero, Quintilian, and Aristotle.[3] Thus in combining "principles and examples not only from ancient and modern men's rhetoric but from men's and women's conversation [and] French and English belles lettres, . . . it writes women rhetors into the history, definitions, and principles of rhetoric" (Smith 352). Preceding the main text, the bookseller's advertisement states that the goals of *The Lady's Rhetorick* are to "render the rules" of rhetoric to a wide audience of readers outside of schools and "to encourage this useful study amongst the Beautiful Sex" so that they may learn and practice the art (*The Lady's Rhetorick* 1). There are no known reviews or other records about the readers of this text. Smith reports that only one edition was published (353). Although obscure, this work of early eighteenth-century British rhetorical theory is designed to support rhetorical practice for "ladies" and thus constitutes a buried landmark in the history of women's rhetoric.

The Lady's Rhetorick appropriates classical and belletristic rhetoric and revises it into a primer that early eighteenth-century English women might use. In epistolary dialogic style, as a discourse to the Lady Sophia, the text starts with the salutation "*Madam*, I Have at last yielded to your pressing Intreaties, or rather obey'd your just Commands, and given you in this Treatise all the most necessary Rules of Rhetorick in our Mother Tongue" (*The Lady's Rhetorick* 1). The phrase "Mother Tongue" indicates that *The Lady's Rhetorick* agrees with Astell and Drake, echoing the Cartesian stance, in arguing for women's rhetorical use of the English language, without need for Latin or Greek. The usage of "Mother Tongue" is also an example of the feminine metaphors that run throughout the text. The language of the first-person narrator is intimate and charming, such as in this definition given for rhetoric:

> I Cannot approve of the Definition, that Isocrates hath left us, That it is an
> Art which renders Great Things little, and little Things great. Such a mon-
> strous Definition might cause you to fancy in it something of Sorcery, and
> that to attain to Eloquence it is needful to be acquainted with the Black Art.
> But I had rather agree with Aristotle to tell you plainly, *That this is the Art*
> *of Speaking Elegantly . . . of All things to the purpose.* (*The Lady's Rhetorick* 6,
> italics in original)

Even when defining terms, the narrator stays in character with a chatty and
affectionate first-person style. At the same time, the organizational structure
in its classification and division of topics signals a direct nod to Aristotle, providing one of many elements showing the unnamed author's familiarity with
and adherence to Aristotelian rhetoric.

Divided into a two-part format, part 1 provides an engaging introduction
to the classical model of rhetoric interspersed with colloquial editorial commentary and an emphasis on particular feminized uses and features of rhetoric. The narrator enlivens classical and belletristic definitions with examples
that would be relatable and interesting to eighteenth-century women readers.
Beginning with the three "genders" of rhetoric (*judicial, demonstrative,* and
deliberative), the narrator describes them as subject types and as tools of discourse, and he provides practical advice of when and how ladies might employ
these in their own lives. The author goes on to note that the judicial gender
is useful for observing time, place, persons, and causes of those things we
would "condemn or defend"; the demonstrative gender works for relating the
"Virtues and Vices of Persons"; and the deliberative gender applies when a lady
needs "to Persuade or to Dissuade" (8–9). When giving advice on the practical
application of the three genders of rhetoric, the narrator conveys confidence
that ladies possess the common sense, propriety, and wit to customize them for
feminine purposes. As Smith notes, *The Lady's Rhetorick* "feminizes rhetoric
by downplaying its warlike, agonistic traditions and emphasizing its ethical
uses in public and private" (363). Although its prescriptions limit women's
rhetoric to interpersonal, not professional communication, the narrator grants
that women have need of rhetoric and, therefore, are entitled to the tools customized for their situations.

Moving through the basics of classical rhetorical theory, part 1 proceeds to
cover the five canons (*invention, disposition, style, memory,* and *pronunciation*
or *action*), the four parts of oration (*exordium* or *beginning, narration* or *narrative, confirmation,* and *conclusion*), and, initially, three styles (*lofty* or *heroic,*
middle or *moderate,* and *plain*). However, the narrator later adds a fourth style,

burlesque or *jesting,* which "none of our Authors, neither French nor English, have treated to any purpose, though it is`. . .` useful to correct Vice, by representing it in a ridiculous shape" (65). This addition of the burlesque style invites women to engage in the eighteenth-century penchant for satire employed judiciously for didactic purposes. However, use of the jesting or burlesque style should not be "sharp or offensive" and "must be seasoned with a dainty and pleasant Wit" designed to produce laughter but not embarrassment or shame (*The Lady's Rhetorick* 74). These recommendations, as Smith notes, provide "a courtly woman . . . witty ways of dealing with the faulty reasoning of impertinent admirers" and prescribe "brevity and satire, or humility and politeness, as the situation demands" (365). *The Lady's Rhetorick* prescribes that feminine wit should consist of clever and well-spoken remarks delivered with sensitivity and devoid of invective.

The prescriptions of the text take the form of friendly advice, which the narrator infuses with plenty of feminine and female-focused imagery. One example of feminized figurative language appears in the discussion of invention, which introduces a maternal metaphor comparing well-conceived discourses to "perfect children" while disturbingly characterizing unplanned speeches as "half-shaped, as those that come into the World as Miscarriages" (31). (Pregnancy metaphors for composition and writing had been in use in the previous century by early modern poets, such as Margaret Cavendish, John Dryden, and Sir Philip Sidney.) The maternal metaphor for invention in *The Lady's Rhetorick* conforms to neoclassical notions of the importance of discovering fit content for composition through a distinct research and design phase, and it also implies that creativity, or creation, is a female-gendered process, thereby building ethos for women's rhetorical practices.

The narrator's appeals to feminine wit continue in part 2, "Treating of the Figures," which moves into a discussion of the modern application of the sixteen classical figures that the narrator claims are most efficacious in imparting eloquence to English speech and literary works. In a playful tongue-in-cheek style, the narrator states, "If among these Rhetorical Flowers you meet with some that seem useless to you, you may in such case imitate the bees, that survey and smell all the Flowers, but draw not from every one that Quintessence which turns into Hony" (*The Lady's Rhetorick* 79). Through this tone of light-hearted metaphorical language and pleasant natural imagery, the text aims to "disarm" the traditional treatment of figures and tropes found in scholastic rhetoric, which the narrator mocks and purposely "turns to jest" (Smith 370–71). In doing so, the narrator demonstrates the burlesque style. Appropriately, the first two figures in part 2 are hyperbole and irony. In its emphasis on vernacular

English usage, its wit and jesting, and its examples from British poets and personages, *The Lady's Rhetorick* signals a move away from classical examples of copious figures and ornamentation, common in humanist rhetorical theory, to a more modernized approach grounded in the English language, still cognizant of classical principles but more aesthetically driven by the experience of British people, and particularly crafted for the personal taste of British women. This light jesting style remained popular throughout the eighteenth century (and beyond).

Almost a century later, light and witty feminine conversation provides an entertaining method for ironically conveying women's rhetoric to an audience of women readers in *Letters for Literary Ladies* (1795), an eclectic collection of creative nonfiction by Anglo-Irish author and educational theorist Maria Edgeworth. While not strictly a work of rhetorical theory, Edgeworth presents a tongue-in-cheek miscellany to instruct women readers on improper embodied, spoken, and written rhetoric; thus *Letters for Literary Ladies* functions as a narrative of negative capability consisting in empirical demonstrations of bad behavior. Through vignettes about the improper actions and poor judgments of ridiculous female characters, Edgeworth shows women readers what not to do. Parts 1 and 2 present ironic fictitious epistolary dialogues focused on the kind of education young ladies should not receive to properly fulfill their gender roles, while part 3 consists of an absurd satire, "An Essay on the Science of Self-Justification," to ironically illustrate the role of the wife.

Part 1 of *Letters for Literary Ladies* combines a dialogic question-and-answer format with a deferred thesis—what we now call a Rogerian style of argument. It begins with a letter from a "Gentleman to his Friend upon the Birth of a Daughter," which raises many questions about girls' education, and concludes with a lengthy reply from the friend, which serves to satirically deconstruct the dangers, vices, and negative consequences of educating a girl to be a learned lady (a term that Edgeworth humorously renders as derogatory). Through this dialogic format, Edgeworth's satire works to critique the uselessness of frivolous and superficial education. Building on this same theme and structure, part 2 consists of a correspondence between two fictitious young women, Julia and Caroline. Julia writes only the first letter, which shows her to be driven by emotion and completely oblivious to reason. All subsequent letters are from Caroline urging Julia to use common sense. Each letter responds to a bad decision of Julia's—in courtship, marriage, and marital separation. Nevertheless, Julia defies Caroline's advice, abandons her family, and flees to France. Through their dialogue, Edgeworth provides an argument by example in which Caroline's letters explain Julia's mistakes. On one hand, Edgeworth seems to be chastising the patriarchal system, but she ultimately upholds its hegemony by disciplining her character Julia in the ways of the world. The last letter from Caroline expresses a gruesome outcome: she writes to Julia's estranged husband, Lord V———, telling him first of Julia's return to England in an emaciated state and then informing him of her eventual death. The dialogue demonstrates patriarchal double standards but also counsels women to make good decisions.

Switching up her style in part 3 of *Letters for Literary Ladies,* "An Essay on the Noble Science of Self-Justification," Edgeworth delivers her didactic message indirectly, but with obvious sarcasm, through an extremely exaggerated and ironic list of advice directed to her stated audience of new brides. The entire essay consists of statements of direct address, such as "Candid pupil, you will readily accede to my first and fundamental axiom—that a lady can do no wrong." She admonishes her readers to "Obtain power . . . by all means: power is the law of man; make it yours." This advice for young women to seize power can be interpreted several ways: on the one hand, Edgeworth is sarcastically criticizing young ladies who act too bossy and controlling; but she also implies that—although and even because women lack physical power over men—new wives need to establish a modicum of rhetorical power. Her humorously ironic instructions for empowering "timid brides" include these methods for successful argument:

> At the first hint of a discovery that you are anything less than infallible: contradict, debate, justify, recriminate, rage, weep, swoon, do anything but yield to conviction. . . .
>
> If then, reasonable pupils, you would succeed in argument, attend to the following instructions. Begin by preventing, if possible, the specific statement of any position . . . Depend upon the sympathy of the spectators. . . . Whilst you have it yet in your power, rise with becoming magnanimity, and cry, "I give it up! . . . I do so hate disputing about trifles. I give it up!" Before an explanation on the word trifle can take place, quit the room with flying colours. (Edgeworth)

Clearly outrageous, Edgeworth's recommendations—to use crying, raging, and swooning as rhetorical devices—mock the hyperbole of literary sensibility. (The witty exaggeration of feminine histrionics is also taken up by a teenage Jane Austen with great glee in her satiric novella *Love and Friendship.*) However, the action of leaving the room demonstrates the rhetorical device of absence, a nonconfrontational and nonviolent tool of feminine rhetoric, which critics commented on as a tactic of Queen Anne (see chapter 1). Edgeworth's essay makes the point that, for many eighteenth-century women, particularly young brides who have just entered into the powerless position of wife, physical demonstrations of frailty and simply walking away might be the only persuasive appeals they had at their disposal, especially if they lacked education and rhetorical training.

Women's Published Arguments on Education

Education, particularly the education of girls, was the central topic of British women's Enlightenment rhetoric. Those advocating for large-scale education and intellectual improvement for girls faced a wall of patriarchal resistance. By the late seventeenth century, women "were almost completely excluded from university education, where the most advanced education in rhetoric took place" (Bizzell and Herzberg 749).[4] After the decline of the humanist movement, its legacy of classical education and formal training in rhetoric continued in the masculine domains of universities and grammar schools; however, females were not admitted to these institutions. Academic study for girls and women throughout the seventeenth and eighteenth centuries occurred informally, for the most part. Nevertheless, eighteenth-century British women writers moved beyond the basic arguments of the humanist *querelle des femmes* (or woman question) in which, from the fifteenth to the seventeenth centuries, as Judith Zinsser explains, "Elite men and women argued over whether or not females could learn, reason, and contribute to the intellectual culture of the era" (123).[5]

After the early modern era of humanism, the Enlightenment produced the next wave of arguments about education. By the early eighteenth century, John Locke, in *Essay Concerning Human Understanding* (1689) had posited that all humans enter the world with relatively equal cognitive capabilities, regardless of their social class or gender, as *tabulae rasae* (blank slates), who are then molded by individual perceptions, circumstances, and life experiences. Lockean empiricism held great authority in early eighteenth-century education theory; however, in his treatise for parents, *Some Thoughts Concerning Education* (1693), Locke does not extend his egalitarian cognitive framework to his philosophy of gendered education. Rather he privileges boys as future political citizens requiring academic preparation for public life, and he upholds the subordination of girls as noncitizens relegated to private domestic roles. Despite this distinction, Locke favors the private domestic setting as the ideal learning environment for younger boys, as well as for girls of all ages.

Locke's program of domestic education strongly influenced the domestic pedagogy movement in eighteenth-century Britain. The Lockean education model also gave rise to a debate centering on what his contemporaries called "the famous question": Should girls be educated separately from boys? (Cohen 226). The famous question received a variety of answers from women intellectuals. One of the most immediate and direct responses came from Mary Astell in *Serious Proposal, Part I* (1694), in which she argues for separate but intellectually rigorous education for young women—not at home but in a school environment. After Locke and Astell, much of British Enlightenment education theory advocates literacy training for both males and females, but most often separately. Even with the gendered double standards in Enlightenment education theory, Locke's views of individual reasoning, rights, and liberties helped debates on education move beyond the question of whether or not females had the mental capacity to learn intellectual subject matter, and throughout the eighteenth century writers published arguments about the optimal environments and models for teaching girls and young women.

British Enlightenment arguments about girls' education appear in a diversity of genres—from traditional humanist dialogues and plans to domestic, empirical, and egalitarian models of teaching and learning. The two major issues addressed were: the benefits of gender-segregated versus co-educational learning models; and the propriety of domestic versus institutional (school) education. Even for girls, domestic education did not refer primarily to lessons in housewifery and household management but rather to regular and structured home-schooling with an organized curriculum, which included various liberal, fine, and domestic arts, and sometimes included the sciences as well. As diaries and other personal mementos of eighteenth-century British women show, "Far from being haphazard, roaming wildly without any plan or method, their home education was highly regulated, following a strict and often self-imposed discipline" (Cohen 231). Families who educated their daughters at home often incorporated what they knew of classical pedagogical methods along with empirical homeschooling practices, such as Locke advises in his treatise. (For an example of Locke's influence in domestic education, see my description of Jane Johnson and her nursery library in chapter 1.) The amount of instruction a young woman received in reading aloud, elocution, and the practice of written argumentation depended on many variables, including the values and resources of her family; her social class and future vocational prospects; and the abilities, religious and political beliefs, and gender of her teachers, as well as the venue where the learning took place.

Throughout the eighteenth century, theorists continued to debate questions concerning the ideal education venues for women (domestic or public) and the need for rhetorical training based on gender, social class, and the future occupations of students. Weighing in on these debates, women writers addressed gendered education at various levels in the class structure, focusing at first on the upper classes, and then giving some consideration to the middle class and, less frequently, to the lower working classes, as the century progressed. The following sections cover the types of proposals and plans that eighteenth-century British women writers published regarding appropriate learning environments, curricula, and distinctions of social class in relation to girls' education.

ARGUMENTS OF GENTILITY

Arguments of gentility by seventeenth- and eighteenth-century women focus on the skills and behaviors necessary for a woman to possess in order to maintain polite decorum and an exemplary feminine image, which would ensure her success as a lady (otherwise known as a "woman of quality"). Many (but not all) arguments of gentility appropriate the genre of the humanist dialogue, and its use of named fictional characters as speakers and auditors, to dramatize and thereby prescribe particular activities as the proper course of learning for the prototypical gentlewoman. Jane Donawerth categorizes the humanist dialogue as a form of conversational rhetoric, which she argues was the predominant form of women's rhetoric from the seventeenth through the nineteenth centuries (*Conversational Rhetoric*). Arguments of gentility use dramatized dialogues between fictitious women characters as devices for modeling women's intellectual curiosity and making the case for learning as women's noble duty. The primary logical appeal of genteel education rests on a historical tradition of feminine nobility, virtue, and morality (countering the misogynistic Christian patriarchal narrative of womanly weakness deriving from Eve's original sin). This does not mean that all arguments of gentility are limited to women of the aristocratic class but rather that feminine virtue and dedication to learning may be construed as a form of moral nobility and purity.

In detailing the education of a lady and the skills she should possess, arguments of gentility synthesize a claim of definition and a claim of value: to be a lady, one must have had instruction in ethical and moral behavior, and this attainment by women, in turn, helps society. Writers of these types of arguments also apply the logic of past precedent by basing their claims on previous standards of women's learning and virtue from earlier times. For example, Bathsua Makin, in *Essay to Revive the Antient Education of Gentlewomen, in Religion, Manners, Arts, & Tongues* (1673), advocates a rebirth of classical academic education for young women in the upper-class echelons of society following the earlier examples of learned ladies from the humanist tradition. Janet Todd describes Makin's essay as the first English publication to "advocate the serious education of girls," noting that Makin argues for the benefits to family, nation, and individuals, and attributes "women's intellectual deficiencies to social conditioning, not inherent inferiority," a rhetorical stance Todd calls "remarkably modern" (Todd and Dow).[6] Following Makin, arguments of gentility persisted throughout the eighteenth century in model curriculums addressing the rhetorical education of girls and women of the upper and middle classes. Works by Hester Chapone, Hannah More, and Clara Reeve all prescribe education models involving rigorous programs of academic study for women of the upper classes. In advocating for girls' education, their arguments take a protofeminist stance to learning, but they do not embrace an egalitarian philosophy toward the social classes.

A popular treatise arguing for the upper-class education of girls, Hester Chapone's *Letters on Improvement of the Mind* (1773) went through twenty-eight editions. The self-educated daughter of a gentleman, Chapone was a member of Montagu's Bluestocking circle. In delineating her ideal curriculum, Chapone employs the humanist style of dialogic address in a collection of letters from herself to her fifteen-year-old niece. Through the narrative device of the didactic letter, Chapone adopts the voice of a concerned advice-giver and provides her rationale for taking the liberty of speaking at length. Chapone's letters emphasize Locke's philosophy of education by stating that females, as members of the human race, possess innate intellectual capacity; by warning against the dangers of ignorance; and by advocating a domestic model in which the mother is the primary teacher of children. Chapone recommends a broad curriculum of academic and sociable subjects, including reading and writing, geography, European history, dance (needed for social interaction), French (for literary conversation), and arithmetic (for practical purposes). Chapone also stresses women's Christian duty and proper moral behavior in society, including responsibilities pertaining to romance and marriage; controlling one's temper; following proper etiquette; and living and traveling economically. She warns her niece not to "waste in trivial amusement the next three or four years . . . the prime season of improvement," stating directly that, without education, "you come to feel yourself inferior in knowledge to almost every one you converse with—and, above all, if you should ever be a mother, when you feel your own inability to direct and assist the pursuits of your children—you will then find ignorance a severe mortification and a real evil" (208). Through these negative pathetic appeals, Chapone argues that ignorance due to lack of education leads to poor mothering by upper-class women.

Although Chapone's curriculum only slightly modifies women's traditional domestic gender role by adding academic study to their responsibilities, her rhetoric—the way in which she argues—models women's engagement in public philosophical debate. For example, in her plan she outspokenly critiques Samuel Johnson's Hobbesian view of human nature as pessimistic and detrimental to society. Defending virtue as the quintessential human goal, Chapone chastises Johnson for describing humans as naturally evil creatures who are only civilized by fear. Rather, she aligns her education model with the theory of natural benevolence outlined by the eighteenth-century philosopher Anthony Ashley Cooper, third Earl of Shaftesbury, a well-known protégé of Locke.[7] In her appropriations of Shaftesbury and Locke, Chapone outlines educational practices that align with progressive Enlightenment philosophies even as she espouses traditional views of the feminine gender role of the lady.

Like Chapone, Clara Reeve in *Plans of Education with Remarks on the Systems of Other Writers* (1792) applies classical, humanist, and contemporary precedents to argue for academic education for girls. The middle-class daughter of a curate, Reeves received a broad and academically rigorous education from her father, including readings in English and classical Greek and Roman history, and she later became a poet and author of gothic novels. Eschewing arguments for domestic and co-educational models, Reeve describes a comprehensive female academy. The main section of *Plans of Education,* titled "Essay on Education and Manners," takes the form of a long humanist dialogue presented in a series of letters between two fictitious characters: a governess, the accomplished Mrs. Danforth, and Lady A——, a woman of rank interested in hiring the governess. The epistolary device is itself a pedagogical act, which Reeve uses to demonstrate a writing-to-learn teaching method. As the character of Mrs. Danforth explains, in her process of composing letters to Lady A——, she involves the labor of her female students by having them transcribe excerpts of exemplary ancient and modern pedagogical theory, which she then incorporates into her correspondences with Lady A——. The device of embedding interspersed transcriptions into her correspondence not only models Mrs. Danforth's pedagogical technique but also shows how student activities can rise beyond classroom exercises and work as a form of service learning.

The fictitious persona of Mrs. Danforth provides Reeve a lively narrative voice through which she critiques landmark theories, arguments, and plans for education from the past and from her contemporaries. Observing that "all knowledge is progressive; and in tracing the errors of former writers, we advance step by step towards perfection" (13), Reeve reviews the pedagogical theories of Locke, Fenelon, Rousseau, Macaulay, and others, weaving what she approves from them into her own plans. In her first chapter, which contains observations of the ancients on youth and age, Reeve adopts a lofty tone and delivers an argument on the civic responsibility to educate youth. As support, she includes historical and philosophical allusions from ancient and early modern authorities, including the "Sacred Scriptures" and Shakespeare. The next several chapters examine the educational practices of the Moderns, including Locke, Rousseau, and Madame de Genlis. Beyond these famous pedagogical theorists, Reeve provides (mostly negative) anecdotes about ineffective girls' boarding schools, which teach subjects either too grandiose or superficial to be of benefit. Reeve's plan includes provisions for the middle and lower classes (as I describe later in the chapter); however, she preserves rigid class distinctions, guarding the higher intellectual subject matter and activities as the provenance of upper-class young ladies.

In yet another elitist argument for girls' education, Hannah More's *Strictures on the Modern System of Female Education* (1799) incorporates social class, religion, obedience, and duty into an instructive treatise in which she discusses female education in the past and present times and argues for the superiority of reason over imagination. Ascending from a middle-class background, Hannah More (1745–1833) became a published poet, playwright, and member of the elite Bluestocking circle of Elizabeth Montagu. In her early years, she worked as a schoolteacher, and through both her writing and religious activism, she championed girls' education and other social reforms, such as abolition. In the introduction to her *Strictures on the Modern System of Female Education*, More addresses herself to the "multitudes of the young and the well-disposed" ladies of England, to whom she offers stern Christian instruction on education and habits of life (xii-xvii).

In chapter 1, More issues a rallying cry, using direct address, calling women of quality and piety to recognize that their "talent is influence" and to "come forward, and contribute their full and fair proportion towards the saving of their country" (1, 4). More locates the influence of upper-class British women in what she sees as their traditional roles as arbiters of virtue and manners for their "civilized" nation (5). She forcefully argues that adherence to proper behavior and polite manners is paramount to a lady's ethos. As More says, "Propriety is to a woman what the great Roman critic says action is to an orator" (6). More's strong language, frequent citing of Christian values, and appeals to authority resonated with readers, making her treatise one of the most popular and influential works of her era on the education of girls and young women.

More begins with an epigraph from William Cowper: "Domestic Happiness, thou only bliss / Of Paradise that has surviv'd the Fall!" Channeling Cowper's sentimental ode to motherhood, More appropriates his comparison of mothers in their domestic sphere to Eve in prelapsarian Eden. More continues her strong emotional appeal to feminine Christian virtue by directly addressing mothers and future mothers:

> The great object to which you who are, or may be mothers, are more especially called, is the education of your children. . . . On YOU, depend in no small degree the principles of the whole rising generation. To your direction the daughters are almost exclusively committed; and . . . to you also is consigned the mighty privilege of forming the hearts and minds of your infant sons. By the blessing of God on the principles you shall . . . infuse into both sons and daughters, they will hereafter arise and call you blessed. . . , May every Christian mother be enabled through divine grace to say, with humble confidence to her Maker and Redeemer, Behold the children whom thou hast given me! (52–53)

More's call links motherhood and domestic education to Christian duty, as she exhorts mothers to become active agents of their children's education. She was not the first to make this move. Domestic education yoked with Anglicanism had been the idealized model for teaching young children and girls of all ages ever since the publication of John Locke's *Some Thoughts Concerning Education* (1693). Along with arguments supporting the wide practice of domestic education in homes across eighteenth-century Britain, maternal ethos grew significantly within Enlightenment discourse; the mother became an important rhetorical trope in eighteenth-century British education theory and the essential worker in domestic education models.

ARGUMENTS FOR DOMESTIC EDUCATION

Proponents of domestic education argue for its value to inculcate morals and common sense through nurture and practical experience. Adding to Locke's influential education treatise, Jean Jacques Rousseau famously formulated a theory of natural domestic education, which he delineated in his novel *Emile* (1762). Rousseau's ideas for teaching young children through natural experience, rather than structured lessons and rote exercises, appealed in some ways to progressive educators, such as Catherine Macaulay, Maria and Richard Edgeworth, and Mary Wollstonecraft. Macaulay's *Letters on Education* (1790) and the Edgeworths' *Practical Education* (1798) both espouse progressive domestic models of education that follow Rousseau's empirically based approach to experiential learning, but they reject his bias of female inferiority as well as the looseness of his pedagogical model. Macaulay pronounces Rousseau's view of the female mind as incapable of rational thought to be an "absurdity," which has "lowered the man of genius to the licentious pedant" (206). The Edgeworths, who saw Rousseau's methods fail in the education of Maria's elder brother, find fault with its lack of a structured curriculum. In her review of *Emile*, Mary Wollstonecraft calls Rousseau's pedagogical model "extravagantly idealistic"; however she supports his ideas of teaching children via "active experience"—even though in her *Vindication of the Rights of Women* (1792) she "relentlessly attacks Rousseau for limiting such an education to boys" (Richardson 29, 33). At a conceptual level, however, Macaulay, the Edgeworths, and (at first) Wollstonecraft approve of Rousseau's naturalized domestic model of education.

More importantly, they acknowledge the role of the mother in domestic education models as the primary monitor and motivator of her children's progress. Even Mary Wollstonecraft, who eventually favored public education over domestic, upheld the importance of mothers in education. Along with their acknowledgement of mothers as key figures in education, many progressive educators also weighed in on the benefits of gender-separate versus co-educational models, as well as the diversity of educational needs based on social class.

Catherine Macaulay's *Letters on Education* (1790) delineates a co-educational model of domestic education. Although she writes in the humanist style of dialogue in a fictitious address to a friend named Hortensia, Macaulay's text veers away from an argument of gentility by recommending a common education for the middle as well as the upper classes and advocates teaching boys and girls together. Macaulay's curriculum begins with educational toys and tactile experiences for young children and gradually progresses to instruction of elementary age children in moral behavior and rational thought. Macaulay outlines a program of male education, but she advises that boys and girls must learn and conform to the same universal set of ethics. Macaulay states that physical strength, the only natural superiority that man has over woman, "in the barbarous ages of mankind, was abused to such a degree, as to destroy all the natural rights of the female species, and reduce them to a state of abject slavery," and the lesser situation of education for females results from "a false notion of beauty and delicacy" in which "their system of nerves is depraved before they come out of the nursery" (206). In the invective tone of her protofeminist rhetoric, she prefigures Mary Wollstonecraft and John Stuart Mill. Macaulay's work, as Gillian Dow points out, inspired Mary Wollstonecraft with its admonition to "discourage coquetry and foster a taste for serious learning and rational reflection" (Dow, *Rooms of Our Own*). Wollstonecraft would go on to advocate for the inclusion of girls in a national public education system. However, Macaulay argues strongly against large-scale public education and in favor of domestic education because, she believes, morals are best inculcated at home by devoted parents or in a small homeschool setting with comparable dynamics. For those parents who are "opulent idlers who have neither the capacity or inclination to fulfill . . . the most important of parental duties," she recommends they entrust their children's education to "enlightened persons . . . who insist on limiting their pupils to a small number" (20). Macaulay's plan illustrates the idealization with which many people viewed domestic education during the eighteenth century.[8]

Accordingly, *Practical Education* (1798), a rationalist pedagogical manual, cowritten by Maria Edgeworth and her father Richard Lowell Edgeworth with notes from Maria's stepmother Honora Edgeworth, presents a comprehensive, empirically based, co-educational homeschool curriculum for toddlers through teenagers.[9] Similar to Macaulay's, the Edgeworths' curriculum foregrounds moral behavior and rational thought, but whereas Macaulay presents her program in a dialogue, *Practical Education* takes the form of an educational manual.[10] Based on methods the Edgeworths used to homeschool their very large family and children in their community circle, and integrating both empirical methods and a rationalist emphasis on logic, *Practical Education* describes a form of domestic pedagogy in which learning is structured, hands-on, and experiential. Establishing the home as the seat of learning, *Practical Education* directly targets mothers as its primary audience. The Edgeworths clearly identify their audience when they write, "We must entreat the teacher to have patience; to fix firmly in her mind, we say *her* mind, because we address ourselves to mothers" (1:46). They appeal to maternal pride, love, and sense of responsibility, asserting that a mother is her children's best teacher because she has intimate "knowledge of their minds, . . . judgment, . . . affection, . . . superintending intelligence, [and] will be of inestimable value to her children" (2:124). In their pedagogical model, the Edgeworths grant unprecedented managerial power to the mother and provide very detailed do-it-yourself guidelines for teaching children of all ages.

Aiming for the plain language of a report with case-study style notes, their preface states, "We have chosen the title of Practical Education, to point out that we rely entirely upon practice and experience" (Edgeworth and Edgeworth iii). The Edgeworths explicitly present their text as guidelines for teaching at home. The comprehensive curriculum of *Practical Education* is organized into two volumes and twenty-five chapters as follows:[11]

Habits of mind and moral behaviors, the main focus in volume 1, hold primacy as prerequisites for the discipline-specific pedagogy of volume 2. The placement of a separate chapter on female accomplishments in chapter 20 might suggest that *Practical Education* adopts the gender-divided curriculum recommended by Rousseau, but unlike Rousseau, the Edgeworths promote scientific and mechanical studies for girls as well as boys (Porter 344). Furthermore, the Edgeworths clearly reject Rousseau's stance against the use of structured lessons in educating elementary age children, but they also critique the rote aspects of classical education.

However, *Practical Education* is not completely devoid of humanist-style conversation, which is apparent in many of its anecdotes. For example, in its critique of pedagogical excesses, *Practical Education* enacts a narrative of dramatic emotional appeal infused with straightforward commonsensical advice. Early in volume 1, the Edgeworths write:

> The age of learning begins, and begins in sorrow. . . . Some people, struck with a panic fear, lest their children should never learn to read and write, think that they cannot be in too great a hurry to teach them. Spelling-books, grammars, dictionaries, rods and masters, are collected; nothing is to be heard of in the house but tasks; nothing is to be seen but tears. (1:41)

After presenting this high-pressure academic scenario, the Edgeworths then stage an exaggerated debate between naturalistic and classical pedagogy. Starting with the Rousseauian voice of the naturalist, they write:

No tears! no tasks! no masters! nothing upon compulsion . . . Children must be left entirely at liberty; they will learn everything better than you can teach them; their memory must not be overloaded with trash; their reason must be left to grow. (1:41)

Responding with the voice of the classicist, they continue:

Their reason will never grow, unless it be exercised . . . Their memory must be stored whilst they are young, because, in youth, the memory is most tenacious. If you leave them at liberty forever, they . . . will never learn Latin grammar; yet, they must learn Latin grammar, and a number of other disagreeable things; therefore, we must give them tasks and task-masters. (1:41)

In response to this dramatic dialogue, the Edgeworths then give their own practical point of view, stating, "In all these assertions, perhaps, we shall find a mixture of truth and error; therefore, we had better be governed by neither party, but listen to both, and examine arguments unawed by authority" (1:41–42). Thus, *Practical Education* rejects practices that do not incorporate common sense. Rather, they consider the merits of earlier approaches, but they rely on their own experiences and observations as teachers as main sources of evidence for their curricular prescriptions. They do not throw away all principles of classical learning, including the study of rhetoric, but rather embed lessons on rhetoric within their primarily empirical curriculum.

Volume 2 of *Practical Education* covers academic subjects, including effective methods for teaching the skills of rhetoric. Chapter 21, Memory and Invention, explains how rhetorical skills help students, scholars, and other professionals and provides methods for memorization and arrangement of detail. The Edgeworths back their methods with real-world applications and examples, such as how an attorney uses rhetorical skills to present evidence (2:151). Stressing the artful application of memory, selection, and arrangement, *Practical Education* describes how careful observations, clear arguments, and sound judgments form the basis of any discipline and serve as the means by which future practitioners build upon existing knowledge and make new discoveries. The Edgeworths praise methodical recordkeepers of their time, such as Benjamin Franklin, Samuel Johnson, and Joseph Priestly, and note that "a good memory for business depends upon local, well arranged associations" (2:158). Hence, the Edgeworths show the practical role of rhetoric and composition in the development of disciplinary knowledge bases and canons.

The prescriptions in *Practical Education* appear to apply universally to the teaching of both boys and girls—although the examples almost always discuss boy students. The one section dedicated specifically to discussion of girls' education, chapter 20, "On Female Accomplishments, Masters, and Governesses," argues that fine arts and crafts, singing, and dancing, while worthwhile, are not essential to women's success, nor to their virtue or happiness. The main reason for practicing and performing an art, they say, is because it is enjoyable and fulfilling, not because it is a proper fashionable pastime. The ability to dance, they argue, does not confer good manners or sophistication, nor does it increase one's chances of finding a suitable husband, a career, or a successful life (Edgeworth 2:121–22). To some of their contemporaries, this view of dancing as frivolous and nonessential would have seemed shocking. However, the Edgeworths clearly express that "ornamental accomplishments" in young ladies are of little use without essential abilities of reasoning and critical thinking. Furthermore, they stress that cognitive skills and academic proficiency can only be attained through concerted hands-on instruction, managed and delivered primarily by parents, or a dedicated governess, who also closely oversee any discipline-specific lessons delivered by masters and tutors (Edgeworth 2:129–31). Above all, *Practical Education* favors maternal guidance and hails domestic education as the ideal for middle- and upper-class British families in the eighteenth century.[12]

Scholars have construed the Edgeworth family's domestic agenda and support for paternalism as marks of conservatism and have interpreted Maria Edgeworth's diverse works and ideas as counter to the progressive protofeminism of some of her peers, such as Mary Wollstonecraft and Mary Hays. However, this blanket characterization downplays and misrepresents Edgeworth's views of educating the masses, and her innovations in education theory, which feminist scholars have more recently begun to acknowledge. The Edgeworths believed education was necessary for all, and that it belonged with the family in the home. They were devoted to removing impediments to home education, and in this mission Maria and her father were progressive educators of their times who clearly supported women's rhetorical education.

PROGRESSIVE PLANS FOR INSTITUTIONAL EDUCATION

Despite the predominance of domestic education in eighteenth-century education theory, a wide variety of day schools and boarding schools for girls existed in eighteenth-century England but without any standardization or consistency. In 1709, for example, Mary Astell, Lady Catherine Jones, Lady Elizabeth Hastings, and Lady Ann Coventry started a charity school for daughters of pensioners in the Royal Hospital at Chelsea, which operated for over a century. Ann Fisher, the first female author of an English grammar book, ran a school for girls in Newcastle in 1750 (Percy 44). Cultural historians note that historical evidence of eighteenth-century British girls' schools is fragmented and still in the process of being collated (Cohen, Simonton). Nevertheless, published plans for female academies show that women writers and educational theorists argued for improvements in institutional education particularly for women and, in some cases, for the middle and lower classes. While many recognized that literacy was increasingly important to all, some developed theories proposing that the specific types of education and training needed by girls and women varied by social class. Knowledge valuable for courtship and marriage was the primary focus of the upper-class young woman's education, and it was also important for middle-class women, while domestic management skills were considered most crucial for the middle class and vocational skills for the laboring classes. A variety of solutions for educating the poor and disenfranchised were envisioned by eighteenth-century British women authors in a number of genres, from treatises to fiction. For example, in her novel *Millenium Hall* (1762), Sarah Scott describes a benevolent female intellectual community that incorporates refuge, training, jobs, and housing for the indigent—progressive social services even by today's standards.

The hallmark of progressive education is the discover of new ways to open up opportunities for learning. One of the earliest progressive treatises on education for British women, Mary Astell's *Serious Proposal, Part I*, calls for upper-class women to switch from the frivolous pursuit of fashion and idle luxury to a life of scholarly study and moral improvement, and she asserts the value of female-only academic communities.[13] Astell, who proclaimed her own celibacy, saw cloistered female communities as a solution to many of the problems women faced, including lack of educational and intellectual opportunities and their need for a respectable alternative to marriage (Perry 361). Eighteenth-century rhetoric about female cohabitations positioned them as platonic arrangements driven by like-mindedness, benevolence, and the need for feminine support systems.[14] Astell's ideas on formal institutions of education for ladies' education called for a retreat-like environment promoting study and contemplation. Hers was not a large-scale plan for the general female populace but rather reflected the model of a studious circle. Astell introduces her plans gradually with nonthreatening language: first providing positive images of learning as a means for a woman to shine socially above others; then promoting "the delights of intellectual and spiritual life" as a new feminine fashion that, in fact, helps break the chains of patriarchy; and finally arguing for the establishment of formalized, female-only institutions of learning as intellectual retreats where women could spend time voluntarily improving themselves for a duration of their own choosing (Sutherland 55–56). Astell's vision assumed that, after a period of solitary study, women would be better prepared for integration into the world.

Models for widely accessible practical institutions of learning for girls and young women came in the latter half of the eighteenth century, perhaps stemming from the influence of Vicesimus Knox who advocated on behalf of public education. In *Liberal Education* (1781), Knox counters Locke's view that domestic education provides the best moral models for both genders, stating first that "private education, rather than shielding youths from vice actually predisposed them to it" and, secondly, that public schooling "fostered virtue and manliness" while domestic education "promoted idleness and vice, both signifiers of effeminacy" (Cohen 226–27). Knox advocates a progressive agenda for public education but not for gender equality; however, women educational theorists, picking up on Knox's arguments for public education, also began to question the need and benefit of separate education for girls and boys. Some argued in favor of a public co-educational model. For example, Elizabeth Hamilton's *Letters on the Elementary Principles of Education* (1801) offers a practical method of teaching and learning that "rarely differentiates between the male and female child" (Dow). Hamilton's memoir describes that, as a young child in Scotland, she was encouraged to play outside along with boys and to experience nature, and from the age of eight to thirteen, she was enrolled at a co-educational boarding school where she studied writing, geography, dancing, French, drawing, and music under the direction of the schoolmaster. Co-educational elementary schools, as Hamilton explains in her memoir, "may shock the fastidiousness of modern refinement to hear . . . but . . . about fifty years ago this practice prevailed universally in Scotland, Ireland, and . . . some parts of England; nor was it unusual to see boys and girls associated in their tasks, with no other separation than the being seated on different forms"; to this she adds a footnote advocating for small, female-led co-educational day schools in which "two or three distinguished women might confer an essential benefit on society" as teachers (Benger 36). Thus, for Hamilton, a co-educational model proliferating through many small local schools was the ideal educational environment.

In contrast to Hamilton, Clara Reeve's vision in *Plans of Education* does not include a co-educational model, but it does address the educational needs for girls of various social classes. As stated earlier in this chapter, Reeve's *Plans of Education* centers on an argument of gentility in providing academic, domestic, and character education for upper-class girls, but it also incorporates vocational training for girls and young women of middling and lower-class families. Her plan incorporates an extensive multitiered support structure, providing a variety of job opportunities and apprenticeship programs for middle-class girls and women, including orphans and widows of professional and gentry families, as well as a proper servant training program for girls of working-class families. Reeve also envisions instruction on ethics, morality, and appropriate domestic, academic, and social skills to promote girls' chances for autonomy and fair treatment within the patriarchal structure of their times. The progressive aspects of Reeve's vision contrast starkly with her conservative views of social and racial constructs as revealed in her severely prejudicial statements about class privilege, racial inequality, and other social inequities prevalent in late eighteenth-century British culture. While its prejudicial and racist statements are extremely problematic and should not be overlooked, *Plans For Education* is "fascinating for the way it brings together a plan for a female community with a discussion and advocacy of women's paid work" (Bagchi). Published the same year as Wollstonecraft's *Vindication of the Rights of Women*, part 1 of Reeve's plan agrees with Wollstonecraft's on the need for schools and formal environments for vocational training, but Reeve upholds rigid class distinctions that Wollstonecraft vehemently rejects, and the two authors differed greatly in their views of gendered social constructs.

After working for years in her twenties as a teacher and private tutor, Mary Wollstonecraft initially supported a program of domestic education for girls, which she outlines in her *Thoughts on the Education of Daughters* (1786). While reviewing Catherine Macaulay's *Letters on Education,* Wollstonecraft reached what Alan Richardson (citing Gary Kelly) describes as "the 'turning point' in her intellectual career," and shifted her thoughts in favor of a co-educational model of domestic education (Richardson 32). By the 1790s, in the aftermath of the French Revolution, Wollstonecraft further shifted her thinking away from the dominant education models of her times. The radical development of her ideas on education is apparent in *Vindication of the Rights of Women* (1792), which revises Wollstonecraft's earlier preference for private domestic education in favor of a national program of co-education in public day schools.

Wollstonecraft justifies her new pedagogical model by exposing problems she finds with private education, both in domestic settings and private institutions of learning. Wollstonecraft appropriates the logic of Vicesimus Knox (who makes a similar point but about males only) in her argument that, for girls and boys alike, the isolation of learning at home tends to retard the development of virtue, a quality that must grow from experiences of public social interaction. Furthermore, she finds even less benefit in the temporary and artificial living environments of private boarding schools where children bide their time until the next break and then spend their vacations in "total dissipation and beastly indulgence" (Wollstonecraft 299). Moreover, Wollstonecraft rejects the utility of the training of upper-class boys in classical Latin and Greek (remnants of humanist education), a standard practice by schoolmasters in boarding schools, because most people of her era, including male aristocrats, did not pursue careers as Latin or Greek scholars, and so they had little use for this skill (Wollstonecraft 303). Wollstonecraft's alternative educational vision, radical for her time, presages the direction of English education in the coming century.

Wollstonecraft's vision of public co-education was inspired by Charles-Maurice de Talleyrand-Perigord who, in the aftermath of the French Revolution, published a report advocating education for all citizens in France, including women, but limiting women to private education while men would have access to public education. In the 1791 constitution of the new French government, women were not recognized as citizens; thus, Wollstonecraft begins her *Vindication* with a dedication imploring Talleyrand to reconsider "the rights of women and national education"; as she notes, "I plead for my sex, not myself. Independence I have long considered as the grand blessing in life—the basis of every virtue" (Wollstonecraft 103). Wollstonecraft directly declares her main argument: a society's failure to educate women will "stop the progress of knowledge and virtue" (102). While this logic seems similar to the argument of gentility posed by humanist-influenced women theorists, such as Bathsua Makin and Hester Chapone, Wollstonecraft extends her plea beyond upper-class women to include the entire national population, male and female, at all levels of the social structure. Essentially, she argues, a civil society is responsible for educating all of its members, and this responsibility is requisite for intellectual growth and healthy civic development.

Wollstonecraft uses forceful and masculine imagery to portray the negative effects of dominance and subservience brought about by gendered and class-based education. She describes the controlling parent whose demand for filial obedience without nurturing or explanation "shackles the mind and prepares it for slavish submission" (293). She compares women in their present state to soldiers who "acquire manners before morals," possessing only knowledge of what they are supposed to do but not why they need to do it; she compares both soldiers and women to ignorant cogs who must "blindly submit to authority" (132). This will not do for Wollstonecraft; she demands a system in which standardized and consistent pedagogy will propagate a climate of egalitarian teaching and learning. As Alan Richardson states, "For Wollstonecraft, . . . only a national system of day schools has the capacity to fundamentally change social relations between the sexes" (35).

Wollstonecraft's model hinges on the formation of free, national, year-round day schools where boys and girls of all classes, rich and poor, from the ages of five to nine years old work together in mixed-gender groups on shared goals and projects in efforts to solve problems jointly (298, 310–11). She argues that day schools should provide lessons of discovery and experience, which should be nationally administered to ensure consistent curricula and to avoid the whims of local parents and schoolmasters stuck in antiquated or narrow practices, such as rote drills of memorization (305). In addition to a curriculum of reading, writing, arithmetic, history, and "natural philosophy" (science), Wollstone-craft's model calls for students to wear uniforms and engage in daily outdoor exercise; the top priority should be outdoor activities, and students "should not be confined to any sedentary employment for more than an hour at a time" (311). According to her plan, after age nine, children graduate from the unisex elementary school and move to the next level of education, in which their placement is based on aptitude, as well as social class and gender. In the mid-level schools, Wollstonecraft recommends that boys and girls who show academic inclinations continue together to study languages (living and dead), history, politics, and polite literature, but girls and boys destined for trades and domestic vocations study together only in the morning and attend separate training in the afternoon (311). According to Wollstonecraft, this model would promote a common understanding and sympathy between the sexes; increase the frequency and success of early marriages based on choice and mutual consent, which she sees as a major goal of society; and eradicate the false behaviors of gallantry and coquetry, which she believes undermine virtue (311–12). Ultimately, Wollstonecraft argues, equal educational opportunities transcending gender and social class are essential for a society to develop rational thinkers, a necessary condition of true virtue and the ultimate aim of humanity.

In contrast to the calls for equal opportunity presented in Wollstonecraft's radical proposal, in the early nineteenth century, many women pedagogues of the late Enlightenment still published works in favor of separate schooling for girls, such as Mary Lamb's *Mrs. Leicester's School: Or, the History of Several Young Ladies, Related by Themselves* (1809) and Elizabeth Appleton's *Private Education: Or a Practical Plan for the Studies of Young Ladies, with an Address to Parents, Private Governesses, and Young Ladies* (1815). However, arguments and models for co-education had become more common. By the century's end, Alan Richardson points out that "for the rise of a revolutionary generation of rational, freethinking, independent women, education reform was crucial" (25).

Conclusion

Delivered across a wide range of polite, popular, and intellectual publications, the performance and reception of eighteenth-century women writers exemplify the cultural activities of a counterpublic coalescing into a coherent voice and appropriating the literary genres and devices of its times to gain a collective identity in the public rhetorical ecology. Within this environment of rising literacy, treatises and plans about education theory written by women intellectuals offer some of the earliest English examples of British women's public deliberative argumentation—prefiguring the rhetorical activity of nineteenth-century women abolitionists and suffragettes.

Furthermore, a growing concern for the lack of any national education standards in eighteenth-century England provoked debate about the educational needs of girls and boys at all levels of the social class structure. Progressive pedagogical theory concerning the idealized female learner moved her from a genteel, gender-segregated domestic space to a pragmatic and (sometimes) mixed-gender domestic space, or to a communal and, in some cases, co-educational public space. However, throughout the eighteenth century, the vast majority of educated Britons viewed a domestic education as most suitable for females.

By century's end, the education of females in Great Britain was a national concern. Education had become a discipline in which women intellectuals wrote and published as rhetorical theorists, and many women, especially mothers, acted as rhetorical practitioners in their roles both as mentors and teachers. Groundbreaking educational theorists, such as Bathsua Makin, Mary Astell, Hester Chapone, Mary Wollstonecraft, Elizabeth Hamilton, Catherine Macaulay, and Maria Edgeworth, saw the education of girls and women as intrinsic to the betterment of British society. These and other women writers contributed to Enlightenment debates on the role of mothers in education; on vocational, academic, and class-based curricula; and on arguments for co-education. Through these debates, women gained voice and agency as they developed and extended models for education, rhetoric, and civic participation. Furthermore, their proposals and plans have had lasting effects on modern co-educational models, including programs of classical learning, domestic education, and public schooling.

Notably, the most astonishingly visionary curriculum of its time, Wollstonecraft's *Vindication of the Rights of Women,* is forceful in its equalizing rhetoric and nationalized model of pedagogy. The egalitarian model for public education that Wollstonecraft proposed foreshadows the nineteenth-century emergence of standardized national programs of education in co-educational day schools. Wollstonecraft's ideas on education in *Vindication* have proven to be forward thinking on so many points; her educational vision largely came true in the twentieth century in the education systems of many developed nations across the globe. Like her female forerunners, Wollstonecraft appropriated the predominant male-oriented pedagogical models and re-visioned them for the support and improvement of women's education.

British women writers significantly revised masculine theories of rhetoric and developed new education models in the age of Enlightenment, a fact that is evident in the variety of their groundbreaking treatises, proposals, defenses, and plans. Through their writings, eighteenth-century British women intellectuals brought issues of gender to the forefront of emerging education theory and sought to broaden academic opportunities for the benefit of women. Publications in rhetoric and education theory by Mary Astell, Judith Drake, Hester Chapone, Maria Edgeworth, Elizabeth Hamilton, Mary Wollstonecraft, and others prefigure the work being done today by feminist scholars in the fields of rhetoric and composition. This type of work is characterized by the use of writing to increase women's professional opportunities, improve the quality of women's education, and identify methods of gaining rhetorical power for women. The diversity of ideas, genres, and styles with which these women theorists approached their shared goal of improving women's intellectual opportunities also reflects the numerous and evolving methodologies that feminist scholars are employing today. An understanding of early protofeminist ideas about rhetoric and education can provide food for thought as we reflect on current debates, models, technologies, and venues of public, private, charter, and homeschool education and their related challenges in our own culture.

Conclusion

*D*URING THE LONG eighteenth century, from 1660 to the turn of the nineteenth century, major economic and social changes in British Enlightenment culture resulted in increased opportunities for British women's rhetoric. Some of the new feminine rhetorical venues and roles became permanent while others were later suppressed. Throughout the long eighteenth century, however, protofeminist topics and activities played an important part in the intellectual dialogue performances of the British Enlightenment, sometimes in serious and direct treatises, proposals, and arguments, but other times cloaked in indirect and ironic forms. Besides women's participation in traditional and nontraditional written rhetorical genres, women's Enlightenment rhetoric included performative displays of nontraditional gendered behaviors, as well as open and veiled critiques of entrenched patriarchal attitudes in sociable mixed-gender sites.

Care must be taken to accurately represent—neither understate nor overstate—the ground truth and accretive effects of British women's Enlightenment rhetoric. Ever since the nineteenth century, the story of feminine domesticity, women's apparently designated place in the private sphere, has persisted as the dominant narrative about eighteenth-century British women. In the twenty-first century, the notion of eighteenth-century society adhering to strictly separate gendered spheres has been questioned, reassessed, and significantly revised, if not debunked. Eighteenth-century British women did not have any legal status as citizens; they could not vote, hold parliamentary positions, or teach in universities, and their civil rights were far inferior to those of British men. However, British women were visibly engaged in the public sphere in many ways in the eighteenth century; they were not cloistered in their homes.

In this book, I have argued that documented acts of persuasion by Restoration and eighteenth-century British women are ubiquitous. Evidence of these acts is accessible to scholars today yet remains grossly understudied in the field of rhetoric. In my approach to studying British women's Enlightenment rhetoric, I have attempted "moving beyond the fashioning of presence in the master narratives of rhetorical history . . . toward the renegotiation of the paradigms" that are currently in place, and as Royster and Kirsh suggest, "not just celebrating the recognition of women's lives and contributions but understanding rhetorical agency itself in new, more-dynamic terms" (132). For me, this renegotiation required breaking away from the fivefold paradigm of British Enlightenment rhetoric (including the recently rediscovered feminine paradigm of conversation) in order to expose more and greater details of the protofeminist rhetorical landscape, which lay hidden in plain view, and to see it with new eyes. To discern the scattered seeds of protofeminism—artistic, intellectual, domestic, and activist—requires a broad ecological approach. Women's Enlightenment rhetoric did not have a name at the time it was happening in England and throughout Great Britain, nor was it part of an organized movement, but like many Enlightenment ideals, it permeated a wide spectrum of British society across many rhetorical venues, from theaters, salons, and debate clubs to print publications of many genres, and even in unpublished textual genres such as the letter and homeschool curricula.

Key Findings

Consistent with the values and aesthetics of eighteenth-century Britain, *wit, virtue,* and *emotion* were the primary appeals of protofeminist British Enlightenment rhetoric. Wit, a masculine-gendered characteristic and the most common appeal for verbal and written argumentation during the Restoration, was also adapted by women rhetors in writing and speech. Restoration actresses and playwrights helped develop spoken protofeminist rhetoric through theatrical representations of the witty couple, the female libertine, and the suffering heroine. In the early 1700s, when wit was joined by an increasing emphasis on politeness and decorum, women essayists such as Mary Astell, Sarah Kirkham Chapone, and Judith Drake published arguments dealing with feminine morality and practices of sociability, in a variety of literary forms, including treatises, dialogues, and defenses, as well as the ephemeral genres of the pamphlet, petition, and periodical editorial. By mid-century, famous authors such as Eliza Haywood and unknown women were contributing protofeminist arguments in magazines. Beyond theatrical and textual forms of rhetoric, symbolic appeals of wit and virtue predominated throughout eighteenth-century Britain in female emblems of fidelity, motherhood, decorum, and manners, which challenged earlier stereotypes of the woman as wanton and morally weak. Maternal virtue, the mother's duty, was a cornerstone of many plans, proposals, and published letters on education.

In the latter half of the century, a wide diversity of women writers—progressives and conservatives—were employing the ethos of feminine virtue and their increasing literacy skills to engage in moral and logical argumentation in a range of literary and nonfiction genres. The infusion of literary trends, such as sentimentalism and sensibility, and the emphasis on taste in spoken and written rhetoric and rhetorical theory, illustrates the increasing importance of emotion and the further feminization of belletristic rhetoric. Elite women, such as Bluestockings Elizabeth Montagu, Elizabeth Vesey, Hester Thrale, Elizabeth Carter, Catherine Talbot, and Catherine Macaulay assumed the role of arbitresses of taste in their salon meetings and their published assessments of culture and history. By century's end, another factor contributing to the place of emotion in women's Enlightenment rhetoric was fervor for the raging Jacobin and anti-Jacobin political debate in England in the wake of the French Revolution, which brought the question of women's rights, made most famous in the work of Mary Wollstonecraft, to the forefront of public discourse in debating societies and in Jacobin novels. These multifarious discussions, which increasingly involved voices of middle-class women and included activist appeals for gender parity, clearly prefigure the British abolitionist, social reform, and suffragette movements of the nineteenth century.

Protofeminist contributions to British Enlightenment rhetoric came from women at many levels of the social hierarchy: royal women and court ladies, government-sponsored actresses, socialites and club members, professional women authors, and other learned ladies. Many and varied practices of persuasive communication affected traditional women's roles, including the grand roles of queen and courtier, as well as common roles of mother and wife, and helped launch new, highly rhetorical gendered identities, such as the professions of actress and author, and the receptive roles of women as consumers, spectators, and readers. British women became a significant factor in many rhetorical venues, participating as hostesses, members, theorists, practitioners, and audiences, and these roles were often intertwined.

In the age of Enlightenment, the identity of the British woman took on new associations of public virtue. With the conjugal family unit increasingly occupying the center of British culture, motherhood became a more authoritative cultural position and thus an open concern of public discussion. The role of wife gained little rhetorical ground, but that of mother gained power and recognition in the area of education, especially in the moral education of children and as the primary source for the teaching of basic literacy, according to domestic models of education. While this development brought recognition and a liminal increase of women's rhetorical power, any suggestions that women could hold professional or public positions were fraught with criticism.

Nevertheless, with increased literacy and the rise of the commercial literary market, learned ladies and professional women writers (known in less flattering terms as "scribblers") became recognized and marginally accepted in British culture. Educated women expanded the practices of women's performative and written rhetorics, even though women's access to rhetorical venues, their ethos, and their legacies were limited by the laws and deep rhetoric of Enlightenment patriarchy. Thus Bluestocking salons, circles of literati, debate societies, and even tea tables offered women intellectual spaces for sharing protofeminist rhetorics.

Much protofeminist rhetorical activity was performative, embodied, and ephemeral, occurring during everyday activities as nuanced gender citations; however, direct evidence of everyday eighteenth-century life is difficult to ascertain and will require the development of customized historical methodologies for specific sites of rhetoric. Data on performative women's Enlightenment rhetoric may be found in surviving letters, diaries, newspapers, reviews, and other mundane accounts, which tend to be more factual and realistic, and less embellished than formal treatises and works of literature and art. Information about performative protofeminist rhetoric is also found in theater history. From critical accounts, we know that the theatrical performances of the first Restoration actresses, such as Elizabeth Barry and Ann Bracegirdle, brought greater attention and realism to women's issues. Famous actresses in signature roles performed memorable dramatic enactments of protofeminist themes, including the commodification of women in courtship and the powerlessness of wives and daughters.

The surprising upside of female commodification was that, with the rapid growth of capitalism in the bourgeois society of eighteenth-century Britain, women's everyday material and embodied rhetorical practices, including socializing and reading, gained more notice, influence, and in some cases economic worth. The size of the British female target audience, with pin money in hand, was not insignificant. Thus, British women slowly became educated consumers and gained a collective voice for the first time, albeit as a large and largely unorganized counterpublic. A variety of published works in a variety of genres describe the venues and protocols for feminine sociability and critique the proper decorum for conversation, behavior, fashionable dress, courtship, friendship, marriage, motherhood, dancing, and many other female- and mixed-gender customs. Serious and satiric treatises, dialogues, and defenses interrogate the definitions of virtuous lady, proper conversation, and gossip. Furthermore, the growing body of protofeminist texts continually questioned and pushed the boundaries of separate gendered spheres and other restrictions on women, especially in the area of education.

Implications

More than a few years ago, when I started writing this book, my working title was "*She Was There*." I began my study by analyzing the rhetorical impact of the Restoration actresses whom I knew were an important and missing piece in the history of women's rhetoric, but I soon saw that they were only the "tip of an iceberg," as Tania Smith has stated (349). In this work, I have attempted to contribute to a "disciplinary transformation," as suggested by Royster and Kirsch, and to downplay the recovery of "elite" figures in "traditional and highly institutionalized arenas" in favor of studying groups of women as they "function in social spaces" and to renegotiate the terms for evaluating rhetoric as a "multidimensional human asset" with "a more broadly based multivariant arena of action" (133). The feminist renegotiation of rhetoric as a field offers great potential in the study of women's Enlightenment rhetoric. This expansion does not invalidate the traditional paradigms, nor the venues of rhetoric of the Western white male elite. Those remain delimited, and intact; but new methods allow researchers to transcend the limitations and deep rhetoric of traditional histories and see the more inclusive and sociable *ground truth rhetoric* of women in the long eighteenth century.

The kairos of studying British women's Enlightenment rhetoric in the current moment of twenty-first century scholarship on feminist rhetoric invokes consideration of several factors: the parallels between the explosion of print publication in the eighteenth-century literary public market and digital publication in our current rhetorical ecology; the new digital tools that provide a larger number of scholars easier access to exploring eighteenth-century women's voices and lives; and new feminist methods for studying the history of rhetoric.

New Directions

Scholars of eighteenth-century studies have already made great inroads into the vast corpus of primary materials by and about eighteenth-century British women, and this work is continuing at a rapid pace. As I write, studies of eighteenth-century women's sociability and ephemera, the bluestocking Enlightenment, women satirists, and the multitudes of women writers of noncanonical texts are but a few areas of scholarly investigation currently under way. Enlightenment rhetoric as a whole, and protofeminist rhetoric of the British long eighteenth century in particular, are ripe and ready subjects for feminist rhetorical study.

While my work here has focused solely on middle- and upper-class white British women, during the long eighteenth century, Britain was a major hub of cosmopolitan culture and a transnational destination. Further research can and will uncover opportunities to study the gendered rhetorics of immigrants; people of different ethnicities, races, and faiths; and other marginalized groups, strangers, and individual outsiders who participated in the colonial counter-flow of people to Britain in the age of Enlightenment. Furthermore, across all inhabitants, including immigrants and the native British population, there are opportunities to study protofeminist rhetoric among religious dissenters, the working-classes, servants, and the poor, as well as women working in various professions, such as medicine, science, the book trade, and even in promiscuous and antisocial sites such as gaming houses, brothels, and criminal courts.

To more fully understand the history of women's rhetorics, feminist researchers in the history of rhetoric must examine women's counterpublic contributions to British Enlightenment culture, especially in the areas of sociability and social reform. This is a missing piece in our history. Besides identifying and analyzing feminine rhetorical venues and roles, another method for accessing this history could be to follow various threads of heated public debate about woman's rhetorical capabilities and place in specific areas of society during the age of British Enlightenment. I would also suggest looking for protofeminist women's rhetoric just beyond the chronological margins of my study, back to the British Commonwealth era of the 1640s and 1650s, further into the British Romantic period during the early part of the nineteenth century, and forward to the Victorian era of the mid- to late-nineteenth century. Also, further research could zoom closer in on the rhetorical ecologies of particular decades and locations within the British long eighteenth century; women were learning, practicing, and theorizing rhetoric in many arenas and subject areas beyond what I have touched on. I close this study knowing that there is much more to be done. I have tried some new paths and surveyed a few sites within the rhetorical ecology of the British long eighteenth century. My hope is that other feminist researchers will join in continued study of women's rhetorics in this historical landscape.

APPENDIXES

NOTES

WORKS CITED

INDEX

Appendix A: Eighteenth-Century
Terminology for Sex and Gender Identity

This appendix explains terminology related to notions of sex and gender identity in eighteenth-century Britain and points out differences in the usage of these same terms today.

In this book, I generally use *male* and *female* as biological designations and *man, woman, masculine,* and *feminine* as terms referring to socially constructed gender roles and qualities. However, in eighteenth-century primary sources, the usage does not always conform to this paradigm, partially because the meanings and connotations of these terms have changed over the last three hundred years—but also because biological and sociological connotations can overlap. In the literature of the period, the terms *female* and *woman* (or *girl*) are used interchangeably. Furthermore, phrases such as "the fair sex" suggest that the word *sex* was not just a biological label but sometimes referenced social identity as well.

While the terms *woman* and *man* generally function as nouns (both then and now), they can occur as adjectives to indicate a socially constructed identity, such as "woman writer," or "man child." In contrast to this social emphasis, the adjective *female* or *male* emphasizes the explicit association of biological sex, when needed for clarification, such as in "male child" and "female child," and especially when biological sex is different from what is normally associated with a social role, such as in "female orator" or "male nurse." The adjectives *feminine* and *masculine* indicate a socially constructed quality associated with gender, such as "feminine style" or "masculine style"—and are similar to the adjectives *womanly* or *girlish* and *manly* or *boyish*. It is important to note that adjectival word forms for indicating biological sex and for indicating sociological gender are both valid and acceptable usages in standard written English. For example, "woman poet" and "female poet" are both meaningful terms but hold different connotations. The term "woman poet" emphasizes the socially constructed intersectional identity of woman and poet; on the other hand, the term "female poet" emphasizes the biological sex of a particular poet and also suggests that this sex differs from that usually associated with the identity of "poet." In the eighteenth century, the default biological sex associated with "poet" was male, just as in the twentieth century the default biological sex of a nurse was female. Hence the usage of "female poet" and "male nurse" are terms that accentuate biological differences from expected gender norms.

Because eighteenth-century British society adhered to patriarchy as a political and cultural model, the absence of gender identifiers for material objects and human occupations indicated the item or role as normed to the default, masculine gender identity. The term "female" had to be prefixed as a marker to distinguish femininity or the female sex. This is obvious in periodical names, such as the *Spectator* versus the *Female Spectator,* and in professional identities, such as "the poet" versus "the female poet" or "novelists" versus "women novelists." When we talk about "women's literature" or "women's history," we need to note the lack of a comparably distinct term as "men's literature" or "men's history"; the lack of the latter terms shows that masculine identity (associated with the male biological sex) is still the default in academic and popular usage. In its masculine defaults, the English language is still patriarchal.

People in eighteenth-century British society did not use the phrase "gender roles" exactly as we do today. The *Oxford English Dictionary* (*OED*) lists a long and diverse etymology for the word *gender* as a noun. The history of this term includes meanings referring to biology and social construction, including "Males or females viewed as a group" and "The state of being male or female as expressed by social or cultural distinctions and differences, rather than biological ones; the collective attributes or traits associated with a particular sex, or determined as a result of one's sex" ("Gender"). The *OED* indicates that, in the mid-twentieth century when "sex came increasingly to mean sexual intercourse ... gender began to replace it (in early use euphemistically) as the usual word for the biological grouping of males and females." The *OED* etymology gives many examples of the term *gender* as it has appeared in a variety of contexts, literary and scientific, dating back to the fifteenth century. The *OED* supports that *gender* as a term has long held a dual meaning: first, the biological sex of a person, as in "the female gender" and "the male gender," and secondly as a set of established norms of sociability that historically has been associated with the two biological sexes.

Although *gender fluidity* is a term we hear now that wasn't heard in the eighteenth century, many cases of eighteenth-century gender fluidity in terms of dress, mannerisms, and matters of taste can be found throughout many written genres, both of fact and fiction. It was generally recognized that people of one biological sex could possess opposite gender traits, such as the foppish male as an effeminate type or the learned lady as a manly figure. For the most part, textual evidence shows that engaging in behaviors deemed opposite one's biological sex was considered abnormal and impolite—but not unheard of.[1]

Appendix B: Table of Precedency among Ladies

Dating back to medieval times, the social construction of the feminine gender intersected with the British social class system to produce very specific ranks for female members of the upper classes of the social hierarchy. Under the general umbrella term "lady," these ranks persisted strongly in British society during the long eighteenth century as shown in this "Table of Precedency among Ladies," which appears in the *Ladies Pocket Journal; Or Toilet Assistant: For the Year 1791* (145–46). A widely known and memorized chart among the people of eighteenth-century Britain, the table details the hierarchy of Britain's aristocratic women.

During the long eighteenth century, this hierarchy was meticulously observed in practices of sociability:

The queen
  The princess of Wales
  Princesses of the royal family
    Duchesses of the blood
    Duchesses
    Wives of the eldest sons of dukes of the blood
    Daughters of dukes of the blood
      Marchionesses
        Wives of the eldest sons of dukes
        Daughters of dukes
          Countesses
          Wives of the eldest sons of marquises
          Daughters of marquises
          Wives of the younger sons of dukes
            Viscountesses
            Wives of the eldest sons of earls
            Daughters of earls
            Wives of the younger sons of marquises
              Baronesses
              Wives of the eldest sons of viscounts
              Daughters of viscounts

Wives of the younger sons of earls
Wives of the eldest sons of barons
Daughters of barons
Wives of the younger sons of viscounts
Wives of the younger sons of barons
   Wives of baronets
   Wives of privy counselors, commoners
   Wives of judges of the law, according to their
      husband's rank
   Wives of knights of the garter
   Wives of knights of the bath
   Wives of knights of the thistle
   Wives of knights bachelor
   Wives of general officers and admirals
   Wives of eldest sons of baronets
   Daughters of baronets
      Wives of eldest sons of knights of the garter
      Daughters of knights of the garter
         Wives of eldest sons of knights of the bath
         Daughters of knights of the bath
            Wives of eldest sons of knights bachelor
            Daughters of knights bachelor
               Wives of youngest sons of baronets
               Wives of esquires by creation
                  Wives of esquires by office
                    Wives of gentlemen
                    Daughters of esquires
                    Daughters of gentlemen
                      Wives of citizens
                        Wives of burgesses

Notes

INTRODUCTION

1. Throughout this study, I use *male* and *female* as biological terms and *man, woman, masculine,* and *feminine* as terms referring to socially constructed gender roles and qualities. For the dual purpose of clarity and accuracy, I strive to adhere to twenty-first century usage of gendered terms while also honoring eighteenth-century beliefs about gender and sex identity. When this has proven an imperfect process (and at times it has), I have been guided by my overarching intention of shedding light on rhetorical constructions of gender as they appear in British women's Enlightenment rhetoric. For more discussion of sex and gender terminology usage in this text, see appendix A.

2. Francis Bacon's *Essays* (1597) and *Nova Organon* (1605) advocate learning based on observation and inductive reasoning, Descartes's *Discourse on Method* (1637) foregrounds individual rational thought as the only accurate method for achieving knowledge, and Hobbes's *Leviathan* (1660) argues that humans are innately competitive and that the role of the political ruler is not ordained by God but rather born out of the essential need for a head to maintain civil order among the body politic.

3. Published in 2005, Taylor and Knott's edited collection, *Women, Gender, and Enlightenment,* is the culmination of the large-scale "Feminism and Enlightenment" research study, conducted from 1998 to 2001 and sponsored jointly by the University of London and the University of East London.

4. In my usage of the term *Bluestocking* versus *bluestocking,* I follow Gary Kelly's explanation: the capitalized version of the term refers to women who were members of the original Bluestocking circle that gathered around Elizabeth Montagu and her friends, while the lower case "bluestocking" refers to any woman intellectual beyond that circle from the eighteenth century to the present ("Bluestocking Work" 175).

5. Glenn defines feminist rhetoric as "a set of long-established practices that advocates a political position of rights and responsibilities that certainly includes the equality of women and Others . . . [and] also focuses on the rights, contributions, expertise, opportunities, and histories of marginalized groups and supports coalitions across and among these groups" (3). She defines rhetorical

feminism as a constantly evolving "theoretical stance" and "set of tactics" that include dialogue, listening, and respect for marginalized others and their vernacular languages, silences, experiences, and feelings—and recognizing all of these as "sources of knowledge" (4).

6. As a famous author and feminist activist, Mary Wollstonecraft has been the subject of numerous articles since the 1970s. Several recent collections focused on Wollstonecraft in British women's history, gender studies, and eighteenth-century literature include *The Cambridge Companion to Mary Wollstonecraft* and *Called to Civil Existence: Mary Wollstonecraft's A Vindication of the Rights of Women*. For studies focused on Wollstonecraft and rhetoric, see Julia Allen's "Uses and Problems of 'Manly' Rhetoric: Mary Wollstonecraft's Adaptation of Hugh Blair's Lectures in her Two Vindications" and Miriam Brody's "Vindication of the Writes of Women: Mary Wollstonecraft and Enlightenment Rhetoric."

7. The terms *woman* and *women* stand in a binary relationship to the counterpart gender identity of *man* and *men*. These terms also relate to the adjectives *feminine* and *masculine,* which I use to refer to the common perceptions of a variety of activities, behaviors, and emotions as typical of one or the other gender. For further reading on gendered terminology, see appendix A.

8. Toward the end of the eighteenth century when Enlightenment belletristic theory gives way to Romanticism, exaggerated sentimentalism and the related trait of sensibility—both of which refer to a superfluity of feeling and emotion—begin to seem rhetorically artificial and also indicative of feminine frailty.

9. Feminization is apparent in eighteenth-century British literature especially in the sentimental mode; in sentimental, domestic, and gothic novels; and in theatrical delivery in a variety of genres, including the she-tragedy and the sentimental and humane comedy.

10. In *Conversational Enlightenment: The Reconceptualization of Rhetoric in Eighteenth-Century Thought*, David Randall discusses the effect of feminization on Enlightenment rhetoric, which he analyzes in relation to the increasing popularity of conversation as a main channel of rhetoric.

11. Deep rhetoric consists of those hegemonic beliefs that are so firmly ingrained in the ideology of the dominant culture that the majority accepts those beliefs as undisputable and fixed facts of nature rather than as socially constructed practices. At each historical moment, deep rhetoric not only reflects the beliefs and institutions of the current culture but also foreshadows the possibilities of the future. As James Crosswhite explains in *Deep Rhetoric: Philosophy, Reason, Violence, Justice, Wisdom,*

Rhetoric has both a horizontal, historical axis in which it assumes the specific institutional shapes by which it seems to be constrained, and also a vertical axis along which it generates ideals of freedom and reason and nonviolence, and the humane formation of human beings, ideals which reach beyond specific situations and generate motives for changing them. (28)

12. For overviews of recent scholarship on Enlightenment rhetoric, see Ferreira-Buckley, Gaillet and Tasker, and Thomas Miller.

13. Although medieval scholasticism had splintered classical rhetoric by recasting its canons of invention and arrangement as sub-branches of logic, the classical five-canon model of rhetoric returned in the fifteenth and sixteenth centuries when humanist educators grafted these first two canons back together again with style, memory, and delivery.

14. One of the great classical works influencing this movement was Longinus's *On the Sublime*. The French embraced belletrism even before the English in Bernard Lami's *L'Art de Parler* (1675) and Charles Rollin's *De la Manière d'Enseigner et d'Étudier les Belles Lettres* (1726).

15. Smith took examples from literature as forms and models for rhetorical style and eloquence. In his *Theory of Moral Sentiments* (1748), Smith writes, "We must imagine ourselves not the actors but the spectators of our own character and conduct" (Golden and Corbett 12). In *Of the Standard of Taste* (1757), Hume posits that standards of taste are universal, but particular tastes about beauty are individual. Thus we must rely on ideal critics, who are experienced in judging a particular art form and *touchstones,* or works of beauty and art that have stood the test of time and are generally agreed to be great. The principles of taste were further applied to rhetoric by Hugh Blair who was known equally as a rhetorician and a literary critic. In his *Lectures on Rhetoric and Belles Lettres,* Blair calls taste "the power of receiving pleasure from the beauties of nature and art" and says that taste is a natural sensibility that is improved and perfected by reason (10).

16. Although Campbell calls persuasion the ultimate aim of rhetoric, he significantly expands the scope of rhetoric in the area of moral reasoning and extends it to encompass communication for a variety of purposes, including informing, entertaining, and exciting the passions.

17. Feminist scholars of Renaissance rhetoric have examined Parisian salonnièrre, Madeleine de Scudery as the main rhetorical theorist for what has become known as salon rhetoric. They cite Scudery as an "other" rhetorical voice of the late Renaissance—one with more authority and influence than

previously realized (Donawerth; Goldsmith; Newman). In *Serious Proposal to the Ladies, Part II*, Mary Astell recommends Scudery as one of the five authors that women should read for their education.

18. As Miller points out, the fourfold model excludes the work of major eighteenth-century orators, such as John Witherspoon, Edmund Burke, and Richard Brinsley Sheridan.

19. At a core level, socialized gender identity bears some connection to the two most common biological sex identities—male and female—aligning with, combining, redefining, rejecting, and endlessly complicating the basic presence of sexual genitalia, hormones, reproductive functions, and genetic markers.

CHAPTER 1. A REVOLUTION IN MOOD

1. For an overview of Masham, see Sarah Hutton, "Lady Damaris Masham." For an overview of Cockburn, see Patricia Sheridan, "Catharine Trotter Cockburn."

2. A well-known and established literary trope, the emblem consisted of a visual image accompanied by an epigram, which encapsulated positive or negative exemplars of cultural values, such as virtue, piety, true love, and contentment, as well as vanity, idleness, foolishness, sin, and other vices. Emblems held political and moral symbolism and often carried gendered connotations— as in the female personification for fickleness. The term *emblem* also came to mean the embodiment of a moral or aesthetic concept in a real person, place, or thing. For more on eighteenth-century emblems, see The English Emblem Book digital archive project at Pennsylvania State University at https://libraries .psu.edu/about/collections/english-emblem-book-project/emblem-books.

3. The Glorious Revolution of 1688 was a Whig-backed government takeover that ousted James II and the Tories. Also called the Bloodless Revolution, it was viewed by supporters as proof that, through a peaceful political coup, unpopular monarchs could be replaced according to the will of the people.

4. While providing a peaceful alternative to military revolution, the reign of William III and Mary II did not alleviate the tension between the Tories, who desired to maintain an aristocratic, land-based economy, and the Whigs who sought to strengthen the interests of the middle class through mercantilism and trade.

5. It makes sense to me that a woman who experienced at least fifteen full-term pregnancies would have eating as a hobby!

6. The relationship of Anne and Sarah is (somewhat inaccurately) dramatized in the movie, *The Favourite* (2018), for which actress Olivia Colman who played Anne won the 2018 Academy Award for Best Actress. The actress's performance

of Anne embodies the queen's multifaceted identity as a regal, shy, and physically disabled female monarch, but the film sexualizes Anne and Sarah's relationship, for which there is no verifiable evidence. The film also omits Anne's husband and royal consort, Prince George of Denmark and Norway, from the story of Anne's reign altogether.

7. Habermas wrote and published his dissertation, *The Structural Transformation of the Public Sphere: An Inquiry into a Category of Bourgeois Society* (1962) in German; it was translated and published in English in 1989. Since then, his theory of the public sphere has been highly influential but hotly debated, and feminist scholars across the humanities have taken issue with his treatment of gender and social class.

8. As Michael Warner explains, "A counterpublic maintains at some level, conscious or not, an awareness of its subordinate status. The cultural horizon against which it marks itself off is not just a general or wider public but a dominant one. And the conflict extends not just to ideas or policy questions, but to the speech genres and modes of address that constitute the public." (Warner 423–24).

9. The subtitle, as Bottin points out, suggests that the work may have influenced Mary Wollstonecraft's later publication of her two vindications—of the rights of men and the rights of women. In addition, the work was translated into French and revised by Madeleine de Puisieux in 1750.

10. Johnson's nursery library now resides in the archives of the Lilly Library in Muncie, Indiana. For the fascinating story of how these documents of Jane Johnson came to be discovered, see *Reading Lessons from the Eighteenth Century: Mothers, Children, and Texts* by Evelyn Arizpe, Morgan Styles, and Shirley Brice Heath. As these authors describe, Heath's uncle discovered this text inside a hatbox, along with Johnson's nursery book and other pedagogical ephemera, in the Muncie home of the Ball family, and he called in "Justin Schiller, New York expert on antiquities of children's literature" who validated the authenticity and historical value of the material (vi). Johnson also wrote one of the first English fairy tales, *A Very Pretty Story* (1744), which is held in manuscript at the Bodleian Library and was published by them in facsimile in 2001.

11. As Elizabeth Eger notes, the *bluestocking* label originated as a derogatory moniker for "the Puritans of Cromwell's Little Parliament in 1653, . . . [and] was revived in 1756 when the eccentric scholar Benjamin Stillingfleet appeared at one of Elizabeth Montagu's assemblies wearing blue worsted stockings" (11–13).

12. For an excellent introduction to the historical querelle des femmes in Western culture, see King and Rabil's introduction to *The Other Voice in Early Modern Literature* series.

13. On Mary Hays's contributions to Enlightenment discourse, see Gina Luria Walker's carefully contextualized and detailed "Mary Hays (1759–1843): An Enlightened Quest."

14. In contrast to the London coffeehouse as a masculine, mixed-class public space, the coffeehouses of Bath and Tunbridge appear to have catered to a mixed-gender upper-class clientele (Cowan 248). For an extended discussion of coffeehouses and gender, see Brian Cowan (246–54).

15. "gossip, n." *OED Online*, Oxford University Press, June 2019, www.oed .com/view/Entry/80197. Accessed 14 June 2019.

16. The *Lady's Mercury* was introduced by the publisher and founder, John Dunton, because the *Athenian Mercury's* innovation of the first-ever advice column was so popular with women. These two weekly periodicals, published by the Athenian Society, were among the earliest magazines in England. The format of both consisted of questions and answers on popular subjects addressed to a mixed-gender audience. The *Ladies Mercury* announced in its first issue that it would not infringe on the subject domains (learning and religion) of the *Athenian Mercury* and instead would deal only with topics of love and marriage, and legal questions related to those subjects (1:3.2).

17. For rich discussions of eighteenth-century women's periodicals, see Jennie Batchelor and Manushag N. Powell's edited collection, *Women's Periodicals and Print Culture in Britain, 1690–1820s: The Long Eighteenth Century.*

18. At the time *The Female Spectator* was published, Haywood was a well-known author of risqué amatory fiction. Hailed as "the most prolific British woman writer in the eighteenth century," Haywood was also an actress, playwright, journalist, publisher and translator, among other occupations (Saxton 2). After her first novel, *Love in Excess* (1719), became one of the three most popular works of fiction in the first half of the eighteenth century—along with Daniel Defoe's *Robinson Crusoe* and Jonathan Swift's *Gulliver's Travels*—Haywood went on in the 1720s to write amatory novellas at the rate of one every three months. However, when her risqué "bodice ripper" stories went out of style, she turned to journalism in the 1730 to 1740s, serving as the editor of the *Female Spectator*. Her sexually scandalous writings and conservative Tory political activities have led Kirsten Saxton to call Haywood a "slightly vexed feminist foremother" (3). Haywood returned to novel writing in the 1750s, producing works in the moralistic and polite tone of sentimental fiction, such as *The History of Miss Betsy Thoughtless* (1751), in response to public demand for more polite literature.

19. See Shaftesbury's (Anthony Ashton Cooper) *Characteristicks of Men, Manners, Opinions, Times* (1711–14), Frances Hutcheson's *Inquiry into the Original*

of Our Ideas of Beauty and Virtue (1725), and Alexander Pope's "Epistle to Burlington" in *A Miscellany on Taste* (1732).

20. For more on eighteenth-century theories of taste, see Thomas Gilmore's *Early Eighteenth Century Essays on Taste,* George Dickie's *Century of Taste,* and James Noggle's *Temporality of Taste in Eighteenth-Century British Writing.*

21. Crawford also reports that Mrs. Crespigny was an accomplished archer who competed in archery contests.

22. Evidence of women's rhetorics among the eighteenth-century British working classes is much less common.

CHAPTER 2. ON THE STAGE

1. For the circumstances that led Charles II to grant to Killigrew and Davenant exclusive theater charters, as well as the policies and procedures governing the charters, see Van Lennep, Howe, or the biographical entries for Killigrew and Davenant in Highfill, Burnim, and Langhans.

2. Although the identity of the first English actress to appear in a public production is unknown, theatrical records show the two theater companies signing a number of actresses in 1660, including Katherine Corey, Anne Marshall, Mrs. Eastland, and Mrs. Weaver in the king's company and Hester Davenport, Mary Saunderson, Jane Long, Anne Gibbs, Mrs. Jennings, and Mrs. Norris in the duke's company (Howe 24). Some of the better known of the earliest actresses were Moll Davis, who became a mistress of Charles II, Mary Saunderson, and the Marshall sisters, Anne and Rebecca (Howe 25; Pope 30–31).

3. In the early 1660s, men such as Edward Kynaston continued to play women's roles, but the royal patent of 1662 effectively shut the door for male actors who specialized in female roles.

4. See Cibber; Langbaine; Summers; Van Lennep; Staves; Holland; Weber; Styan; Highfill, Burnim, and Langhans; Howe; Lowenthal; Marsden.

5. Staves's excellent study connects innovations of Restoration theater to concurrent developments in British society as she "tries to understand how changes in ideas about authority were shaped by common cultural experiences shared by late seventeenth-century English philosophers, dramatists, . . . and the less distinguished ladies and gentlemen who were their audience" (xvi).

6. Despite its title, *The Life of Mr. Thomas Betterton* (1710) is not a biography of Betterton but rather an extensive manual on delivery "devoted to rules for the stage that can also be applied to the bar and pulpit" (Glen 101).

7. Later in the eighteenth century, Hugh Blair's *Lectures on Rhetoric and Belles Lettres* (1779) theorizes the rhetoric of drama with focus on classical Greece and Rome, early modern France, and Restoration England. In *Philosophy*

of Rhetoric (1779), George Campbell draws examples from drama in his discussions of both wit and humor as a means for exciting pity and fear in an audience.

8. Jeremy Collier's pamphlet *A Short View of the Immorality, and Profaneness of the English Stage* (1698) concerns how indecency on the stage was affecting the audience, particularly the female audience. Collier argues that the London theater was enacting lewd performances, which insulted female virtue and corrupted the young. Collier's protest is representative of early eighteenth-century criticism on the unseemly influence that overtly sexual themes might have on the female population. Marsden describes the paranoia of ecclesiastics in early eighteenth-century British society who saw theatrical licentiousness as a slippery slope in which "uncontrolled female [sexual] appetites could result in the downfall of the emerging British Empire. Dramatic representation of transgressive sexual behavior could, it was feared, set a bad example and influenced otherwise virtuous women in the theater audience, in effect shattering national security" (5).

9. The *Biographical Dictionary* lists Susannah Percival Mounfort Verbruggen as having lived from 1667 to 1703.

10. After Mountfort's murderer, Captain Richard Hill, who was a crazed male fan of Anne Bracegirdle's, was acquitted. Mrs. Mountfort apparently appealed the verdict but then decided to drop her appeal in exchange for her father's release from a death sentence (Highfill, Burnim, and Langhans 15:137). Further details of the murder are available under the entries for Susannah Verbruggen, William Mountfort, and Anne Bracegirdle in Highfill, Burnim, and Langhan's *Biographical Dictionary*.

11. In "Sarah Siddons and Her Place in Rhetorical History," Lindal Buchanan discusses late eighteenth-century actress Sarah Siddons's (1755–1831) pregnant performances as a startling fact, but it was the norm for eighteenth-century actresses to continue performing throughout their pregnancies.

12. The breeches role—the term for a woman's role in which the actress disguises herself as a man by wearing pants—was a comic form originally used in the medieval romance plays of France and Italy. It was imported to the London stage in the Elizabethan era and became a popular device for women's roles in English theater.

13. *The Western Lass* is also known as *The Bath* (1701), which is how it appears in the appendix titled "Major Actresses and Their Roles in New Plays" of Elizabeth Howe's *First English Actresses*.

14. According to Evans's editorial note in Cibber's apology, a Joan Trot is "a female John Trot, i.e., a bumpkin; cf. Trot, John in OED" (98).

15. My analysis of Elizabeth Barry in this section necessarily repeats some of the points I make in the article.

16. For discussion of Bracegirdle's celebrity status and its effects, see Erin M. Keating's "Secret History and Restoration Drama" and Joseph Roach's *It*.

17. In *Female Playwrights and Eighteenth Century Comedy: Negotiating Marriage on the London Stage*, Misty Anderson notes that legalities about primogeniture and inheritance were not concerns for most women because most people in England were poor; however, in the rising capitalist system, married women became more economically powerless than they had been in the system of aristocratic patriarchy.

18. Aphra Behn's *The Rover* still fits the bill as an outrageous and simultaneously libertine and protofeminist play, as I witnessed in a February 2019 production of the play by the Hidden Room theater company in Austin, Texas. See http://hiddenroomtheatre.com/past/the-rover/.

19. Behn purposefully gave Willmore a name similar to Barry's real-life lover and patron, John Wilmot, a notorious rake who was married to another woman. Just as Hellena enticed Wilmore, Barry attracted Wilmot, but unlike Hellena, Barry did not marry Wilmot; rather she became his mistress for a number of years.

20. Otway's tortured passion for Barry is proven beyond doubt in five letters written to her sometime in the early 1680s, which were first published anonymously in 1697 and later attributed to Otway in 1713.

21. Millamant's concerns for women in marriage reflect the lack of marriage laws from the period 1653 to 1753. See the discussion of wives in chapter 2.

22. Nussbaum's study of second-generation actresses includes: "Anne Oldfield (1683–1730), Catherine Clive (1711–85), Margaret Woffington (1720?–60), Frances Abington (1737–1815), and George Anne Bellamy (c. 1731–88)" (9).

23. Garrick's techniques are well documented in many mid-century works on acting and elocutionary theory, including Aaron Hill's *Art of Acting*, John Hill's *Actor, a Treatise on the Art of Playing*, and Denis Diderot's *Le Paradoxe sur le Comedien*.

CHAPTER 3. IN SOCIABLE VENUES

1. Assessing contributions of women intellectuals to eighteenth-century British narratives of progress, O'Brien also explores the influence of ancient Roman matrons and Germanic female warriors on that narrative. She traces the Gothic past and the Germanic custom of chivalry as the source of the revival of gallantry that began in the latter half of the eighteenth century and rose as the dominant narrative of gender in nineteenth-century Victorian England.

2. For more discussion of national reform in late eighteenth-century Britain, see Arthur Burns and Joanna Innes's edited collection, *Rethinking the Age of Reform: Britain 1780–1850*.

CHAPTER 4. ON THE PAGE

1. The authorship of *Ladies Library* (1714), a collection of miscellaneous prescriptions on female communication and behavior, is unclear; the title page credits it to "a lady," and the text was published by the famous eighteenth-century periodicalist Richard Steele.

2. Judith Drake was married to James Drake, a Tory pamphleteer and fellow of the Royal Society and College of Physicians who was supportive of his wife's writing and publication. Following his death, Drake edited her deceased husband's writings on anatomy (1707); she may have co-authored the work, *Anthropologia Nova*, and she practiced unlicensed medicine for which she was called to the Royal Society and defended herself (Todd and Dow).

3. Tania Smith reports the top-cited theorists, and number of references, as follows in descending order: Cicero, 22; Balzac, 18; Quintilian, 12; Aristotle, 10; Demosthenes, 8; Emperor Augustus, 7; Malherbe, 7; Ménage, 6; Seneca, 6; Homer, 6; Isocrates, 5; and Plutarch, 5 (Smith 350).

4. Even though Renaissance women were rarely allowed to use their rhetorical education for any type of public speaking, in the humanist schools of the fifteenth through the seventeenth centuries across Europe, aristocratic girls had been educated along with boys (Bizzell and Herzberg 562). Up through the fifteenth century, cloistered convents in England had provided formal venues for women's higher academic studies until Henry VIII dismantled monastic Catholic education (Perry 361). The privileged domain of the university and the public grammar schools, with their rigorous daily exercises in grammar recitation, written composition, and Latin, both modeled in the humanist style of classical learning, were considered the ideal intellectual sites of rigorous education, suitable only for males (Cohen 231–36).

5. Italian women Christine de Pizan and Laura published humanist arguments on education in the fifteenth and sixteenth centuries, as did Bathsua Makin in England, and Anna Marie Shurman in Holland in the seventeenth century.

6. Bathsua Makin was reportedly a child prodigy who was fluent in Greek, Latin, and French and who also studied Hebrew, Spanish, German, and Italian. Makin tutored Princess Elizabeth, daughter of Charles I around 1640, and in 1662 established a school for girls at Tottenham High Cross outside of London, which included a curriculum in needlework, singing, dancing, accounting,

English grammar, French, Latin, geography, arithmetic, astronomy, natural philosophy, and options of Greek or Hebrew.

7. For more on Shaftesbury's theories of moral benevolence from his *Characteristicks of Men, Manners, Opinions, Times* (1714), see https://oll.libertyfund.org/titles/shaftesbury-characteristicks-of-men-manners-opinions-times-3-vols.

8. Jane Austen's novels, especially *Emma*, reflect the viewpoint that domestic education was superior to day schools and boarding schools for girls.

9. Maria Edgeworth was an articulate advocate and pioneer of education reform. In addition to publishing numerous works of fiction and nonfiction, Edgeworth collaborated with her father, Richard Lovell Edgeworth, and her stepmother, Honora Edgeworth, in developing a holistic, domestic, co-educational curriculum by which they taught her twenty younger siblings and other children of Edgeworthstown, the Irish village of which their family was the center.

10. The contrast in format from the Platonic form of the dialogue to the more Aristotelian form of the manual reflects the movement away from humanist genres and modes to rationalist directly empirical didactic genres in the eighteenth century.

11. Although *Practical Education* is a collaborative work involving not only Edgeworth and her father but also her stepmother and other members of the Edgeworth family, Maria Edgeworth is acknowledged as the primary author of chapters 3 through 7 in volume 1 and chapters 18 through 25 in volume 2.

12. In contrast to the detailed pedagogical methods presented in *Practical Education*, Edgeworth's unpublished manuscript "On the Education of the Poor" (1800) proposes a serious and formal plan for educating Ireland's lower classes. Currently archived at the Bodleian Library, "On the Education of the Poor" exists only in draft form as a classical argument exhorting readers with powerful rhetorical appeals and logical justifications. In this formal treatise, Edgeworth analyzes the societal causes and effects of ignorance among the poor, refutes counterarguments that the lower classes are innately inferior, and recommends the implementation of a radical education vision involving the redistricting of labor and land. Edgeworth's utopian vision is based on a paternalistic model similar to Edgeworthstown, the Irish estate of which their family was the center, in which an executive body oversees the community, and community members all contribute to the production of goods, earn wages, and either own, rent, or possess the rights to farm small tracts of land. This vision depends on the fairmindedness and honesty of the leaders, as well as the work ethic of the community, and it underlines Edgeworth's support for paternalism and staunch opposition to any type of subversive or revolutionary activity.

13. The female-only community was not a new idea of the Enlightenment. According to Margaret Hunt, during the eighteenth century, throughout Europe, there was an increase in groups of single women of all social classes living together in "economic and cultural partnerships." Some areas reported nine or ten percent of households as female-headed, and some very poor Italian and Spanish towns reported eighteen to twenty percent of households as female-headed; in England specifically, insurance records show that single women not only cohabitated but also maintained joint insurance policies on their possessions, including their book collections (79–81).

14. The possibility of sexual relationships between women in female-only households was not broached publicly.

APPENDIX A

1. For a person of one biological sex to openly identify themselves as completely adopting the identity of the opposite sex was unusual, but it happened. For example, actress and author Charlotte Charke dressed and conducted herself as a man.

Works Cited

Addison, Joseph, and Richard Steele. *Spectator.* 1711–14.

Allen, Julia. "The Uses and Problems of 'Manly' Rhetoric: Mary Wollstone-craft's Adaptation of Hugh Blair's Lectures in Her Two Vindications." *Listening to Their Voices: The Rhetorical Activities of Historical Women,* edited by Molly Meijer Wortheimer, U of South Carolina P, 1997, pp. 32–336.

Anderson, Misty G. *Female Playwrights and Eighteenth Century Comedy: Negotiating Marriage on the London Stage.* Palgrave, 2002.

Andrews, Donna T. *London Debating Societies, 1776–1799.* London Record Society, 1994.

Anne, Queen of Great Britain. *Queen Anne's Reasons for Her Conduct, Both with Respect to the War and Peace: And Her Majesty's Characters of King William III and His Majesty K. George the French King and the Pretender.* Publish'd for the Use of the Late Ministery. London, 1715. Eighteenth Century Collections Online. Gale. Trial Site Database. 30 May 2019.

———. "Popular Culture and Public Debate: London 1780." *Historical Journal,* vol. 39, no. 2, 1996, pp. 405–23.

Apetri, Sarah. *Women, Feminism, and Religion in Early Enlightenment England.* Cambridge UP, 2010.

Arizpe, Evelyn, Morag Styles, and Shirley Brice Heath. *Reading Lessons from the Eighteenth Century: Mothers, Children, Texts.* Pied Piper Publishing, 2006.

Astell, Mary. *A Serious Proposal to the Ladies, Parts I and II.* 1694, 1697. Edited by Patricia Springborg, Pickering and Chatto, 1997.

———. *Some Reflections upon Marriage.* London: Printed for John Nutt, near Stationers-Hall, 1700 [first edition]. http://digital.library.upenn.edu/women /astell/marriage/marriage.html.

Austen, Jane. *Emma.* 1815

———. *Love and Friendship.* 1790.

———. *Sense and Sensibility.* 1811.

Avery, Emmet. L., editor. *London Stage 1660–1800: Part 2: 1700–1729.* Southern Illinois UP, 1960.

Bacon, Francis. *Essays.* 1597. Penguin Books, 1985.

———. *The Feign'd Curitizans. The Works of Aphra Behn,* vol. 6, edited by Janet Todd, Ohio State UP, 1996.

———. *Nova Organon.* 1605. Cambridge UP, 2000.

———. *The Rover. The Broadview Anthology of Restoration and Early Eighteenth Century Drama,* edited by Douglas Canfield, Broadview Press, 2001.

Bagchi, Barnita. "'Instruction a Torment'?: Jane Austen's Early Writing and Conflicting Versions of Female Education in Romantic-Era 'Conservative' British Women's Novels." *Romanticism on the Net,* no. 40, 2005, id.erudit .org/iderudit/012463ar.

Batchelor, Jennie, and Manushag N. Powell, editors. *Women's Periodicals and Print Culture in Britain, 1690–1820s: The Long Eighteenth Century.* Edinburgh UP, 2018.

Behn, Aphra. *The Lucky Chance,* edited by Jane Spencer, Oxford UP, 1995.

Benger, Elizabeth. *Memoirs of the Late Mrs. Elizabeth Hamilton,* 1818.

Bizzell, Patricia, and Bruce Herzberg, editors. *Rhetorical Tradition: Readings from Classical Times to the Present.* 2nd ed., Bedford/St. Martin's, 2001.

Blair, Hugh. *Lectures on Rhetoric and Belles Lettres.* 1783. Edited by Linda Ferreira-Buckley and S. Michael Halloran, Southern Illinois UP, 2005.

Bottin, Eileen Hunt. "Human Stories: Wollstonecraft, Mill and the Literature of Human Rights." *Wollstonecraft, Mill, and Women's Human Rights,* Yale UP, New Haven; London, 2016, pp. 204–248. *JSTOR,* www.jstor.org/stable/j .cttikft8kh.9.

Brody, Miriam. "The Vindication of the Writes of Women: Mary Wollstonecraft and Enlightenment Rhetoric." *Feminist Interpretations of Mary Wollstonecraft,* edited by Maria J. Falco, Penn State UP, 1996, pp. 105–123.

Brooks, Helen E. M. *Actresses, Gender, and the Eighteenth-Century Stage: Playing Women.* Palgrave Macmillan, 2015.

Broomhill, Susan. *Spaces for Feeling and Sociabilities in Britain 1650–1850.* Routledge, 2015.

Buchanan, Lindal. *Regendering Delivery: The Fifth Canon and Antebellum Women Rhetors.* Southern Illinois UP, 2005.

———. *Rhetorics of Motherhood.* Southern Illinois UP, 2013.

———. "Sarah Siddons and Her Place in Rhetorical History." *Rhetorica,* vol. 25, no. 4, 2007, pp. 413–34.

Bucholz, Robert O. "Queen Anne: Victim of Her Virtues?" *Queenship in Britain: 1660–1837: Royal Patronage, Court Culture and Dynastic Politics,* edited by Clarissa Campbell-Orr, Manchester UP, 2002, pp. 94–129.

Burney, Frances. *Evelina.* 1778.

Burns, Arthur, and Joanna Ines, editors. *Rethinking the Age of Reform: Britain 1780–1850.* Cambridge UP, 2003.

Bush-Bailey, Gilli. *Treading the Bawds: Actresses and Playwrights on the Late-Stuart Stage*. Manchester UP, 2006.

Butler, Judith. "From *Gender Trouble.*" *Norton Anthology of Theory and Criticism*, edited by Vincent B. Leitch, Norton and Company, 2001, pp. 2485–2501.

Campbell, George. *Philosophy of Rhetoric*. 1776. *Rhetoric of Blair, Campbell, and Whatley*, edited by James L. Golden and Edward P. J. Corbett, Southern Illinois UP, 1990, pp.145–272.

Canfield, Douglas, editor. *Broadview Anthology of Restoration and Early Eighteenth Century Drama*. Broadview Press, 2001, pp. ix–xviii.

Chapone, Hester. *Letters on Improvement of the Mind*. 1773. Weed and Rider, 1820.

Chapone, Sarah Kirkham. *The Hardships of the Laws in Relation to Wives*. London, 1735.

Cibber, Colley. *A Critical Edition of an Apology for the Life of Colley Cibber, Comedian*. 1740. Edited by John Maurice Evans, Garland Publishing, 1987.

Cicero. *On the Ideal Orator*. Translated by James M. May and Jakob Wisse, New York: Oxford UP, 2001.

Clark, Anna. "Women in Eighteenth-Century British Politics." *Women, Gender, and Enlightenment*, edited by Barbara Taylor and Sarah Knott, Palgrave Macmillan, 2005, pp. 570–86.

Clark, Peter. *British Clubs and Societies, 1580–1800*. Oxford UP, 2000.

Cohen, Michele. "'To Think, To Compare, To Combine, To Methodise': Girls' Education in Enlightenment Britain." *Women, Gender, and Enlightenment*, edited by Barbara Taylor and Sarah Knott, Palgrave Macmillan, 2005, pp. 224–42.

Collins, Margo. "Centlivre v. Hardwicke: Susannah Centlivre's Plays and the Marriage Act of 1753." *Comparative Drama*, vol. 33, no. 2, 1999, pp. 179–98.

Collins, Vicki Tolar. "The Speaker Respoken: Material Rhetoric as Feminist Methodology." *College English*, vol. 61, no. 5, 1999, pp. 545–74.

Conboy, Martin. "The Print Industry—Yesterday, Today, and Tomorrow: An Overview." *Print Journalism: A Critical Introduction*, edited by Richard Keeble, Routledge, 2005, pp. 3–21.

Cowan, Brian. *The Social Life of Coffee: The Emergence of the British Coffeehouse*. Yale UP, 2005.

Crawford, Elizabeth. "Mariana Starke: The Mystery Of The Bodleian Diary." *Woman and Her Sphere*, https://womanandhersphere.com/2012/11/02/mariana-starke-the-mystery-of-the-bodleian-diary/, November 2, 2012. Accessed May 15, 2018.

Crosswhite, James. *Deep Rhetoric: Philosophy, Reason, Violence, Justice, Wisdom*. U of Chicago P, 2013.

DeLucia, JoEllen. *A Feminine Enlightenment: British Women Writers and the Philosophy of Progress, 1759–1820.* Edinburgh UP, 2015.

Descartes, René. *Discourse on Method for Guiding One's Reason and Searching for Truth in Science.* 1637. *René Descartes: Discourse on Method and Other Writings,* Penguin Books, 1999.

Dickie, George. *The Century of Taste: The Philosophical Odyssey of Taste in the Eighteenth Century.* Oxford UP, 1996.

Donawerth, Jane. "Conversation and the Boundaries of Public Discourse in Rhetorical Theory by Renaissance Women." *Rhetorica,* vol. 16, no. 2, 1998, pp.181–99.

——. *Conversational Rhetoric: The Rise and Fall of a Women's Rhetorical Tradition, 1600–1900.* Southern Illinois UP, 2012.

——. "The Politics of Renaissance Rhetorical Theory by Women." *Political Rhetoric, Power, and Renaissance Women,* edited by Carole Levin and Patricia A. Sullivan, State U of New York P, 1995, pp. 257–72.

——, editor. *Rhetorical Theory by Women before 1900.* Rowman and Littlefield, 2002.

Dow, Gillian. *Rooms of Our Own: Lucy Cavendish College.* Chawton House Library, 2009.

Drake, Judith. *An Essay in Defence of the Female Sex in Which Are Inserted the Characters of a Pedant, a Squire, a Beau, a Virtuoso, a Poetaster, a City-Critick, &c. in a Letter to a Lady.* Printed for A. Roper and E. Wilkinson, 1696.

Edgeworth, Maria. *Essay on Education of the Poor.* Bodleain Library. MS Eng. Misc. e. 461, fols 1–77b.

——. *The Life and Letters of Maria Edgeworth.* Edited by Augustus J. C. Hare. Dodo Press, 2013.

Edgeworth, Maria, and R. L. Edgeworth. *Practical Education.* 2nd American ed., Providence: J. Francis Lippitt, 1815. *The Project Gutenberg ebook of Practical Education.* 2009.

Eger, Elizabeth. *Bluestockings: Women of Reason from Enlightenment to Romanticism.* Palgrave Macmillan, 2010.

Ellis, Markman, Richard Coulton, Ben Dew, and Matthew Mauger. *Tea and the Tea-Table in Eighteenth-Century England.* Vol. 1. Pickering and Chatto, 2010. 4 vols.

Enoch, Jessica. "Releasing Hold: Feminist Historiography without the Tradition." *Theorizing Histories of Rhetoric,* edited by Michelle Ballif, Southern Illinois UP, 2012.

Escott, Angela. "The School of Eloquence and "Roasted Square Caps": Oratory and Pedantry as Fair Theatrical Game?, *Women's Writing,* vol. 8, no. 1, 2001, pp. 59–80.

Fell, Margaret. *Woman's Speaking Justified, Proved, and Allowed by the Scriptures.* 1666. *The Rhetorical Tradition: Readings from Classical Times to the Present,* 2nd ed., edited by Patricia Bizzell and Bruce Herzberg, Bedford St. Martin's, 2001, pp. 753–60.

Female Tatler. London. 1709–1710. Edited by Fidelis Morgan, Everyman, 1992.

Ferreira-Buckley, Linda. "The Eighteenth Century." *The Present State of Scholarship in the History of Rhetoric,* edited by Lynée Lewis Gaillet, U of Missouri P, 2010, pp. 114–51.

Fielding, Sarah. *The Governess: Or, the Little Female Academy. Calculated for the Entertainment and Instruction of Young Ladies in Their Education.* 1749. Project Gutenberg e-book #1905, October 10, 2008.

Filmer, Robert. *Patriarcha.* 1680.

Foucault, Michel. *The History of Sexuality, Part 1. An Introduction.* Translated by Robert Hurley, Vintage Books, 1990.

Francus, Marilyn. *Monstrous Motherhood: Eighteenth-Century Culture and the Ideology of Domesticity.* Johns Hopkins University Press, 2012.

Gaillet, Lynée Lewis. "The Nineteenth Century." *The Present State of Scholarship in the History of Rhetoric,* edited by Lynée Lewis Gaillet, U of Missouri P, 2010, pp. 152–84.

Gaillet, Lynée Lewis, and Elizabeth Tasker. "Recovering, Revisioning, and Regendering the History of Eighteenth- and Nineteenth-Century Rhetorical Theory and Practice." *Sage Handbook of Rhetorical Studies,* edited by Andrea Lunsford, Kirt H. Wilson, and Rosa Eberly, Sage Publication, 2009, pp. 67–84.

Gallagher, Catherine. *Nobody's Story: The Vanishing Acts of Women Writers in the Marketplace, 1670–1820.* U of California P, 1994.

Gildon, Charles. *The Life of Mr. Thomas Betterton.* London: Frank Cass and Company, 1969.

Gill, Pat. "The Way of the Word: Telling Differences in Congreve's *Way of the World.*" *Broken Boundaries: Women and Feminism in Restoration Drama,* edited by Katherine M. Quinsey, UP of Kentucky, 1996, pp. 164–84.

Gilmore, Thomas. Introduction. *Early Eighteenth Century Essays on Taste.* Scholars Facsimiles and Reprints, 1972.

Glen, Rochelle. "Charles Gildon." *Eighteenth-Century British and American Rhetorics and Rhetoricians,* edited by Michael Moran, Greenwood Press, 1994.

Glenn, Cheryl. *Rhetorical Feminism and This Thing Called Hope.* Southern Illinois UP, 2018.

———. *Rhetoric Retold: Regendering the Tradition from Antiquity through the Renaissance.* Southern Illinois UP, 1997.

———. *Unspoken: The Rhetoric of Silence.* Southern Illinois UP, 2004.

Gold, David. "Remapping Revisionist Historiography." *College Composition and Communication,* vol. 64, no. 1, 2012, pp. 5–34.

Golden, James L., and Edward P. J. Corbett. *The Rhetoric of Blair, Campbell, and Whatley.* 1968. Southern Illinois UP, 1990.

Goldsmith, Elizabeth C. *Exclusive Conversations: The Art of Interaction in Seventeenth Century France.* U of Pennsylvania P, 1988.

Goring, Paul. *The Rhetoric of Sensibility.* Cambridge UP, 2009.

"gossip, n." *OED Online,* Oxford UP, June 2019, www.oed.com/view/Entry /80197. Accessed June 14, 2019.

Graban, Tarez Samra. *Women's Irony: Rewriting Feminist Rhetorical Histories.* Southern Illinois UP, 2015.

Gregg, Edward. *Queen Anne.* Yale UP, 2001.

Habermas, Jurgen. *The Structural Transformation of the Public Sphere.* 1st ed. 1962. Translated by Thomas Burger, MIT P, 1991.

Hamilton, Elizabeth. *Letters on the Elementary Principles of Education.* 1801. Baldwin, Cradock, and Joy, 1818.

Hannan, Leonie. *Women of Letters: Gender, Writing, and the Life of the Mind in Early Modern England.* Manchester UP, 2016.

Haskins, Ekaterina V. "A Woman's Inventive Response to the Seventeenth-Century Querelle des Femmes." *Listening to Their Voices: The Rhetorical Activities of Historical Women,* edited by Molly Meijer Wertheimer, U of South Carolina P, 1997, pp. 288–304.

Haywood, Eliza. *Female Spectator. Selections from the Female Spectator.* Edited by Patricia Meyers Spacks, Oxford UP, 1999.

———. *Tea Table.* 1725.

Heller, Deborah, editor. *Bluestockings Now! The Evolution of a Social Role.* Routledge, 2016.

Highfill, Philip H., Kalman A. Burnim, and Edward A. Langhans. *A Biographical Dictionary of Actors, Actresses, Musicians, Dancers, Managers and Other Stage Personnel in London, 1660–1800.* Southern Illinois UP, 1987.

Hobbes, Thomas. *Leviathan.* 1660.

Holland, Peter. *The Ornament of Action: Text and Performance in Restoration Comedy.* Cambridge UP, 1979.

Holloway, Sally. "Materializing Maternal Emotions: Birth, Celebration, and Renunciation in England, c. 1688–1830." *Feeling Things: Objects and Emotions through History*, edited by Stephanie Downes, Sally Holloway, and Sarah Randles, Oxford UP, 2018.

Howe, Elizabeth. *The First English Actresses*. Cambridge UP, 1992.

Hughes, Derek. *Eighteenth-Century Women Playwrights*. Pickering and Chatto, 2001.

———. *The Theatre of Aphra Behn*. Palgrave, 2001.

Hulquist, Aleksondra. "Bringing Order to the Passions: Eliza Haywood's Fiction, 1719 and 1748." *Spaces for Feeling and Sociabilities in Britain 1650–1850*, edited by Susan Broomhill, Routledge, 2015.

Hume, David. *On the Standard of Taste*. 1757. *The Rhetorical Tradition: Readings from Classical Times to the Present*, 2nd ed., edited by Patricia Bizzell and Bruce Herzberg, Bedford St. Martin's, 2001, pp. 830–40.

Hunt, Margaret. *Women in Eighteenth-Century Europe*. Routledge, 2010.

Hutton, Sarah, "Lady Damaris Masham," *Stanford Encyclopedia of Philosophy*, Winter 2016, edited by Edward N. Zalta, plato.stanford.edu/archives /win2016/entries/lady-masham/.

Immel, Andrea, and Lissa Paul. "Poems in the Nursery." *Oxford Handbook of Poetry, 1660–1800*, edited by Jack Lynch, Oxford UP, 2016.

Jarratt, Susan C. *Rereading the Sophists: Classical Rhetoric Refigured*. Southern Illinois UP, 1991.

———. "Sappho's Memory." *Rhetoric Society Quarterly*, vol. 32, no. 1, Winter 2002, 11–44.

Johnson, Jane. Copies and drafts of letters to friends, 1739–55. Oxford, Bodleian Library, MS. Don. c. 190 fols. 11–24.

———. Two letters to her son Robert, 1753–1755. Oxford, Bodleian Library, MS. Don. c. 190 fols. 7–10.

Johnson, Nan. *Gender and Rhetorical Space in American Life, 1866–1910*. Southern Illinois UP, 2002.

Jordan, Robert, and Harold Love. *Works of Thomas Southerne*, Vol. 1. U of Virginia P, 1988.

Keating, Erin. "Secret History and Restoration Drama." *The Secret History in Literature, 1660–1820*, edited by Rebecca Bullard and Rachel Carnell, Cambridge UP, 2017.

Keeble, N. H. *Restoration: England in the 1660s*. Wiley-Blackwell, 2002.

Kelly, Gary. "Bluestocking Work: Learning, Literature, and Lore in the Onset of Modernity." *Bluestockings Now! The Evolution of a Social Role*, edited by Deborah Heller, Routledge, 2016, pp. 175–208.

———. *Women, Writing, and Revolution, 1790–1827*. Clarendon, 1993.

King, Margaret, and Albert Rabil Jr. "The Other Voice in Early Modern Europe." Introduction. *Story of Sapho*, by Madeleine de Scudery. *The Other Voice in Early Modern Europe*, edited by Karen Newman, U of Chicago P, 2003.

Knox, Vicesimus. *Liberal Education*. 1781. London, 1782.

Kreis-Schink, Annette. *Women, Writing, and the Theater in the Early Modern Period: The Plays of Aphra Behn and Suzanne Centlivre*. Associated UP, 2001.

Ladies Mercury. London, 1693. Vol. 1.

The Lady's Rhetorick: Containing Rules for Speaking and Writing Elegantly. Printed for J. Taylor, 1707.

Locke, John. *Essay Concerning Human Understanding*. 1689.

———. *Some Thoughts Concerning Education*. 1693.

———. *Two Treatises on Government*. 1690.

Loftis, John, editor. *Works of John Dryden*, vol. 9, Berkeley, U of California P, 1966.

Logan, Shirley Wilson. *We Are Coming: The Persuasive Discourse of Nineteenth-Century Black Women*. Southern Illinois UP, 1999.

Longaker, Mark Garrett. *Rhetorical Style and Bourgeois Virtue*. Pennsylvania State UP, 2015.

Lowenthal, Cynthia. *Performing Identities on the Restoration Stage*. Southern Illinois UP, 2003.

———. "Sticks and Rags, Bodies and Brocade: Essentializing Discourses and the Late Restoration Playhouse." *Broken Boundaries: Women and Feminism in Restoration Drama*, edited by Katherine M. Quinsey, UP of Kentucky, 1996, pp. 219–33.

Lunsford, Andrea A., editor. *Reclaiming Rhetorica: Women in the Rhetorical Tradition*. U of Pittsburg P, 1995.

M.C. *An Account of the Fair Intellectual-Club in Edinburgh: In a Letter to a Honourable Member of an Athenian Society There. By a Young Lady, the Secretary of the Club*. J. McEuen and Company, January 1, 1720.

Macaulay, Catherine. *Letters on Education with Observations on Religious and Metaphysical Subjects*. 1790. Garland Publishing, 1974.

Makin, Bathsua. *An Essay to Revive the Ancient Education of Gentlewomen, in Religion, Manners, Arts, & Tongues*. 1673.

Marsden, Jean. *Fatal Desire: Women, Sexuality, and the English Stage, 1660–1720*. Cornell UP, 2006.

———. "Rape, Voyeurism, and the Restoration Stage." *Broken Boundaries: Women and Feminism in Restoration Drama*, edited by Katherine M. Quinsey, UP of Kentucky, 1996, pp. 201–218.

McAfee, Helen. *Pepys on the Restoration Stage.* Benjamin Blom, 1916.

Mellor, Anne K. "The Debate on the Rights of Women: Wollstonecraft's In-fluence on the Women Writers of her Day." *Called to Civil Existence: Mary Wollstonecraft's A Vindication of the Rights of Women,* edited by Enit Karafili Steiner, Rodopi, 2014.

Merrens, Rebecca. "Unmannered with Thy Words: Ungendering Tragedy in Manley and Trotter." *Broken Boundaries: Women and Feminism in Restoration Drama,* edited by Katherine M. Quinsey, UP of Kentucky, 1996, pp. 31–53.

Miller, Thomas. "Eighteenth-Century Rhetoric." *Encyclopedia of Rhetoric,* edited by Thomas Sloane, Oxford UP, 2001, pp. 227–37.

Monroe, Julie A. "A Feminist Vindication of Mary Wollstonecraft." *Iowa Journal of Literary Studies,* vol. 8, 1987, pp. 143–52, ir.uiowa.edu/ijls/vo18/iss1/34.

Montagu, Elizabeth. MO 3258, "Letter to Elizabeth Carter, 1769, October 10." Elizabeth Robinson Montagu papers, Huntington Library, San Marino, California.

Moran, Michael G. *Eighteenth-Century British and American Rhetorics and Rhetoricians.* Greenwood Press, 1994.

More, Hannah. *Strictures on the Modern System of Female Education With a View of the Principles and Conduct Prevalent among Women of Rank and Fortune.* London, 1799. http://name.umdl.umich.edu/004902140.0001.001.

More, Mary. "The Woman's Right: Or Her Power in a Greater Equality to Her Husband." 1680. British Library, Harley 3918, fols 46r.

Munns, Jessica. "Theatrical Culture 1: Politics and Theater." *Cambridge Companion to English Literature: 1650–1740,* edited by Stephen N. Zwicker, Cambridge UP, 1998, pp. 82–103.

Muthu, Sankar. *Enlightenment against Empire.* Princeton UP, 2003.

The New Art of Speaking, or, A Complete Modern System of Rhetoric, Elocution, and Oratory. Printed for Alex Hogg, 1785.

Newman, Karen. "The Other Voice." Introduction. *Story of Sapho,* by Madeleine de Scudery. *The Other Voice in Early Modern Europe,* edited by Karen Newman, U of Chicago P, 2003, pp. 1–12.

Noggle, James. *The Temporality of Taste in Eighteenth-Century British Writing.* Oxford UP, 2012.

Nussbaum, Felicity. *Rival Queens.* U of Pennsylvania P, 2010.

O'Brien, Karen. Introduction to section 1, "Sexual Distinctions and Prescriptions." *Women, Gender, and Enlightenment,* edited by Barbara Taylor and Sarah Knott, Palgrave Macmillan, 2005. pp. 3–7.

———. *Women and Enlightenment in Eighteenth-Century Britain.* Cambridge UP, 2009.

Ó Gallchoir, Clíona. *Maria Edgeworth: Women, Enlightenment, and Nation.* U of Dublin P, 2005.

Orr, Clarissa Campbell. "Aristocratic Feminism, the Learned Governess, and the Republic of Letters." *Women, Gender, and Enlightenment,* edited by Barbara Taylor and Sarah Kent, Palgrave Macmillan, 2005, pp. 306–325.

———. "Introduction: Court Studies, Gender, and Women's History: 1660–1837." *Queenship in Britain 1660–1837: Royal Patronage, Court Culture and Dynastic Politics,* edited by Clarissa Campbell Orr, Manchester UP, 2002.

———. "The Sappho of Gloucestershire: Sara Chapone and Christian Feminism." *Bluestockings Now! The Evolution of a Social Role,* edited by Deborah Heller, Routledge, 2016, pp. 91–110.

Osell, Tedra. "Tatling Women in the Public Sphere: Rhetorical Femininity and the English Essay Periodical." *Eighteenth-Century Studies,* vol. 38, no. 2, 2005. pp. 283–300.

Pearson, Jacqueline. *Prostituted Muse: Images of Women and Women Dramatists 1642–1737.* Harvester Wheatsheaf, 1988.

Percy, Carol. "Women's Grammars." *Eighteenth-Century English: Ideology and Change,* edited by Raymond Hickey, Cambridge UP, 2010.

Perry, Ruth. *The Celebrated Mary Astell.* U of Chicago P, 1986.

Pocock, J. G. A. *Barbarism and Religion,* 6 vols. Cambridge UP, 1999–2015.

Porter, Roy. *Enlightenment.* Penguin Books, 2000.

Powell, Manushag N. *Performing Authorship in Eighteenth-Century English Periodicals.* Bucknell UP, 2012.

Quintilian. *Orator's Education.* Edited and translated by Donald A. Russell, Harvard UP, 2001.

Randall, David. *Conversational Enlightenment: The Reconceptualization of Rhetoric in Eighteenth-Century Thought.* Edinburgh UP, 2019.

Reeve, Clara. "An Account of Clara Reeve." 1792. *Monthly Magazine,* vol. 24, 1808, p. 601.

———. *Plans of Education with Remarks on the Systems of Other Writers.* 1792. Garland, 1974.

Richardson, Alan. "Mary Wollstonecraft on Education." *Cambridge Companion to Mary Wollstonecraft,* edited by Claudia L. Johnson, Cambridge UP, 2002, pp. 24–41.

Richardson, Samuel. *Pamela in Her Exalted Condition.* 1742.

———. *Pamela; or Virtue Rewarded.* 1740.

Ritchie, Joy, and Kate Ronald, editors. *Available Means: An Anthology of Women's Rhetoric(s).* U of Pittsburgh P, 2001.

Rizzo, Betty. "Male Oratory and Female Prate: 'Then Hush and Be an Angel Quite.'" *Eighteenth-Century Life,* vol. 29, no.1, 2005, pp. 23–49.

Roach, Joseph. *It.* U of Michigan P, 2007.

Ronald, Kate. "Feminist Perspectives on the History of Rhetoric." *Sage Handbook of Rhetorical Studies,* edited by Andrea Lunsford, Kirt H. Wilson, and Rosa Eberly, Sage Publication, 2009, pp. 139–52.

Rosenthal, Laura J. "Reading Masks: The Actress and the Spectarix in Restoration Shakespeare." *Broken Boundaries: Women and Feminism in Restoration Drama,* edited by Katherine M. Quinsey, UP of Kentucky, 1996, pp. 201–218.

Rousseau, Jean Jacques. *Emile.* Amsterdam, 1762.

Royster, Jacqueline Jones, and Gesa Kirsch. *Feminist Rhetorical Practices: New Horizons for Rhetoric, Composition, and Literacy Studies.* Southern Illinois UP, 2012.

Ryan, Kathleen J., Nancy Myers, and Rebecca Jones, editors. *Rethinking Ethos: A Feminist Ecological Approach to Rhetoric.* Southern Illinois UP, 2016.

Salzman, Paul, editor. *Expanding the Canon of Early Modern Women's Writing.* Cambridge Scholars, 2010.

Saxton, Kirsten. Introduction. *Passionate Fictions of Eliza Haywood: Essays on her Life and Work,* edited by Kirsten Saxton and Rebecca Bocchicchio, UP of Kentucky, 2000, pp. 1–18.

Scouten, Arthur J, editor. *London Stage 1660–1800: Part 3: 1729–1747.* Southern Illinois UP, 1960.

de Scudery, Madeleine. "Of Conversation." 1683. *Rhetorical Tradition: Readings from Classical Times to the Present,* 2nd ed., edited by Patricia Bizzell and Bruce Herzberg, Bedford St. Martin's, 2001, pp. 767–72.

———. *Selected Letters, Orations, and Rhetorical Dialogues.* 1650–1680. *The Other Voice in Early Modern Europe,* edited and translated by Jane Donaworth and Julie Strongson, U of Chicago P, 2004, pp. 1–43.

———. "The Story of Sapho." *The Other Voice in Early Modern Europe,* edited by Karen Newman, U of Chicago P, 2003, pp. 1–12.

Sheridan, Patricia. "Catharine Trotter Cockburn," *Stanford Encyclopedia of Philosophy,* Spring 2019, edited by Edward N. Zalta, plato.stanford.edu/archives/spr2019/entries/cockburn/.

Sheridan, Thomas. "Lectures on Elocution." *Rhetorical Tradition: Readings from Classical Times to the Present,* 2nd ed., edited by Patricia Bizzell and Bruce Herzberg, Bedford St. Martin's, 2001, pp. 879–88.

Simonton, Deborah. "Schooling the Poor: Gender and Class in Eighteenth-Century England." *Journal for Eighteenth-Century Studies*, vol. 23, no. 2, 2000, pp.183–202.

Siskin, Clifford, and William Warner, editors. *This Is Enlightenment*. U of Chicago P, 2010.

Skinner, Carolyn. *Women Physicians and Professional Ethos in Nineteenth-Century America*. Southern Illinois UP, 2014.

Smith, Adam. *Theory of Moral Sentiments*. 1759.

Smith, John Harrington. *The Gay Couple in Restoration Comedy*. New York: Octagon Books, 1971.

Smith, Tania. "Elizabeth Montagu's Study of Cicero's Life: The Formation of an Eighteenth-Century Woman's Rhetorical Identity." *Rhetorica*, vol. 26, no. 2, 2008, pp. 165–87.

———. "Lady's Rhetorick (1707): The Tip of the Iceberg of Women's Rhetorical Education in Enlightenment France and Britain." *Rhetorica*, vol. 22, no. 4, 2004, pp. 349–73.

———. Learning Conversational Rhetoric in Eighteenth-Century Britain: Hester Thrale Piozzi and Her Mentors Collier and Johnson." *Rhetor: Journal of the Canadian Society for the Study of Rhetoric*, vol. 2, 2007, cssr-scer.ca/journal/volumes/rhetor-vol-2/.

Solomon, Diana. *Prologues and Epilogues of the Restoration Theater: Gender and Comedy, Performance and Print*. U of Delaware P, 2013.

Sophia. *Woman Not Inferior to Man: Or, a Short and Modest Vindication of the Natural Right of the Fair-Sex to a Perfect Equality of Power, Dignity and Esteem with the Men*. London, 1739. https://digital.library.upenn.edu/women/sophia/woman/woman.html.

Southerne, Thomas. *The Fatal Marriage*. Edited by Robert Jordan and Harold Love. *Works of Thomas Southerne*, Clarendon Press, 1988.

———. *Sir Anthony Love. Broadview Anthology of Restoration and Early Eighteenth Century Drama*, edited by Douglas Canfield, Toronto, Broadview Press, 2001, 1215–77.

Spacks, Patricia Meyer. *Imagining a Self: Autobiography and Novel in Eighteenth-Century England*. Harvard UP, 1976.

———, ed. *Selections from The Female Spectator*. Oxford UP, 1999.

Staves, Susan. *Players' Scepters: Fictions of Authority in the Restoration*. U of Nebraska P, 1979.

Steele, Richard. *Ladies Library*. 1714.

———. *Tatler*. London. 1709–1711.

Stone, Lawrence. *Family Sex and Marriage in England, 1500–1800.* Harper and Row, 1977.

Styan, J. L. *Restoration Comedy in Performance.* Cambridge: Cambridge UP, 1986.

Sutherland, Christina Mason. *The Eloquence of Mary Astell.* U of Calgary P, 2005.

Swearingen, C. Jan. *Rhetoric and Irony: Western Literacy and Western Lies.* Oxford UP, 1991.

Tarbuck, Derya Gurses. "Exercises in Women's Intellectual Sociability: The Fair Intellectual Club." *History of European Ideas,* vol. 41, no. 3, pp. 375–86.

Tasker, Elizabeth. "Before Garrick: Elizabeth Barry, Mistress of Emotion on the Restoration Stage." *Re/Framing Identifications,* edited by Michelle Ballif, Waveland Press, 2014.

Taylor, Barbara. *Mary Wollstonecraft and the Feminist Imagination.* Cambridge UP, 2003.

———, and Sarah Knott, editors. *Women, Gender, and Enlightenment.* Palgrave Macmillan, 2005.

Thale, Mary. "The Case of the British Inquisition: Money and Women in Mid-Eighteenth-Century London Debating Societies." *Albion: A Quarterly Journal Concerned with British Studies,* vol. 31, no. 1, 1999, pp. 31–48.

———. "London Debating Societies in the 1790s." *Historical Journal,* vol. 32, no. 1, 1989, pp. 57–86.

———. "Women in London Debating Societies in 1780." *Gender and History,* vol. 7, no. 1, 1995, pp. 5–24.

Thrale, Hester. *Letters of Mrs. Thrale.* Lane, 1926.

Tipper, John. *Ladies Diary: Or, the Womens Almanack.* London, 1709. Harry Ransom Center, University of Texas.

Todd, Janet. *Sensibility.* Methuen, 1986.

———. *Sign of Angellica.* Columbia UP, 1989.

———, editor. *Works of Aphra Behn.* Ohio State UP, 1996.

Todd, Janet, and Gillian Dow. "Margaret Cavendish and the Imagined Female Academy." *Rooms of Our Own Exhibition at Lucy Cavendish College,* 2009. Accessed at Chawton House Library, 2012.

Ulman, H. L. *Things, Thoughts, Words, and Actions: The Problem of Language in Late Eighteenth Century British Rhetorical Theory.* Southern Illinois UP, 1994.

Van Lennep, editor. *London Stage 1660–1800: Part 1:1660–1700.* Southern Illinois UP, 1965.

Walker, Gina Luria. "Mary Hays (1759–1843): An Enlightened Quest." *Women, Gender, and Enlightenment*. Edited by Barbara Taylor and Sarah Knott, Palgrave Macmillan, 2005. pp. 493–518.

Warner, Michael. "Publics and Counterpublics (abbreviated version)." *Quarterly Journal of Speech*, vol. 88, no. 4, 2002, pp. 413–25.

Weber, Harold. *Restoration Rake-Hero*. Madison, U of Wisconsin P, 1986.

Wertheimer, Molly Meijer, editor. *Listening to Their Voices: The Rhetorical Activities of Historical Women*. U of South Carolina P, 1997.

Whyman, Susan. "Letter Writing and the Rise of the Novel: The Epistolary Literacy of Jane Johnson and Samuel Richardson." *Huntington Library Quarterly*, vol. 70, no. 4, December 2007, pp. 577–606.

Wollstonecraft, Mary. *Thoughts on the Education of Daughters*. 1781.

———. *A Vindication of the Rights of Men, In a Letter to the Right Honorable Edmunde Burke; Occasioned by His Reflections on the Revolution in France. The Vindications*, edited by D. L. Macdonald and Kathleen Scherf, Broadview Press, 1997.

———. *A Vindication of the Rights of Women: With Strictures on Political and Moral Subjects. The Vindications*, edited by D. L. Macdonald and Kathleen Scherf. Broadview Press, 1997.

Woman of Colour: A Tale. Edited by Lyndon J. Dominique, Broadview, 2007. (Originally from Black, Parry, and Kingsbury, 1808.)

Wycherley, William. *The Country Wife. The Broadview Anthology of Restoration and Early Eighteenth Century Drama*. Edited by Douglas Canfield, Broadview Press, 2001.

Zinsser, Judith P. "Emilie du Chatelet and the Enlightenment's Querelles des Femmes." *Challenging Orthodoxies: The Social and Cultural Worlds of Early Modern Women: Essays Presented to Hilda L. Smith*, edited by Melinda S. Zook. Routledge, 2014. pp. 123–46.

Index

absence, as rhetoric, 39, 155–56

Addison, Joseph, 70. See also *Spectator*

Allen, Julia, 188.6

Anderson, Misty 43, 195.17

Andrews, Donna, 118, 125–26, 130–39

Anglicanism and Anglicans, 28–29, 32–33, 48, 57, 63, 162

Anne, Queen 33–34, 38; rhetorical performance of 36–39, 151; rhetorical training, 35, 86; and Sara Churchill, 39, 190–91.6

Apetri, Sarah, 34, 57, 75, 145

Aristotle, 13, 17, 66, 119, 144, 151–52, 197.10

Arizpe, Evelyn, 49, 51, 53, 75, 191.10

Asiatic style, 80–81, 91, 119, 124

Astell, Mary, 5–6, 18, 25, 28–29, 119–20, 167, 173–74, 176, 190.17; *Serious Proposal to the Ladies*, 5, 146–49, 157, 168; *Some Reflections Upon Marriage*, 43–44

Athenian Mercury, 61–62, 192.16

Austen, Jane, 46, 72, 155

Bacon, Francis, 3, 18, 187.2

Bagchi, Barnita, 170

Barry, Elizabeth, 78–79, 84–85, 91–94, 97, 178; delivery and elocution, 92–94, 104, 109, 119; as female libertine, 101–2; partnered with Bracegirdle, 97, 107–8; rhetorical training, 92; as victim 104–5

Batchelor, Jennie, 71, 73, 192.17

Beattie, James, 120

Behn, Aphra, 86, 88–89; *The Lucky Chance*, 99; *The Rover*, 101–2; 195.19

belletristic rhetoric: defined, 15–17; and emotion, 177, 188.8, French, 189.14; in *Lady's Rhetorick*, 147, 150–152; and Mary Astell, 147–49; in salons, 121, 141; and sensibility, 79, 188.8; and taste, 69–71

Benger, Elizabeth, 70, 169

Betterton, Mary Saunderson, 33, 35, 84–87, 94–95, 109

Betterton, Thomas, 89, 93–95, 97

Bizzell, Patricia, 15–16, 148–49, 156, 196.4

Blair, Hugh, 3, 17, 144; *Lectures on Rhetoric and Belles Lettres*, 189.15

bluestockings (Bluestockings): and belles lettres, 17; compared to debating societies, 140–41; defined and described, 55–56, 116, *117*, 120, 187.4; early circles, 40; London salons, 113, 116, 121–24, 140, 178; model of conversation, 11, 56, 71; origin of term, 191.11; as patrons, 58; salon rhetoric, 25, 119, 121–25; scholarship on, 8; on Wollstonecraft, 139

Boscawen, Frances, 120, 123

Bottin, Eileen Hunt, 41, 46, 191.9

Boutell, Elizabeth, 84

Bracegirdle, Anne, 78, 84–86, 94–97, 109; as sentimental heroine, 106; partnered with Barry, 107–9; as victim, 104, 194.10

Brady, Nicholas, *The Rape; or, The Innocent Imposters*, 104

Goring, Paul, 40, 59, 79, 83, 93, 111,
117–18
Graban, Tarez Samra, 20
grammar, 16, 64, 165, 166–67, 196.4,
197.6
Gregg, Edward, 35–37
ground truth, 14, 23, 27, 56, 175, 179
Gwyn, Nell, 84, 87–89, *88*, 100, 109; in
Secret Love or The Maiden-Queen,
100, 102

Habermas, Jurgen, 41, 191.7
Hamilton, Elizabeth, 173–74; *Breakfast
Table*, 70–71; *Letters on the Elemen-
tary Principles of Education*, 169
Hannan, Leonie, 47–48
Hart, Charles, 100
Haskins, Ekaterina, 146, 150
Haywood, Eliza, 57, 176, 192.18; *Female
Spectator*, 66–70
Heath, Shirley Brice, 49, 51, 53, 75,
191.10
Heller, Deborah, 8, 56
Herzberg, Bruce, 15–16, 148–49, 156,
196.4
Highfill, Philip, 33, 78, 86–97, 105,
193.1, 194.10
Hobbes, Thomas, 3, 187.2; reflected in
Johnson, 160
Holland, Peter, 82, 98, 100
Holloway, Sally, 52
Howe, Elizabeth, 77–78, 82, 84–86,
90–93, 95, 98, 100–107, 193.1–2
Hughes, Derek, 7, 30, 98
Hultquist, Aleksondra, 67
humanism, 16, 35, 156, 171, 189.13,
196.4–5. *See also* querelle des femmes
humanist style, 147, 149, 154, 166
Hume, David, 3, 5, 17–18, 189.15
Hunt, Margaret, 8, 10, 42, 136, 142–44,
198.13
Hutton, Sarah, 190.1

Immel, Andrea, 48
Innes, Joanna, 196.2

Jacobin movement, 58–59, 139, 177
James II, 33, 86
Jarratt, Susan, 20
Johnson, Jane, 48–55, *50*, *52*, *53*, 191.10
Johnson, Joseph, 58
Johnson, Nan, 20, 23
Johnson, Samuel, 70–71, 89, 160, 166;
Johnsonian literary circle, 120
Jones, Rebecca, 9, 15, 22, 26, 76
Jordan, Robert, 105

Kames, Lord, 120
Keating, Erin, 106
Keeble, N. H., 32
Kelly, Gary, 55–56, 59, 170
King, Margaret, 78, 91
Kirsch, Gesa, 8–9, 22, 113, 175, 179
Knott, Sarah, 3, 8, 58, 187.3
Knox, Vicesimus, *Liberal Education*,
169–70

La Belle Assemblée. *See* debating
clubs and societies
Ladies Library, 63, 143, 196.1
Ladies Mercury, 61, 192.16
Lady's Rhetorick, 147, 150–154
Langhans, Edward, 33, 78, 86–97, 105,
193.1, 194.10
libertinism, 32–34, 40, 81, 108, 110; as
character type, 13, 31, 99–100; decline of, 94–95; female, 87, 101–4,
176
Licensing Act of 1737, 110, 128
Locke, John, 3, 5, 18, 28–29, 45–47, 75,
144, 148–50, 169; and education,
46–47; empiricism, 69, 120, 147, 156;
*Essay Concerning Human Under-
standing*, 28, 149, 156; influence
on bluestockings, 144, 160; social

ELIZABETH TASKER DAVIS is a professor of English and coordinator of graduate studies at Stephen F. Austin State University, where she teaches courses on British literature, satire, and writing. Her scholarship has appeared in *Women's Writing, Rhetoric Review, Peitho, South Atlantic Review, Re/Framing Identifications*, and the *Sage Handbook of Rhetorical Studies*.

Studies in Rhetorics and Feminisms

Studies in Rhetorics and Feminisms seeks to address the interdisciplinarity that rhetorics and feminisms represent. Rhetorical and feminist scholars connect rhetorical inquiry with contemporary academic and social concerns, exploring rhetoric's relevance to current issues of opportunity and diversity. This interdisciplinarity is transforming the rhetorical tradition as we have known it (upper-class, agonistic, public, and male) into regendered, inclusionary rhetorics (democratic, dialogic, collaborative, cultural, and private). Our intellectual advancements depend on such ongoing transformation.

Rhetoric, whether ancient, contemporary, or futuristic, always inscribes the relation of language and power at a particular moment, indicating who may speak, who may listen, and what can be said. The only way we can displace the traditional rhetoric of masculine-only, public performance is to replace it with rhetorics that are recognized as being better suited to our present needs. We must understand more fully the rhetorics of the non-Western tradition, of women, of a variety of cultural and ethnic groups. Therefore, Studies in Rhetorics and Feminisms espouses a theoretical position of openness and expansion, a place for rhetorics to grow and thrive in a symbiotic relationship with all that feminisms have to offer, particularly when these two fields intersect with philosophical, sociological, religious, psychological, pedagogical, and literary issues.

The series seeks scholarly works that both examine and extend rhetoric, works that span the sexes, disciplines, cultures, ethnicities, and sociocultural practices as they intersect with the rhetorical tradition. After all, the recent resurgence of rhetorical studies has been not so much a discovery of new rhetorics as a recognition of existing rhetorical activities and practices, of our newfound ability and willingness to listen to previously untold stories.

The series editors seek both high-quality traditional and cutting-edge scholarly work that extends the significant relationship between rhetoric and feminism within various genres, cultural contexts, historical periods, methodologies, theoretical positions, and methods of delivery (e.g., film and hypertext to elocution and preaching).

Queries and submissions:

Professor Emerita Shirley Wilson
   Logan
University of Maryland
Email: slogan@umd.edu

Cheryl Glenn
Department of English
402 Burrowes Bldg.
Penn State University
University Park, PA 16802-6200
Email: cjg6@psu.edu

Other Books in the Studies in Rhetorics and Feminisms Series